SAGE was founded in 1965 by Sara Miller McCune to support the dissemination of usable knowledge by publishing innovative and high-quality research and teaching content. Today, we publish more than 750 journals, including those of more than 300 learned societies, more than 800 new books per year, and a growing range of library products including archives, data, case studies, reports, conference highlights, and video. SAGE remains majority-owned by our founder, and after Sara's lifetime will become owned by a charitable trust that secures our continued independence.

Los Angeles | London | Washington DC | New Delhi | Singapore | Boston

Orientalism, Terrorism, Indigenism

Orientalism, Terrorism, Indigenism

South Asian Readings in Postcolonialism

Pavan Kumar Malreddy

www.sagepublications.com
Los Angeles • London • New Delhi • Singapore • Washington DC • Boston

First published in 2015 by

SAGE Publications India Pvt Ltd
B1/I-1 Mohan Cooperative Industrial Area
Mathura Road, New Delhi 110 044, India
www.sagepub.in

SAGE Publications Inc
2455 Teller Road
Thousand Oaks, California 91320, USA

SAGE Publications Ltd
1 Oliver's Yard, 55 City Road
London EC1Y 1SP, United Kingdom

SAGE Publications Asia-Pacific Pte Ltd
3 Church Street
#10-04 Samsung Hub
Singapore 049483

Published by Vivek Mehra for SAGE Publications India Pvt Ltd, typeset in 10/12 pts Berkeley by RECTO Graphics, Delhi, and printed at Chaman Enterprises, New Delhi.

Library of Congress Cataloging-in-Publication Data Available

ISBN: 978-93-515-0142-8 (HB)

The SAGE Team: Supriya Das, Sanghamitra Patowary, Nand Kumar Jha, and Rajinder Kaur

Contents

Preface

The End(s) of Postcolonial Theory

In 2012, *New Literary History* hosted a debate on the "future" of post-colonial theory, led by two renowned exponents of the field—Dipesh Chakrabarty and Robert Young—who, despite their divergent theoretical standpoints, arrived at the same conclusion that postcolonial theory had lost its luster, and new conceptual directions were needed. In the wake of the anthropogenic (human-made) global warming, Chakrabarty (2012: 11) argues that there are two ways of historicizing the human subject: "human–human," one who is a geological force, part and parcel of the ontic existence of nature; and "nonhuman–human," one who constructs individual experience through "differently scaled histories of the planet" (ibid., 14).[1] Given that postcolonial theory cannot resolve the ontological predicament of "human–humans," Chakrabarty contends that we need "to think the human on multiple scales and registers and as having both ontological and nonontological modes of existence" (ibid.). Implicit in Chakrabarty's argument is that the struggles of "nonhuman–humans" become secondary to the survival of "human–humans." Although one is left to wonder what happens to the struggles of "nonhuman humans," once we avert the apocalypse, as in Benita Parry's (2012) scathing cri-tique of Chakrabarty, it is entirely possible to conceive that man-made global warming is caused by the "existing", if not the ever-present, ever-contingent inequalities in resource distribution "between" and "among" "nonhuman–humans." Robert Young is least bothered by Chakrabarty's apocalyptic gestures, as he goes on to celebrate the hard-fought victories of the "nonhuman–humans," suggesting that colonial continuities and colonial dependencies "have ceased to exist," and "the 21st century is already the century of postcolonial empowerment" (ibid., 20). This leaves postcolonial theory without a challenge or an object of critique, or rather with new challenges to seek out "the hidden rhizomes of colonialism's historical reach" (ibid., 21): the invisible sites of indigenous struggles and their relation to settler colonialism, illegal workers, and undocumented citizens, and political Islam that has been gaining momentum in the Arab world since October 2011.

These two positions, however, were met with a spate of critical responses by commentators, such as Simon During, Benita Parry, Robert Stam and Ella Shohat, Bill Bell, and Ato Quayson. For Simon During, Young's reading of postcolonial theory in terms of colonial continuities or discontinuities builds on a "moral judgment" of colonialism as an invariably oppressive force. This is not how, During affirms, most post-colonial societies perceive colonial legacy, as they "find a comfortable berth in democratic state capitalism" (2012: 333) which is enabled by colonial domination. Like During, Parry (2012) criticizes both Young and Chakrabarty for underplaying the hegemonic nexus of colonialism, imperialism, and global capitalism, one which not only accounts for the "invisible" legacies of colonialism (political Islam, settler colonial oppression, and so forth) but also human-made global warming. Like the two previous debates that announced the proverbial death of the field (in the 1990s, and again in 2007),[2] this one, too, fails to provide a consolidating platform that could account for a renewed conception of postcolonial theory and its objectives. Instead, it succeeds only by way of rekindling the internal disputes between Marxism (ibid.), indigenism (Stam and Shohat 2012), historicism (Bell 2012; Quayson 2012) and the various poststructuralist tenets of subalternity, and anti-essentialist politics (Chakrabarty 2012; Young 2012).

In 2013, the news service portal Al Jazeera hosted a similar debate which, unlike the "progressive" tenor of the *New Literary History* discussion, followed a rather "regressive" suit. In a response to Zabala's (2012) salutary remark about Slavoj Žižek as "the thinker of our age," Dabashi (2013) wonders why Zabala relegates non-European thinkers to the category of "other philosophers," as though they do not seem to merit "a specific name to be sitting next to these eminent European philosophers," and asks the much anticipated question: "Can non-Europeans think?"[3] Without much ado, Latin American cultural theorist Walter Mignolo joins the debate with a befitting response: "Yes, we can: Non-European thinkers and philosophers" (2013):

> And if behind Zizek there is Derrida in continental philosophy, behind Gordon is Fanon in Africana philosophy; behind Seyyed Hossein Nasr is Ali Shariati in Muslim philosophy, behind Wang Hui there is Liu Xun in Chinese philosophy, behind El Sadawi the legacies of Muslim *falsafa* and behind Dussel is Rodolfo Kusch in Latin American philosophy. (ibid.)

Mignolo takes his nuanced antagonism a step further: "I do not intend to dispute Zabala's evaluation of Žižek as a philosopher. What I am saying is that we, decolonial intellectuals, if not philosophers, 'have better things to do' as Fanon would say, than being engaged with issues debated by European philosophers" (Mignolo 2013). Michael Marder (2013), another European philosopher, intervenes into the debate by declaring that the whole issue is a "post-colonial comedy of errors," for "post-colonial theorists agree that there is no strict division between the coloniser and the colonised; that both colonial and post-colonial structures of power and domination are complex and multilayered."

The wheel, it seems, has turned its full circle. The Al Jazeera debate ends where the *New Literary History* debate begins: the pervasive exhaustion of colonial/postcolonial continuities. The *New Literary History* debate ends where the Al Jazeera debate begins: the unresolved tensions between the colonial continuities and third world emancipation.

"Are the British Coming Back Again?"

The incommensurability of the aforementioned debates merits attention not only because it is relevant to the issues raised in this book, but largely because it gestures toward the scale(s) of diversity, polarity, and even hostilities among the internal practitioners of postcolonial theory today. The chapters presented here are the products of this much contested legacy. A case in point, while ruminating on the theoretical fodder of these two debates, I was reminded of a curious vignette that a student in Canada told me upon his return from India, and that inspired this book in the first place. The vignette involved a Canadian visitor, the student in question, and a group of Telangana villagers under a Neem tree in 2006. On a cold winter evening, the student decided to give his Canadian friend the much awaited tour of his village. A white person is evidently a rare sight in these places, and as they took a few steps from the house, they were greeted by a group of 20 villagers who escorted them to the Neem tree in the village center. Like a politician grilled by a local scribe on failed electoral promises, the villagers began to grill the Canadian bystander, having turned the student into an obedient translator: "Do English people eat much rice?" "Why is it night in Amreeka [*sic*] when it is day here?" But the most astounding question of all came from the depths of a dark corner, like a bullet triggered by a sniper's finger pin with the student's name engraved on it: "Look Anna (brother), are the British coming back again?" "What?" The student shook head in disbelief. "I see so many white people come here after you went to Amreeka, people are saying that the British are coming back again."

The student, no doubt perplexed by the magnanimity of the rumor, did not bother to correct the villager that he had in fact lived in Canada, and for that matter, he had no business with "the British" or "Amreeka." Yet he wondered if he had been accused of staging the return of the British to his village, and perhaps the rest of India. "Well," he tried to reassure the villager, "we were never ruled by the British, you know that, don't you, we were under the *Nizam-ul-Mulk* even after the British left India, the British never set afoot here." "Doesn't matter," retorted the villager, "at least the British built roads and rails wherever they went, look at Andhra people,[4] how well they are doing now, they have irrigation, water, bridges, roads—all built by the British. I have nothing against the British, in fact it is our *Nizam*s and *Patel*s (local elite and rulers) who continue to ruin us, don't tell me that the hat-wearing *tella doras* (white lords) are worse than our own topi-wallas—*nalla doras* (black lords). They are the ones who are ruining our country." "Unbelievable," cried out the Canadian bystander, looking ever more bemused as the student rendered him the translation verbatim. Could the mere presence of a foreign companion instigate this Telangana villager to confront the student as a potential outsider? Or is it the very illusory prospect of "the British coming back again" that exposed him to the fault lines in the local governance? Or could it well be that the 60 years of native rule did little or nothing to allay his fears that the return of the colonizer is just a matter of a rumor coming to life? But perhaps the rumor of the colonizer's goodwill is no longer a ruse, as Simon During (2012: 333) argues in the *New Literacy History* debate:

> No doubt, and unforgettably, colonialism involved expropriation after expropriation, oppression after oppression, atrocity after atrocity. Nonetheless, even among those very aware of this, it has long been recognized that there is also a strong case for arguing that empire brought benefits to its subject peoples too.

During's claims, we must note, are not entirely unsubstantiated. For instance, he goes on to cite the case of the Maori Party in New Zealand, which joined the coalition with a "fiercely neoliberal" National Party that is currently in power to "to protect the considerable capital sums that have accrued to *iwi* (tribes) by virtue of their successful appeal to the 1840 Waitangi treaty by which Maori seceded sovereignty" (ibid.).

Consider, then, the vintage revelation of Manmohan Singh, India's former prime minister: "the 'idea of India as an inclusive and plural society' was inherited from the Raj" (Singh cited in During: 334). This statement, taken together with the Telangana villager's exclamation, raises a number of challenges concerning the perceived "dissolution" (Young 2012: 19) of "the long-lingering aftereffects of imperial, colonial, and neocolonial rule" (ibid., 20) in non-Western countries. First, it challenges what Partha Chatterjee (1986) calls the "derivative" discourse of elite nationalism that is built on anticolonial impulses, a discourse that is conceived by the very Indian National Congress that Manmohan Singh represents, and somewhat ironically, with the very blessings of the heirs of the Gandhi-Nehru family.[5] In "its moment of arrival", as Chatterjee (1986: 132) contends, the derivative discourse is alienated from the nationalistic aspirations of the indigenous masses, thereby widening the gulf between colonial modernity and local traditions. Second, in light of the Telangana villager's anxious exclamation over the return of the British, such an internal rift loses its derivative power: in conceding the perceived benefits of colonialism, the prime minister and the villager join ranks as each other's uncanny doubles. Third, this doubling act, however, does not presuppose the dissolution of the "derivate" discourse, for the prime minister's complicity with the colonial legacy merely anticipates, if not mimics, the villager's "generative" claim, that is, nalla doras have replaced the tella doras.

Rumor's Performance

For the Telangana villager, however, the rumored goodwill of the colonizer no longer pertains to its residual benefits, nor is it a case of naïve lumpenism that toys with the idea of replacing one colonizer with another. On the contrary, it constructs a powerful political idiom that opens him to a "world" of "cosmopolitan exchanges" (During 2012: 334), "a world order which colonialism has shaped and which it continues to haunt, but for which it no longer provides adequate terms of reference" (ibid., 336).

If we were to dismiss the villager's argument over the colonizer's goodwill as a case of unfounded rumor, then we must concede the view that rumor holds a unique place in the contours of subaltern resistance. Whether it is the Hawaiians who took Captain Cook for god, or the villagers of the Gorakhpur district who took Gandhi for a magician, or even the tribals of Dandakaranya who took the Naxalites for dacoits, rumor's enabling function in mass mobilization has been widely documented in anticolonial movements. If, for James Scott, rumor and gossip are "weapons of the weak" (1985: 241–89), for Ranajit Guha, rumor is "a necessary instrument for rebel transmission" (1983: 256). Yet for rumor, fact is always nonfactual, if not inconsequential, just as in the Telangana villager's unfounded claim that he was a British subject, even if he was not, as it "lacks a clear, identifiable origin or source" (Morton 2007a: 105). In Gayatri Spivak's reading of Guha, "rumour is spoken utterance *par excellence*" (Guha cited in Spivak 1988a: 23; emphasis in original), for it has an immediate political function and therefore lacks "any *one* voice-consciousness" (Spivak 1988a: 23; emphasis in original). It is this collective genesis of rumor that makes its (non)narratology inherently deconstructive, in line with Derrida's critique of writing as a structured structure, one that is derived from the putatively unstructured speech. Yet, rumor is not merely passive, which it surely is; in its strategic innocence, factual naïveté, and overcoded memory, it is charged with the "enunciative" function of "communal adhesiveness" (Bhabha 1994: 332). Once the "enunciative" function is fulfilled, rumor then prods into "performative" action spreading fear and panic that is "more dangerous than anger ... beyond the knowledge of ethnic or cultural binarisms and becomes a new, hybrid space of cultural difference in the negotiation of colonial power-relations" (ibid., 292). At least, this is what led the British armed forces to concoct a counter-rumor that the Indian villagers were using chapattis (with a secret message baked on a paper inside) to mobilize support for the 1857 Sepoy Revolt as soon as the rumor of cow-fat coated ammunition (which allegedly was mutton-fat and wax) spread like wildfire among the sepoys.

My interest in the function of rumor, however, is not simply to do with its transformative role in the anticolonial resistance, but its implications to the very memory and reception of colonialism in popular imagination, and the manner in which it is carried over to the present in the guise of a postcolonial condition. If the student were to respond to the Telangana villager's burning question—"Are the British coming back again?"—with a counter-exclamation that the colonizers have indeed come back again, or that they have never left us for that matter, as in Stuart Hall's rendition of postcolonialism as "not the end of colonisation" but "a certain *kind* of colonialism, after a certain moment of high imperialism and colonial occupation" (Hall cited in Drew 1999: 230; emphasis in original), his response would have simply fed into rumor's enunciate function, much to the negation of its performative effect. That is, the villager's implied complicity with the colonizer's return, and his expressive desire for escaping from the domestic pathos of the internal colonizer to the colonizer's model of the world, would not have sustained its intended effect, owing largely to rumor's penchant for auto-deconstruction, let alone the student's own awkward intervention. Here, it may well be the case that, as Bart Moore-Gilbert (1997: 185) contends, "the postcolonial 'moment' has been and gone" or it has reached a point of pervasive "exhaustion" in its "mantric iteration of the embattled past" (Gandhi 1998: 128), but it is the very "failures" of rumor's performative function that open up space for a renewed conception of postcolonialism. Such a renewal, this book contends, requires a move beyond various ports and points of this pervasive exhaustion. These include the derivative discourses built on anticolonial impulses, an obsession with narratives of counter-historiography and anti-Eurocentrism as well as rhetorically overcoded academic claims to "radical re-thinking and re-formulation of forms of knowledge and social identities authored and authorized by colonialism and western domination" (Prakash 1992: 8). Here, rumor's proto-performative function—the "denial" of the colonizer's oppression as the "desire" to replicate the colo-·nizer's model of the world—poses a daunting challenge to the politics of postcolonial theory. Taking this challenge to task more than a decade ago, Akhil Gupta's *Postcolonial Developments* (1998) exposes the disjuncture between postcolonial theory's counter-discursive politics and what he then called the "postcolonial condition." In the latter, Gupta provides ample ethnographic evidence to convince us that there is "a pervasive feeling of being underdeveloped" among North Indian villagers, clearly lagging "behind the West" (ibid., ix). Applied to our Telangana villager, although it is hard to prove whether or not this "derivative" self-negation is the source of the rumor that the colonizer is bound to return; suffice to say that the current state of the postcolony is replete with new forms of Otherness, new sites of alterity that can no longer be explained by the established practices in postcolonial studies. Arguing that postcolonial literature from the second half of the 20th century is "less historically delineated" (ibid., 14), Emma Dawson Varughese, for instance, draws attention to a world of post-globalized, post-internationalized, "post-paradigm" (ibid., 8–15) literary practices (production, circulation, reception) that are far less concerned with articulating power and difference purely in terms of "writing back" to the Empire.[6]

It is here, in the moment of the postcolonial "present," that rumor's proto-performative function finds the object of its critique. As in Aijaz Ahmad's assertion that "[c]olonialism is *now* being blamed not only for its own cruelties, but conveniently enough for *our* cruelties too" (Ahmad cited in Baber 2002: 748; emphasis added), the crimes of nalla doras take precedence over those of the tella doras. But as the conventional wisdom has it, it is not too wise to bend the stick too far in the other direction. In the case of the Telangana villager, then, it is merely the denial of tella doras' dominance that makes the acknowledgment of nalla doras possible. Posed in this way, rumor generates its own populism while undermining populism's status quo—the derivative discourses of anticolonialism and its elite nationalism. Accordingly, if rumor is seen as a populism from below, as in Bhabha's account (1985: 145–47) of the Elderly Man's challenge that the European book cannot possibly be sent by god directly to Hurdwar, it is entirely possible to conceive rumor as a subaltern device that could forge forms of difference and desired alterity even in its denial or selective subjugation of oppression to conventional tropes of (colonial) authority and power. The subjection of subaltern resistance and agency to a palimpsest-like, layered, fissured, and even "endosmotic" ("cellular dissemination" of knowledge "toward the public domain at large and there mutated into a greater concentration") form of postcolonial power structures beyond the prescribed narratives of canonical colonialism and imperialism has emerged as a dominant current in recent criticism (Dabashi 2009: 222).

Hamid Dabashi's *The Arab Spring and the End of Postcolonialism* (2012), for instance, proposes a new theory of subalternity and political globalization based on resistance, one that challenges "the South Asian subaltern" figure who has long occupied the postcolonial margins as the subject figure of all colonial oppression and resistance. The spate of political agitations in the Arab world since October 2011, Dabashi (2012) contends, signals a new wave of postcoloniality that is not necessarily shaped by responsive agency to capital or consumption, but by resistance and renaissance of the Arab Muslim subject who transcends the universalizing tropes of Western metaphysics, including its ideological alternatives set forth in the postcolonial discourse. Extending from his previous work, *Post-Orientalism: Knowledge and Power in Time of Terror* (2009), Dabashi holds that the essentialist discourses of the imperial powers (Orientalism, etc.) have lost epistemological currency, having mutated into new forms of governing techniques and principles that are as elusive as they are endosmotic. Against this, Dabashi announces the birth of new forms of subaltern solidarity, much like Guha's, based on horizontal alliances and new histories of oppression.

Correspondingly, the call for subaltern, vernacular, even abject cosmopolitanisms (Nyers 2003) and political globalization that are based on a shared sense of global resistance rather than shared values of hospitality or acceptance have received significant praise and purchase in contemporary postcolonial discourse (Spencer 2011; Lazarus 2011b). As the military invasions in Afghanistan and Iraq, the war on terror doctrine, and the spate of political upheavals in the Arab world have led to the creation of what Vivienne Jabri (2013: 99) calls the "precariously situated" postcolonial subject, they have also contributed to the weakening of the postcolonial state power.[7] These events, Jabri argues, open up to the articulation of a new postcolonial subject that unfolds between the fissures of dominance and resistance. Within this, Jabri traces the rise of a liberal cosmopolitan discourse to a host of international governing institutions, and the weakening of the postcolonial state power. In what Jabri calls a move from panoptical to post-panoptical power, colonial modernity has evolved into more complex forms of domination that require a careful rearticulation and relocation of the precarious postcolonial subject to political immediacy "that is relational and hence inter-subjective" (Jabri 2010: 10; Malreddy 2015: 5). Jabri's rendition of "late modernity" as "liquid modernity" (Bauman's term), one that is characterized by competing discourses of power and difference (ibid., 4), finds parallels with Hamid Dabashi's (2009) notion of *epistemic endosmosis* (see Chapter 3). In the post-9/11 context, for instance, Susan Koshy (2008) has argued that the internal fissures within the dominant discourses of racism and minoritization have led to a "serial minoritization" within and among diasporic minorities.

In spite of this internal shift toward "postcolonial moments" and "presents," "selving" and "retrieving history" (Boehmer 1993: 273) has remained a major preoccupation of postcolonial studies since its inception. For Dipesh Chakrabarty, such vexed relationship with the colonial past is a symptom of a "politics of despair" (2008 [2000]: 45) by which postcolonial theory is confronted with the impossible task of tracing resistance in the uniform translation of cultures into foreign semiotic systems in a dead history, and that too, in a world of academic protocols that are not independent from the academic globality instituted by European modernity (ibid., 45–46). For a less intemperate critic, however, "the *post* in *postcolonial* must not only recognize and articulate its connectedness to the past but see how the past impinges on the present in order to transform colonial archival knowledge into a politics of contemporaneity" (Afzal-Khan 2000: 25; emphasis in original).

The Scope of the Book

In examining these new developments, this book attempts to rescue the enabling impact of postcolonialism's passage that courses through diverse claims and counterclaims over its origins, disjunctures, and emancipatory pathways. In that sense, this book echoes similar concerns raised in the *New Literary History* debate, although it does not necessarily concede that "long-lingering aftereffects" of colonialism and imperialism have either ceased to exist or have assumed "residual" forms (Young 2012: 20–21). Instead, it turns to the various transfigurations and translocations of the "aftereffects" of colonialism in their current, precarious forms. By challenging the conventional antinomies set forth by early postcolonial theory—Eurocentrism/indigenism, humanism/nativism, universalism/ localism—each individual theme of the book is geared toward a renewed articulation of post-essentialist, transformative, and even mutative qualities of the discourses involved. These include, but are not restricted to, the transition of literary Orientalism to endosmotic post-Orientalism; the post-Eurocentric turn forged by postcolonial theory's internal disputes and disjunctures, and new sites of agency and emancipatory politics imparted therein: "locopolitanism" as opposed to metropolitan cosmopolitanism, indigenous humanism in the absence of universalism, and the politics and poetics of minor writing that resist institutional forces of assimilation.

The South Asian focus remains at the heart of the analysis for a host of reasons. Since the 1960s, not only did the English literature from the Indian subcontinent play a decisive role in shaping the field of post-colonial studies at large, but the writings of Raja Rao, Mulk Raj Anand, R.K. Narayan, and Kamala Markandaya also provided a strong literary platform for the ensuing theoretical currents on nationalism, or critiques of Orientalism and Eurocentrism from a distinctly anticolonial perspective. This approach has changed considerably with the intervention of the subaltern studies group in the 1980s, the influence of postmodern criticism and the writers of diasporic origin. Subsequently, the postmodern turn in South Asian literature posed a formidable challenge to earlier approaches based on anticolonial ideological impulses. The ensuing theoretical currents built on diasporic quest for identity, longing, and belonging were greeted with a great deal of suspicion and skepticism in the intellectual circles within the subcontinent. It was believed that the theories and concepts that celebrated hybrid identities, imagined communities, transnational, and traveling cultures were ill-equipped to grasp the vernacular diversity of South Asian literary and cultural landscapes. This book situates the contemporary debates in South Asian literary studies in the larger context of postcolonial theory, while uncovering their methodological inconsistencies, theoretical limits and argumentative fallacies. In particular, by challenging the legacy of the postmodern discourse that appropriates a select body of writings from the postcolony that are conducive to the needs of the Western academy, and from a provisionally post-Eurocentric perspective, this book turns to the current developments in DalitBahujan literature and popular fiction that remain underrepresented in postcolonial studies despite the modest success they enjoy in Indian academic circles.

The thematic division of the book into three sections—"Discourses," "Disjunctures," and "Indigenism(s)"[8]—provides the space necessary for an adequate treatment of literary texts, theoretical contexts, and a multidisciplinary genesis of the themes featured in this book. Starting with Edward Said's pioneering contributions to the field, the first section of the book "Discourses" attends to the methodological inadequacies of *Orientalism* uncovered by his recent critics, while relocating Orientalism's compliance with the discourses on terrorism, necropolitics, and pulp literature, among other pertinent aspects of popular culture. Consequently, by counterpoising postcolonialism's "residual" humanism with the misconceived partisanism of *Orientalism*, the second section of the book "Disjunctures" features an "interdiscursive," transgressive strategy to postcolonial theory's ambiguous affiliation to Eurocentrism, universalism, anti-disciplinarity, and interdisciplinarity. Extending these views to the disjuncture between Marxism and poststructuralism, nationalism, and cosmopolitanism, the third section of the book "Indigenism(s)" proposes a mediating ground between ethics and agency on the one hand, and solidarity and criticism on the other. Accordingly, the book retraces postcolonial emancipations to the fissured passages of "ethno-humanism," "alter-humanism," and cultural nationalism ("nationalogues") that lay the groundwork for a post-Eurocentric discourse.

In postcolonial studies, there is a specific ground for literary and disciplinary comparison wherein "[c]omparison is overdetermined at both ends of colonialism's culture" (Melas 2007: 36). Against this, taking its cue from Natalie Melas, this book proposes "a ground clearing exercise" that aims to investigate forms of difference, alterity, and equivalence that do not quite unify, but "must underlie the 'multiplied poetics of the world'" (Glissant cited in Melas 2007: 37). In that sense, my approach to the texts and contexts selected for analysis is driven by a theoretical commitment to "ground their own authority," without assuming the ideological innocence endemic to textual formalism or social functionalism.

Leipzig, October 2014

Notes

1. Although Chakrabarty does not deny the ontological genesis of "nonhuman–humans," he concedes that humans are prone to ontological collectivity, and such collectivity has played an instrumental role in staging anticolonial struggles since Frantz Fanon.

2. Postcolonial theory's "limits" and "ends" were first brought to attention following the critical acclaim of Gayatri Spivak's essay "Can the Subaltern Speak?" (1988a), and again in the late 1990s when a plethora of texts appeared (Gandhi 1998; Moore-Gilbert 1997), and more recently in a roundtable discussion published by *PMLA* journal titled "The End of Postcolonial Theory?" (2007). It is also worth noting that the much celebrated subaltern studies group has been disbanded since its last publication over a decade ago.

3. All subsequent citations without page numbers refer to Internet sources. Please see the list of cited works at the end of the book for a full reference to the relevant Internet links.

4. The Telangana region has been part of the federal state of Andhra Pradesh since 1956. But the region is noted for its underdevelopment under the Nizam's tyrannical rule. Once the Nizam's rule came to an end with the military intervention in 1948, the Hyderabad state was annexed into the Union of India under the directive of Jawaharlal Nehru. Subsequently, the Telugu speaking regions of Andhra areas, previously part of the Madras Presidency under the British rule, were merged with the Telangana region, forming a united Andhra Pradesh. Nevertheless, the regional disparities continued, as Telangana people suffered from a lack of access to agrarian and economic resources, and were subjected to decades of internal colonialism. At the time of writing this book, Telangana was declared the 29th state of India, after a decade-long separatist movement led by political parties and activist groups.

5. It is a well-known fact that Manmohan Singh was handpicked for the prime minister post by the current president of the Indian National Congress, Sonia Gandhi—the grand daughter-in-law of India's founding prime minister, Jawaharlal Nehru.

6. This is reflected in Varughese's choice of literary texts for analysis, which consists of relatively unknown writers to the Western readers: Chetan Bhagat (India), Shamini Flint (Malaysia/Singapore), Nii Ayikwei Parkes (UK), and Ali Sethi (Pakistan) to name a few.

7. These views do not necessarily align with the institutional-centric, state-based alternatives suggested by Robert Young to the question of "Political Islam" (2012: 26–28).

See also Simon During's (2012) critique of Young on the pitfalls of state-centric alternatives to democratic practices.

8. I define indigenism as a variant of nativism, an ideological collective based on a group's claims over place, cultural heritage, and their subjection to subalternity and subjugation. My view builds on the contestations produced by the various marginalized groups—from the Tuaregs of Sahara to the *girijans* (hill people) of Srisailam—to the normative discourses of homogeneity and cultural unity. As such, it is not the authenticity of claims, but the contestation itself that becomes the locus of any given indigenous subject position.

Acknowledgments

I am most thankful to Diana Brydon for her feedback on a number of chapters presented in this book. My special thanks to Maria-Belen Ordonez, Arun Chaudhuri, and Melissa Kennedy for their editorial assistance. I have also benefited from discussions with Alex Tickell, Enrique Galván Álvarez, Frank Schulze-Engler, Astrid Erll, Ole Birk Laursen, Ashok Kumbamu, and Ines Detmers. I thank Sakej Henderson, Marie Battiste, and Len Findlay for introducing me to the world of indigenous theory. I am deeply indebted to friends, academics, and family members for their unwavering support in all my professional and non-professional endeavors over the years: Madhu Sripathi, Paul Hamilton, Daniel DeLury, Melanie Graichen, Terry Wotherspoon, Peter Stoicheff, Sunitha Anmanagandla, and Praveena Sripathi. This book grows out of my doctoral dissertation titled "Postcolonial Predicaments: Contexts, Disjunctures, and Emancipations," and it has benefited immensely from the academic guidance of Cecile Sandten, Muiris Ó Laoire, Klaus Stolz, and Winfried Thielmann.

A number of chapters in this book have appeared in the following journals in their full and partial forms: Chapter 1 as "Introduction: Orientalism(s) after 9/11" in *Journal of Postcolonial Writing* 48 (3), 2012: 233–240; Chapter 2 as "Imagining the Terrorist: Racialization of Asian Identities since 9/11" in *Kasarinlan: Philippines Journal of Third World Studies* 22 (2), 2007: 4–21; Chapter 3 as "Pulp Orientalism: Endosmotic Banality, *terra necro*, and *homo ludens* in Dan Fesperman's *The Warlord's Son*" in *Journal of Postcolonial Writing* 48 (3), 2012: 265–277; Chapter 4 as "Humanism and Its Other: Difference and Disjuncture in Postcolonial Theory" in *Distinktion: Scandinavian Journal of Social Theory* 17 (2), 2009: 87–99; Chapter 5 as "Postcolonialism: Interdisciplinary or Interdiscursive?" in *Third World Quarterly* 32 (4), 2011: 653–672; Chapter 6 as "Cosmopolitanism Within: The Case of R.K. Narayan's Fictional Malgudi" in *Journal of Postcolonial Writing* 47 (5), 2011: 558–570; and

Chapter 7 as "(An)other Way of Being Human: Indigenous Alternative(s) to Postcolonial Humanism" in *Third World Quarterly* 32 (9), 2011: 1557–1572 (www.informawold.com). My thanks to the editors and publishers for allowing me to reprint the aforementioned essays in this book.

I dedicate this book to Birte Heidemann, without whose selfless interest, care, and companionship it would not have been completed.

Introduction

A Saidian Affair

A decade after Edward Said's death, his legacy and legend seem to have hit a cul-de-sac. Yet the tributes continue to pour in, as do critiques, in myriad renditions of his life and work—posthumous publications, monographs, edited anthologies, dictionaries, art work, musicals, and archives. The adjective "Saidian" became almost synonymous with his peculiar brands of "humanism" and "contrapuntality," paving the way to new conceptual pathways on the questions of agency, the dialectics of imperialism, and post-Eurocentrism in the works of Michel Foucault, Joseph Conrad, and Rudyard Kipling. For some, there is much more to Said's work than the enduring legacy of *Orientalism*, while for others, it is entirely possible to read "Said *against* Said: to accentuate the resources contained in his work to develop more self-conscious but still politically engaged ways of thinking" (Spencer 2011: 165; emphasis in original). And it is for a good reason that Said's *Orientalism* is regarded as the departure point in postcolonial theory, in spite of other foundational contributions of Frantz Fanon, Aimé Césaire, Albert Memmi, Amílcar Cabral, and Mahatma Gandhi among others. Nonetheless, over 30 years since its publication and 10 years after the death of its author, it is perhaps the despairing fate of the "authorial death" that one is bound to learn much more (about Said) from his critics, rather than his interlocutors.

"[C]olonial rule," Said wrote, "was justified in advance by Orientalism, rather than after the fact" (2003 [1978]: 39), implying that Orientalism as a discourse provided an "a priori" moral justification for colonial domination, including the violence it required to discipline and transform Oriental subjects through militant action. Here, Said's overemphasis on "synchronic essentialism," that is, the distortion of the Orient in literary imagination and the ensuing attempts by the colonizers to transform the Orient in tune with such imagination suffer from inadequate attention to the resistance (which Said has later termed "diachronic" instability [ibid., 240]) to the Orientalist discourse at large. As Philip Mellor (2004: 110) points out, a major flaw of *Orientalism* is its "failure to grapple satisfactorily with the relationship between representation and reality that colours Said's contradictory and unsympathetic account of religion," human agency, diversity of Oriental regionality, and scholarship.

By extension, Said's methodic, if not mantric, claims over the (in)authenticity of the Orient are further exacerbated by his uneasy relationship with conventionalist and realist modes of textual representation. In declaring that the Orient is "almost a European invention" (Said 2003 [1978]: 1), therefore a textual construction, Said negates the Oriental reality outside of its textual discourse.[1] According to critics, this leaves Said's methodology seamlessly adrift between the authenticity of the Orient and the inauthenticity of its representation. For instance, opposing Bill Ashcroft and Pal Ahluwalia's (1999: 4) claim that Said's position in *Orientalism* is properly conventionalist, owing largely to Said's concession that the existence of a real Orient outside of its discursive misrepresentations is impossible to trace or prove, Neil Lazarus (2011a: 195–96) points out the tactical fallacy in Said's own statements: "[t]here were—and are—cultures and nations whose location is in the East, and their lives, histories, and customs have a brute reality obviously greater than anything that could be said about them in the West" (Said 2003 [1978]: 5). Here, notwithstanding Said's later claim that *Orientalism* was less concerned with "a correspondence between Orientalism and Orient" than "with the internal consistency of Orientalism and its ideas about the Orient" (ibid.), his vexed conception of discourse as "[a]ll representation is misrepresentation of one sort or another" (2002 [2001]: 237) raises more eyebrows over *Orientalism*'s methodological inconsistency than it could afford. For instance, as Aijaz Ahmad (1992: 172) holds, since *Orientalism* is primarily concerned with the crisis of textual representation in the West, it fails to acknowledge "how these textualities might have been received, accepted, modified, challenged, overthrown, or reproduced by the intelligentsias of the colonized countries ..." Hence, for Said's critics, if *Orientalism* cannot sustain its methodological premise, it then accounts for the unclaimed failures of the postcolonial discourse at large. Thus, as in Lazarus's observation (mediated through Timothy Brennan), "*Orientalism* is simply two texts at once: the book that Said wrote and the book that his "post-" theoretical interlocutors read and appropriated" (Lazarus 2011a: 187). The first section of this collection "Discourses: Orientalism, Terrorism, and Popular Culture" sets out to re-examine Orientalism's sustained influence on postcolonial theory by carefully acknowledging Said's critiques, while extending their implications to the post-9/11 context. Arguing that the rigid demarcation of the imaginary Orient in Said's work requires further scrutiny, the chapters in this section account for the transition of literary Orientalism into endosmotic forms of post-Orientalism, pulp Orientalism, "new terrorism," and the necropolitics of war in the South Asian context (India, Pakistan, and Afghanistan). Chapter 1, "Orientalism(s) After 9/11," attends to the methodological inadequacies of *Orientalism* uncovered by Marxist critics. The first part of the chapter builds on Hamid Dabashi's notion of "post-Orientalism," one that marks the transition of literary Orientalism to an *epistemic endosmosis*, having been characterized by a charade of multiple, competing, often disposable Orientalisms ("techno-Orientalism," "internal Orientalism," etc.) that ceaselessly collide with contemporary discourses on terrorism. Accordingly, Chapter 2, "Imagining the Terrorist: A Post-Orientalist Inquiry," uncovers the genealogical complicity between (post)Orientalism and terrorism in the discourses of anthropology and anthropometry in colonial India. Extending this analysis to the emergence of scientific geography and the geopolitics of the post-independence era, the chapter maps the journey of literary and scientific Orientalism from 19th-century colonialism to the post-9/11 context. While conceding that Said's literary Orientalism may have lost its primacy, the chapter maintains that the discourses on post-9/11 terrorism cannot be understood in isolation from the Saidian framework. Chapter 3, "'Pulp Orientalism': Representations of Afghanistan and Pakistan in Popular Fiction" situates the relevance of post-Orientalism within a contemporary South Asian context. Drawing from Dabashi's notion of *epistemic endosmosis* and Achille Mbembe's work on "necropolitics," the chapter advances the conceptual exposition of "endosmotic banality," *terra necro*, and "splintered subjects" in Dan Fesperman's novel, *The Warlord's Son*. In due course, the chapter takes the post-Orientalism thesis a step further by uncovering the discursive complicity between popular fiction and terrorism. Like all pulp fiction that simply reaffirms the populist notions about the Orient, Fesperman's novel can be read as an exemplary case of pulp Orientalism, one that depicts every conceivable aspect of Afghani and Pakistani biosphere as the exegeses of civilizational, if not congenital, difference. Furthermore, unlike the cultural Orientalism of canonical fiction, Fesperman's Orientalism forges an endosmotic "style" of Othering by reducing the entire Afghani and Pakistani topographies into death worlds (terra necro), while depicting subcontinental Muslim subjects as inherently splintered, unstable, and mutable.

Postcolonial Disjunctures

By the late 1990s, with concepts such as liminality, conviviality, and contrapuntality gaining momentum, postcolonial theory became more preoccupied with "the lived *condition* of unequal power sharing globally and the self-authorization of cultural, economic, and militaristic hegemony than with a particular historical phenomenon such as colonialism" (Sheshadri-Crooks 2000: 19; emphasis in original). According to critics, particularly the Marxist proponents, this shift toward a "postcolonial present" was accentuated by the poststructuralist notions of "[i]ndeterminacy, interruption of the signifying chain, aporia, endless displacements, translations, and negotiations" (San Juan 2006: 45). Here, the symbolic treatment of colonialism and imperialism "as a set of deeply patterned 'structures of attitude and reference'" (Said cited in Lazarus 2011a: 37) is often attributed to Said's ambiguous relationship to Marxism and poststructuralism. Although Said sought to showcase the cumulative effects of Anglo-Saxon cultural criticism, anticolonial liberation movements, Western Marxism, and Foucault's ethnocentrism where he saw potential for humanism and agency—the implications of discourse in the knowledge-power nexus to the histories of oppression (Parry 2004: 6)—he remained more or less complicit with the poststructuralist iterations of Orientalism in the postcolonial discourse. If *Orientalism* is recognized for its brilliant synthesis of "the rhetorical power of textual readings offered by discourse analysis" and "a 'real' world of domination and exploitation, usually analyzed by a Marxism hostile to poststructuralism's epistemological scepticism" (Hulme 1989: 3), his subsequent works, especially *The World, the Text, and the Critic* (1983) revealed a deep "suspicion of totalizing concepts," including Western Marxism which, in Said's view, held "the status of a cultural idol or commodity" (Said 1983: 30). On the Marxist front, Said was careful to acknowledge the contributions of Eqbal Ahmad, Mahmoud Darwish, C.L.R. James, Aimé Césaire, Frantz Fanon, and Y.V. Mudumbe to the anticolonial liberation movements. But when it came to the question of agency, he was too quick to abandon Marxism in favor of poststructuralism. Despite the fact that Said advances *Orientalism* as a Foucauldian discourse—the exegesis of the knowledge–power nexus of the colonial project—he remains unfazed by Foucault's own constituent anti-humanism, anti-universalism, and the negation of sovereign autonomy of the subject. Instead, in *Culture and Imperialism* (1993), Said goes on to redeploy Foucault's discourse in favor of humanism and human agency, while reinstating his commitment to humanism and sovereignty of the secular intellectual. In *Culture and Imperialism* and *Reflections on Exile* (2000), for instance, Said calls for a contrapuntal articulation of the emergence of cultural forms by moving beyond the territorial bounds that are conventionally marked as separate between empires and their colonies. In *Humanism and Democratic Criticism* (2004), Said attempts to rescue "critical humanism" from the abuses of Euro-American humanism: "humanism that was cosmopolitan and text-and-language-bound" (Said 2004a: 10–11). Though such text-centric literary humanism is presented as a mere "proleptic gesture," as Rajagopalan Radhakrishnan (2007: 17) holds,[2] it comes as no surprise when "Said turns to literature as a potential spokesperson of that other future that is being occluded, aborted, by forces of division, hatred, and identitarian protectionism" (ibid., 34).

The benefactor of this "potential spokesperson," as E. San Juan (2006: 48) avows, is none other than "the postcolonial intellectual" who is positioned "as middleman-facilitator of colonized subalterns and Western imperial power." Rather than excavating postcolonial literary humanism buried under Western humanist classics and their abuses, Said draws inspiration from predominantly Western literary humanists such as Giambattista Vico, Richard Blackmur, Leo Spitzer, and Erich Auerbach. The result is the figure of the "secular intellectual," who "has authorized powers of one's own society, which are accountable to its citizenry" (Said 1994b: 98).

Regardless of the secular intellectual's dubious authority, who remains more or less immune to "dialectics of privilege" and "filiation" (Lazarus 2011a: 198– 203), *Orientalism*'s epic foray into postcolonial theory has led its various interlocutors to tactfully appropriate Said's inconsistencies to the latter's advantage. If, then, Orientalism (both as a text and as a method) is regarded as the genesis of postcolonial theory, it then follows that postcolonial theory embarks on a critique of human(ist) divisiveness forged by the Orientalist ideology. As Natalie Melas (1999: 14) observes, this discursive legacy is consistent with Said's own views on agency; the Western desire to dichotomize "authentic human reality" into Self and Other distinction(s) was particularly objectionable to Said, as it fuelled self-serving essentialisms in the name of a civilizing mission. Admittedly, Said's demarcation of discursive Otherness opened up a space for postcolonial theory's political program: to rescue the victims of the Orientalist ideology and to revive the(ir) marginalized cultures and knowledges suppressed by Euro-humanism. And despite Said's reservations for nativism, ethnocentrism, and the politics of difference at large, canonizing, revising, rewriting, and celebrating native cultures and traditions became the flagship of postcolonial discourse. Thus, as Lazarus aptly remarks, *Orientalism* is a text that is marked by an overt "disjuncture" between "Said's *position-taking* ... and the *position* that this text came to occupy within the field of postcolonial studies" (Lazarus 2011a: 187; emphasis in original).

This disjuncture between humanism and nativism, by and large, is echoed by postcolonial theory's own anxieties and ambiguities over its relentless institutionalization, disciplinary affiliations, interdisciplinary commitments, and anti-disciplinary politics. Although postcolonial theory boasts English and comparative literature as its disciplinary home, Said's critique of select brands of literary humanism for their "didactic" and "pedagogic" advocacy of Western classics has opened up space for nonliterary, and in that sense, interdisciplinary avenues of inquiry. While this interdisciplinary turn is embraced by the internal practitioners as a welcome challenge to Eurocentric forms of disciplinary knowledge, the assimilation[3] of postcolonial studies into the Western academic curriculum has led critics, such as Gayatri Spivak, to warn of the dangers of sacrificing ethics in the name of politics. In her recent work, *An Aesthetic Education in an Era of Globalization* (2012), Spivak accentuates these concerns in the guise of a "double bind" that calls for saving humanities by "playing" both its ethical and political imperatives without having to settle for one. This, however, cannot resolve the perceived crisis of the "literary" and the "disciplinary" that is exacerbated by the interdisciplinary turn, wherein, for instance, only "experimental texts," or texts that cater for metropolitan tastes (fragmented narratives, resisting closure) are considered properly "textual," therefore "political," while all other "conventional texts" are relegated to a thematic or content-based treatment on the basis of their literary form (Sorenson 2010: 19–26). With literary "form" associated with Eurocentric disciplinarity, and "literary texts" translated into "extra-literary" politics, much of postcolonial literary criticism today is fraught with the same positivist dangers it sought to avoid by resorting to interdisciplinary measures (ibid., 27–30). For more intemperate critics, however, postcolonial theory must resist the urge to "disciplining" its critical discourse, let alone "inter-disciplining" it, if it is to transcend Eurocentricity (Khair 2004; Behdad 1993). Graham Huggan (2002: 264–65), for one, reads Said's rejection of "disciplinary tactics" as essentially anti-authoritarian, therefore "anti-disciplinary." Implicitly, the disjuncture between (inter)disciplinarity and anti-disciplinarity not only embraces, but rather unfolds deep within the epistemic rift between humanism's all-embracing interdisciplinarity and nativism's radical anti-disciplinarity.

The second section of the book "Disjunctures: Humanism and Interdisciplinarity" subjects these internal contradictions of postcolonialism to a critical examination. While acknowledging Said's own shortcomings in forging the transition from a critique of a divisive, in that sense, abused humanism in *Orientalism* to the inculcation of revisionist yet inclusive humanism in his later work, Chapter 4, "After Orientalism: Difference and Disjuncture in Postcolonial Theory," accounts for the diverse ideological geneses of postcolonialism that led to the misconceived partisanism of *Orientalism*. These include the predominantly post-Marxist interventions by the subaltern studies group and Dipesh Chakrabarty's project of "provincializing Europe." Owing largely to the failed legacies of nativism, the chapter traces the emergence of post-Eurocentrism to the writings of Homi Bhabha and Gayatri Spivak. Following Brennan's suggestion that the uneasy conflation of Said's *Orientalism* with postcolonial discourse at large fails to appreciate Said's contributions to humanism, the chapter gestures toward a polyvalent, if not post-Eurocentric, postcolonialism outside of Orientalism's totalizing gaze. Chapter 5, "Postcolonialism: Interdisciplinary or Interdiscursive?" examines the way the disjuncture between humanism and nativism finds a renewed expression in postcolonial theory's ambiguous relationship with Eurocentric (inter)disciplinarity and anti-Eurocentric discourses within the Western academy. The chapter underscores the pitfalls of this ambiguity through a genealogical account of postcolonial theory's disciplinary affiliations. Accordingly, the chapter traces postcolonialism's interdiscursive affiliations to the strategic deployment of what I call the "foundational disciplines"—philosophy, literature, and history—and "supplemental disciplines"—anthropology, geography, and development studies.

The "Now" of the Postcolonial

While postcolonial theory is noted for canonizing forms of domination (Eurocentrism, humanism, capitalism, and globalization), it enjoys a grim reputation in theorizing resistance or "strategies" of resistance. In the mid-1990s, select stands of postcolonial theory sought to refute political strategies based on nativism, essentialism, and other "derivative" narratives inspired by anti-Eurocentrism. This implicit post-Eurocentric move, largely influenced by the success of Gayatri Spivak's essay "Can the Subaltern Speak?" (1988a) and, to some extent, by Dipesh Chakrabarty's

Provincializing Europe (2000), has led a number of commentators to frown upon postcolonial theory's loss of critical and political impulse, and an increasing valorization of nativism and indigenism in the name of anti-essentialism. Marxist critics strongly objected to the way Saidian humanism was appropriated into the sort of anti-nationalist, post-Eurocentric internationalism that effectively silences indigenous agency. Within the Saidian framework which signals "a progression from nativist through nationalist to liberation theory" (Parry 2004: 43) and "a transformation of social consciousness beyond ethnicity and reconceiving the possibilities of human experience in nonimperialist terms" (ibid., 43–44), Parry considers the idea of "cultural nationalism" as conceived by the anticolonial resistance movements still worth preserving (Malreddy 2015: 3). "The multivalencies" of the pan-African, Afro-Caribbean nationalism in Césaire's 'Négritude," and Fanon's pan-Africanism, Parry contends, "pre-empt both closure and fixity, making it available to rearticulations covering other modes of oppression" (ibid., 48).[4]

Yet, Said's conflation of cultural nationalism (exclusive to the Palestinian liberation struggle) with post-nationalist "alignments made across borders, types, nations, and essences" (Said 1994a [1993]: xxviii) has issued an ethical dictum to his more enthusiastic interlocutors to celebrate difference, multiplicity, and indignity "within the field of a pluralist global market" (San Juan 2006: 51). For instance, as Rahul Rao (2012: 184) concedes:

> both cosmopolitanism and nationalism might perform valuable ethico-political work in subaltern resistance, even as hegemonic variants of both can also function to disenfranchise the subaltern. From a subaltern perspective, then, the question is not *whether* cosmopolitanism or nationalism but *when* cosmopolitanism and nationalism. (emphasis in original)

This unhinging nexus of nationalism and internationalism on the one hand, and difference and sameness on the other, has inspired an array of theories on subaltern and indigenous cosmopolitanisms that are based on global alliances over questions of equality, rights, and democracy (Spencer 2011; Dabashi 2012).

Walter Mignolo (2000: 721, 741) for one argues that since "[c]osmopolitanism is not easily aligned to either side of globalization"—globalization of capitalism and globalization of the marginalized—it can accommodate space for "border epistemologies" that are founded upon "colonial difference" as opposed to "cultural difference." Such difference, for Mignolo, is neither semantic nor relational, but is universally constituted by its epistemic "delinking" from colonial modernity (Mignolo 2000: 721, 741). Instead of succumbing to the "inclusionalist" or "reformative" cosmopolitan projects that cast subaltern subjects as the passive recipients of "hegemonic imaginary" (ibid., 726, 736), Mignolo proposes an active dialogue between "colonial modernity" and border epistemologies. Accordingly, Mignolo's radical manifesto rejects the mainstream postcolonial project as passive radicalism, as one that unfolds deep within the fissures and crises (such as of deconstruction or the poststructuralist turn) of the European epistemology. Unlike the nativist, cultural nationalist proclivities in postcolonial theory, Mignolo's "border thinking" is essentially anti-essentialist: "[it is] the ability to speak from more than one system of knowledge ... Being able to speak in and from both systems of knowledge and language is not a rejection of one in favour of the other, but an act of pluralising epistemologies" (Mignolo 2010). In much the same way, Robert Young's thesis on "tricontinentalism"[5] invokes the "insurgent knowledges" of "the three continents of the South—Africa, Asia, and Latin America— ... particularly those that originate with the subaltern, the dispossessed, that seek to change the terms and values under which we all live" (2009: 15). In the *New Literary History* debate, Young (2012: 26) goes on to extend the purview of tricontinentalism to the indigenous struggles (as the "new tricontinental") that received scant attention in postcolonial theory.

However, such political manifestos based on cosmopolitan, pan-continental, and global solidarity movements are met with new challenges presented by the decade-long wars in Iraq and Afghanistan, the continued terrorist threats in the West, and the global financial meltdown in 2008, the rise of Chinese capitalism, the emergence of new regionalisms within Europe, and reverse migration from Europe to former colonies.[6] On the other hand, the Declaration on the Rights of the Indigenous Peoples in 2007 and the demands of some 370 million indigenous peoples around the world for self-determination and separate provision of economic and cultural rights pose a daunting challenge to postcolonial studies' premature celebration of cosmopolitan or globalized alternatives. Since its inception, however, postcolonial theory has maintained an arms-length relationship to the Universal Declaration of Human Rights (1949) for its alleged Eurocentrism which places Western subjects as the subject figure of all histories and societies. The third section of the book "Indigenism(s): Cosmopolitanism, Rights, and Cultural Politics" seizes upon these various internal disjunctures of postcolonialism as outlined in the previous section—post-essentialism, post-Eurocentrism, and interdiscursivity. As such, each chapter in this section gestures a move towards "generative" politics based on polyvalent indigenisms, beyond the "derivative" gaze of the institutionalized postcolonialism. Chapter 6, "Cosmopolitanism Within: The Case of R.K. Narayan's Fictional Malgudi," locates new sites of cosmopolitanism outside its metropolitan conditioning. Drawing from David Harvey's (2000) notion of local geographies as the locus of cosmopolitan experience, the chapter turns to R.K. Narayan's fictional town of Malgudi to unravel the politics of alterity, the hazards of domesticity, conditions of economic and cultural production, and, more importantly, its ethno-humanist underpinnings. Following Anthony Appiah's (1997) assumption that even the very notion of "global" that is typically set off against "local" must be rooted in certain local experiences, the chapter goes on to challenge the binaries of home vs. world, and universal vs. local that precondition the debate on postcolonial cosmopolitanism. Against this, by way of the Malgudi example, the chapter highlights the innate capacity of local worlds to cultivate difference, inclusion, and hospitality outside of their perceived ethnocentrism.

Chapter 7, "(An)other Way of Being Human: Indigenous Alternatives to Postcolonial Humanism," engages with the indigenous peoples' movement leading to the United Nations Declaration on the Rights of the Indigenous Peoples (2007). From a provisionally post-Eurocentric framework, the chapter demonstrates that the indigenous peoples' movement succeeds in what postcolonial theory has conventionally set out to emancipate but has failed to do so. In particular, postcolonial theory challenges all Eurocentric and liberal humanist discourses on rights while appealing for a language that would articulate other ways of being human and humanist. Yet, recent trends in postcolonial theory have come to embrace the very language of (liberal) cosmopolitanism and humanism as viable alternatives for a postcolonial future. Drawing upon the principle thematic of the UN Declaration on the Rights of the Indigenous Peoples, the chapter suggests that the Declaration provides an alternative to postcolonial theory's revisionist humanism. As part of the international legal discourse, the Declaration is particularly noted for its political victories in the legitimization of collective rights in postcolonial societies. Furthermore, as the Universal Declaration of Human Rights remains an integral part of the collective rights of indigenous peoples, the chapter concludes that the indigenous peoples' movement succeeds in negotiating a language that would legitimize other ways of being human that are not necessarily adversarial or antithetical to Euro-American humanism.

As the debates on cosmopolitanism and rights are generally attributed to the dissolution of cultural nationalism and the weakening of the nation-state institutions, Chapter 8, "Margins of India: Kancha Ilaiah's Postcolonial 'Nationalogues'," draws attention to a latent surge of postcolonial nationalism in the newfound genre of "nationalogues." Featuring Kancha Ilaiah's *Why I am Not a Hindu* (1996) and *Post-Hindu India* (2009) as the prime examples of this genre, this chapter explores how Ilaiah's narratives defy the conventions of existing literary genres by virtue of the "ethical bind" they impose upon the reader. In particular, by forging the narrative strategy of a "collective monologue," the chapter suggests that Ilaiah's narratives resist all generic parameters set forth by postcolonial studies as well as autobiographical studies. In the process, the chapter highlights how Ilaiah's indigenism distances from the derivative nationalism of the Indian bourgeoisie that is inspired by anticolonial sentiments. Instead, as the chapter reveals, by turning to the generative forces of indigenous nationalism, Ilaiah's narratives signal a post-Eurocentric move, one that calls for the globalization of national attachments in the name of indigenous solidarity.

Notes

1. If the conventionalist view upholds the discursive complicity between text and real world (Lazarus 2011a: 195), then the realist view denies the imputation of the real world in textual discourse.

2. Here, by positioning the counter-empirical (renewed-literary) against the empirical (abuses of the literary), Said opens up a theoretical space for humanism at the expense of its methodology. See Radhakrishnan (2007).

3. The institutionalization of postcolonial studies today is generally attributed to "a web of professional practices that include publishing, book reviews, syllabus exchange, conferences" which produces "a pattern of privileging texts more readily responsive to 'authorized' questions and pedagogic imperatives" (Bahri 2003: 10).

4. Echoing these concerns from an economic point of view, Bill Ashcroft points to the resurgence of nationalism in an era of transnational economic dependency. The global financial meltdown in 2008, for instance, Ashcroft argues, has rekindled a certain national spirit as nation-states have been called to rescue, and as result, in countries such as India and China, the nation-state's prominence over economic authority has the potential to reshape the disintegrating cultural nationalism of their respective states. Since these nations are invariably linked to the global financial system, Ashcroft contends that they produce an excess of nation (transition), which allows for negotiating cultural nationalism beyond its national perimeter by means of economic power; see Ashcroft (2009: 12–13) and also my earlier discussion in Malreddy (2015: 5).

5. I have benefited from discussions with Frank Schulze-Engler, Goethe University Frankfurt on this aspect.

6. The Euro crisis has reduced economically marginalized countries, such as Portugal, Ireland, Greece, and Spain, to the status of internal colonies within Europe. Not only that these countries have seen a dramatic rise in reverse migration to their formal colonies, such as Brazil, Argentina, and Mozambique since 2009, their economies have grown increasingly dependent on the multinational firms operating from the non-Western world, such as China Three Gorges Corp, Piraeus Container, and Cosco (Marder 2013).

SECTION 1

Discourses: Orientalism, Terrorism, and Popular Culture

1

Orientalism(s) After 9/11*

As we enter the second decade after 9/11, it is becoming increasingly clear that the tragedy of that day has been hijacked into a casus belli for protracted wars and neocolonial geopolitics, and other clandestine operations led by the US and its allied forces around the globe. According to critics, taken together, 9/11 and the redemptive violence the event has since invoked have effectively replaced other major historical precedents of the 20th century (Lazarus 2006), including the Second World War and the Cold War. Orientalism, often colliding with racism, Islamophobia, selective prejudice, model minoritization, and other doctrines of civilizational difference, has been at the crux of these developments. Although the term "terrorism" is said to have undergone some notoriously "non-normative" conceptual mutations (Wheeler 2008), it has come to represent a nameless Oriental collective that stretches from the Saharan Tuareg in North Africa to the Solomon Islands in the Asia Pacific. Thus, if the discourse of terrorism is just another form of Orientalism (Morton 2007b), the Oriental collective that is glutted by seamlessly borderless terrorists can no longer be defined in terms of a fixed geographical entity.

Instead, the new Orient consists of elastic coordinates that are drawn against "terror and torture [that] always refer to the actions of others, never to ourselves" (Gregory 2007: 229). Consider, for instance, the case of Anders Behring Breivik, who is indirectly compared to that of "a caliph ... almost of the Middle Eastern variety" (Fisk cited in Dabashi 2011), but not "quite" a terrorist. Sure enough, hours after the news of Breivik's massacre broke out, media outlets across Europe mulled over a distinctly troubling question: why would Islamic terrorists target such a peace-loving

---

* This chapter was previously published in *Journal of Postcolonial Writing*, 2012. The text has been revised and modified, and edited for typographical errors, stylistic consistency, and sequential organization in order to make it suitable for inclusion in this book.

country as Norway? Four years after the tragedy, Breivik is certified as a "maverick," a "nut-ball," a "crazy-loner"—an excess of modernity and anomie or a combination of both—but not quite a terrorist. So rarely has the term "home-grown terrorist" been used, as in the case of Timothy McVeigh, that it appears as if "home" is congenitally incapable of breeding terrorists, let alone the ideological manure required for it. Thus, by definition, a terrorist is always already "foreign-grown," as it were, lurking "in the dreaded forest, wild steppe, fierce desert, mysterious mountains, and endless untamed darkness of the sea," while "moving surreptitiously across harsh terrain" (Ludden 2003: 1061).

Indeed, the coinage of "new terrorism" has been part and parcel of an incendiary discourse that is designed for the "sole" purpose of relegating "terror" to an alien domain. Unlike "old" terrorism, which is defined as a violent but unlawful form of political resistance, "new" or "categorical terrorism" refers to the nonconventional, nonpolitical, and even "irrational" violence that primarily targets Western civilians (Goodwin 2006). Furthermore, such "irrationality" of violence is said to be motivated by the terrorists' perception that civilian populations in the West are "complicit" with their state policies against them (ibid.). Accordingly, "new terrorism" encompasses all forms of militant resistance in the non-Western world under the sweeping category of terrorism; this now includes civil wars, armed nationalisms, guerrilla movements, and Maoist insurgencies, which were separate categories prior to the 9/11 attacks (Scanlan 2001). Thus, even if by the old account of the term Breivik cannot be considered a "terrorist," the concept of "new terrorism" accounts for precisely this situation: if a Westerner kills his fellow civilians, he is a "crazy-loner;" if an Oriental kills his fellow civilians, he is the good old terrorist; and if the same Oriental kills Western civilians, he is the "new" terrorist. Only Western ways of killing civilians—be it through war, invasion, or military conquest—are deemed superior, proper, and unquestionably legitimate (Porter 2009). The strategic cultivation of "death worlds," by which people in the postcolony are reduced to a perpetual state of "living dead," Achille Mbembe argues, can no longer be articulated in terms of biopower but of "necropower" of the imperial war machinery (Mbembe 2003; Morton 2007b). As war becomes a "potent site of Orientalism," "[i]n and through war, people formulate what it means to be Western or non-Western" (Porter 2009: 2).

This chapter aims to uncover the calibrated links between such resurgent forms of Orientalism and terrorism that course through post-9/11 academic discourses in general, but more specifically in theory (literary and cultural), text (fiction), and image (film and mass media). In literary and cultural theory, *Orientalism* has been the subject of sustained criticism for over two decades, but has become increasingly susceptible to attacks from its detractors and apologists alike, particularly since Edward Said's untimely death in 2003. Among other notable critics, Clifford (1988: 265–66) points to Said's (mis)use of Michel Foucault's "discourse" as a totalizing instrument of power, including his persistence to ascribe agency (as a "moral note") to Foucault's endlessly transgressing ground of both discursive power and agential capacities of its subjects. In what Homi Bhabha calls the "polarities of intentionality" (2004 [1994]: 102), Said's uneasy conflation of latent (content) and manifest (form) Orientalism clearly undermines the effectivity of Foucault's "discourse" (ibid., 103–04). By separating the dominant from the dominated in the process of actualizing the Orientalist discourse, Said turns Foucault's disproportionate position of the subject as both the recipient and an adversary of power into a symmetric, *"Pouvoir/Savoir"* (ibid., 103; emphasis in original), oppositional discourse. This situation, as Hamid Dabashi admits (mediated through Clifford), enables Said to take whatever he wants from Foucault, and abandon him as a "theoretical troublemaker" (Dabashi 2009: 93) when it comes to the question of agency. In Ahmad's (1991) view, Said's attribution of a unified "structure" to European history on the sole account of its literary canon is not only anti-Foucauldian, but it also says nothing about the Oriental subjects themselves. With all representation reduced to "textual representation"—and that, too, European textual representation—*Orientalism* becomes more or less obsessed with, say, what "effects" European re-presentation of Oriental texts may produce, than what Oriental texts themselves say about a given point in Oriental history (ibid., 291–96).

Among other intemperate critics, Ibn Warraq argues that *Orientalism*'s impact has been quite the opposite of what Said "misguidedly" attributes to the West: "[n]o conspiracy or dreams of empire, just a desire to learn" (2007: 161). For Varisco (2007), Said's militant political Orientalism deliberately misreads the satirical, theatrical, and even the self-critical undertones of the European literary canon. Confusing literary scholarship with imperial power, Irwin (2006) argues that Said provides no direct evidence of the implied compliance between Orientalism and colonialism. While Warraq and Varisco go on to dispute Said's mistranslation of Goethe, Habib (2005) challenges Said's uncritical treatment of Goethe's and Hegel's influence on Marx's writings on India and the Asiatic modes of production. Worse still, for Irwin and others, the pages of *Orientalism* are replete with multiple misreadings, mistranslations, and a selective deployment of favored sources that harness Said's ideological predispositions while willfully ignoring German, Hungarian, or Greek Orientalisms that are not directly linked to colonization.

Though most of the objections raised by Said's critics are well justified, it would seem that they serve cross-purposes; for all too often the failures of postcolonial studies are projected as the failures of *Orientalism*. This has largely to do with the biblical status given to *Orientalism* as some sort of "theoretical machine" (Said 2003 [1978]: 340) that churns out an endless stream of "partisan" critiques on account of postcolonial emancipation. As Timothy Brennan observes, this has led to an undue canonization of Said's rhetorical partisanism despite his stated admiration for humanism and anti-foundationalist politics (2000: 558–83). Though none of Said's "serious" critics go so far as denying that *Orientalism* (as an ideology) is an empty rhetoric, their chief bone of contention seems to be the misconceived foundationalism that Said's thesis has advocated by way of its reductionist take on the European literary canon. Nevertheless, postcolonial studies assumed a great deal of responsibility in addressing the limitations of *Orientalism* long before Said's critics had arrived on the scene. For instance, during the 1980s, critics, such as Bhabha, Prakash, and the subaltern studies exponents, carefully reworked Orientalism's "diachronic instability" to better explicate modes of agency and interruptions produced by the colonial subjects within the Orientalist discourse. On the other hand, Said's "multiple" misreadings of Foucault must be (re) read in light of Foucault's own vexed relationship with agency that Spivak has articulated elsewhere. And if Said should be chastised for overlooking Marx's "rhetorical intentions" (Clifford 1988: 270), I wonder why we cannot accord the same rhetorical leverage to Said that we are expected to accord to Marx in the name of the proletariat? In fact, most critics who dissect *Orientalism* from its cover page to index entries are woefully dismissive of Said's rhetorical intentions. After all, is Said's rhetorical partisanism more dangerous than the colonizer's own rhetorical humanism, and the violence it issued in the name of the civilizing mission? This is not to suggest that *Orientalism* is flawless, and when "a canvas [is] so broad and diverse, there is much with which to disagree and question" (Turner cited in Varisco 2007: xvi). Yet, Said's own shortcomings have inspired a plethora of book length studies on German Orientalism, military Orientalism, and internal Orientalism among others. Correspondingly, the notion of "post-Orientalism" emerged as a constellation of multiple

Orientalisms that are cultivated in the absence of a discernible hegemony and empire—"an empire with no hegemony" (Dabashi 2009: 106, 209). The following typology provides a glimpse of the various Orientalisms to have emerged in the past two decades:

Military Orientalism	War as a site of Orientalism, through war, strategies of war; the construction of the "wild east" by which Western fears, identity, and survival are constantly measured and reassessed (Porter 2009: 21).
American Orientalism	Borne out of indirect colonial contact; multicultural anxieties arising from the waves of emigration to the New World ("Yellow peril;" "Islamic peril"). With vested geopolitical interests in t he Middle East ("Islam"), including the post-War, Cold War expansionism in Africa (Liberia), Asia and the far East (Philippines, Vietnam) (Obeidat 1998).
Internal Orientalism	Orientalism cultivated by the Orientals themselves: "self-Orientalism" of the Turks; Turkish Orientalism of the Kurds; Black Orientalism of the Americas; and Tribal Orientalisms of South Asia. Inverted/internal Orientalism does not negate external Orientalism, and is generally cultivated by the well-meaning critics of Orientalism, including Western-educated local elites, monarchs, princely kings, and the postcolonial states themselves (Mazumdar, Kaiwar, and Labica 2009).
Re-Orientalism	Orientalism that is predominantly featured in the fictional works of the authors (such as Anita Desai, Arvind Adiga) from the Oriental societies. Such "Re-Orientalism" rewrites the ideological coordinates of Orientalism in such a way that it critiques the Self/Other distinctions of the classical Orientalism, and allows for repositioning Oriental subjects in "peripheral" positions that serve as "covert vantage points" (Lau and Mendes 2011: 4).
Parallel Orientalism	Orientalism within and among minorities (Koshy 2008), creation of "model minorities"—"good Muslims vs. bad Muslims"
Traveling Orientalism	Orientalism as a traveling theory, as in Brennan's contention that Said's Orientalism cannot be (mis)taken as a foundational text of postcolonialism or an originary critique of Orientalism. By extension, Orientalism as a discourse is received and reapplied well beyond its set geographical coordinates: Black Orientalism, Hispanic Orientalism, Irish Orientalism, etc. (Lennon 2004).

Pulp Orientalism	Orientalism in popular literature, news media, Hollywood blockbusters, pulp magazines, comics, and children books (Irwin 2011); Orientalism that is "dumbed-down" for mass consumption (newspaper reality).
Techno-Orientalism	"A practice of ascribing, erasing, and/or disavowing relationships between technology and Asian peoples and subjects" (Niu 2008: 74) in science fiction films, literature, video games, and cyberspace. Techno-Orientalism is a cult incarnation of pulp Orientalism; it consists of parody adverts, super-imposed images of Oriental figures, characters, and events (lynching videos of Saddam Hussein, re-enacted spoofs of bin Laden's capture) that are circulated across cyberspace.
Virtual Orientalism	Closely affiliated to the above category, "virtual Orientalism" is confined to the representations of Asian religions and its mythical figures of monks, nomads, and ascetics in the "visual forms of media" that "train the consumer to prefer visual representations" (Iwamura 2010: 7). Aesthetically reconfigured to re-present a refined image of the Asian religious figures, visual Orientalism "adds gravitas to the narrative and creates its own scene of virtual encounter" (ibid.).
Counter-Orientalism	Resistance to Orientalism through "diachronic instabilities" produced by the colonial subjects; anti-Orientalism of postcolonial novels (Codell and Macleod 1989; Scanlan 2001).
Economic Orientalism	The (exoticized) exaggerated class disparities as the generic trait of the Orient ("Millionaires vs. slum dogs"); "modernization" of the so-called Tiger Economies (Latham 1999); the perception of emerging Oriental economies as a threat to Western dominance.

Of its many variants, the post-Orientalism thesis generally asserts that (old) Orientalism was conceived, perceived, and analyzed diachronically, that is, the culmination of the self and other identities as the result of centuries of colonial rule and its divisive ideology (Koshy 2008). On the other hand, post-Orientalism is equally attentive to the synchronic formation of the self and other identities as not merely discursive repetition or the reproduction of previous inequalities, but as the outcome of a "serial minoritization" that takes place within and amongst minorities as a result of their oppressive relationship with the majority (ibid.). In other words, the post-Orientalism thesis seeks to explain othering, orientalizing, and racializing beyond the geographical and cultural coordinates set forth by the conventional Orientalist thesis.

According to Dabashi, if Orientalism is seen through the founding principles of the sociology of knowledge that no knowledge is possible "except as articulated within a specific *epistemic* ... frame of reference" (2009: 99; emphasis in original), Said's critique can be (re)read as a sociological exposition of the "integral relation between the social (colonial) conditions in which a mode of knowledge (Orientalism) is presumed valid and set in motion" (ibid., 97). This does not mean that the sociology of knowledge is static; paradigms do "shift" (Kuhn cited in Dabashi 2009: 101) as they set up new epistemic frames of reference. This view, Dabashi asserts, enables us "to make distinction among a variety of phases and mutations of Orientalisms, in plural, that are otherwise treated identically in [Said's] *Orientalism*" (ibid., 102). The Orientalism of the Greek era that is directed at the Persians, Dabashi affirms, is based on rivalry; the confrontation between the Ottoman and the European empires is equally inflected by fear and alien threats. These two phases are categorically different from the sort of Orientalism Said diagnosed under the pretext of colonialism. Yet, by the time Orientalism appeared, the literary Orientalist scholarship has "exhausted its inner creative power," having "done its active or implicit services to European colonialism" (ibid.). In what Dabashi calls *epistemic endosmosis,* the literary phase gave way to post-Orientalism through area studies, think tanks, geopolitics, and so on, that are "conducive to various manners of *disposable knowledge production*— predicated on no enduring or legitimate episteme, ... that provide instant gratification and are then disposed of after one use only" (ibid., 213; emphasis in original).

Correspondingly, Abdulla Al-Dabbagh points out the distinct phases in the development of Orientalist ideology. First, Orientalism of the classical era—from early Greek encounters with Persia to the Enlightenment period—is not solely confined to the East/West distinctions. The classical phase was followed by a proliferation of "oriental studies [that] do not belong to any general frame, but must draw their concepts and methods of analysis from the absolute specificities of the East, whether these be historical or philosophical, religious or national" (Al-Dabbagh 2010: 2). Though this stage did not contribute to a "deliberate distortion intended to insult and to antagonise" (ibid.) the Orient, the third stage is characterized by a certain positivist Orientalism of the colonial advent and Enlightenment: "[T]he works of the orientalists ... [that] provide the *only basis* for understanding the East since the oriental is incapable of scientific study" (ibid., 3; emphasis in original). The more hostile, antagonistic discourse, Al-Dabbagh maintains, "did not begin until the last decades of the last century, as Orientalism entered its declining phase" (2010: 4).

Complementing these two perspectives, Mazumdar et al. (2009) demarcate three specific coordinates of Orientalism. The first coordinate can be traced to 17th-century cartographers, such as John Speed and Nicolo Lombardi among others, who pioneered a certain "metageography (space) and metahistory (time) that function as the space-time coordinates around which the scaffolding of Orientalism is built up" (ibid., 19). This phase of Orientalism identified Eurasia as a "contagious landmass," and initially drew a map of the Americas as the land of "Indias Occidentales" (ibid., 20). The second coordinate is perhaps more "narrowly" linked to colonial rule; it encompasses a diverse body of historical, ethnological, and philosophical writings on the Orient from late 18th century onward. Theories, such as Adam Smith's "moral sentiments," Henry Maine's "ancient law," or Montesquieu's "Oriental despotism," have all paved way to "the quasi-organicist ideas of a hierarchy of human groups according to certain universalizing criteria" (ibid., 26). And not all this was associated with empire building, unlike Said's annexation of organicism to colonial rule (ibid.). Finally, the third coordinate refers to "a set of antinomies that underpin European universalism and everybody else's particularisms that constitute, as it were, the formal structure of Orientalism" (ibid., 19). This structure, in turn, was accepted by the third world elite in the process of postcolonial nation formation.

Thus, a post-Orientalist approach enables a demarcation of the mutating qualities of the dominant discourse that is often confused with the "new Orientalism" of the post-9/11 era, one that is best exemplified in Bernard Lewis' (in)famous exhortation that Islam is a failed civilization (2002 [2001]: 152–158). With Islam as its target, Almond (2007) asserts that new Orientalism is cultivated by the liberal-minded advocates of assimilationist policies who exoticize difference in the name of empathy and solidarity. For Almond, postmodern critics are a good example of this, invoking as they do the cultural symbolism of the Islamicate in the guise of pluralist/anti-essentialist politics. In social theory, Baudrillard's (2003) notion of 9/11 as a spectral moment, Virilio's (2002) image of a de-politicized digital meaning of the event, and Žižek's (2002) allegory of the Other as "the desert of the real" have also evoked an entirely new system of coding and decoding Oriental societies and cultures since 9/11.

Correspondingly, the constellation of new Orientalism, post-Orientalism, and anti-imperialist critiques has emerged as the signature theme of post-9/11 literature, film, mass media, and other venues of popular culture.

Crime fiction, thrillers, and genre novels, such as Slimane Benaissa's *The Last Night of a Damned Soul* (2004), Dan Fesperman's *The Warlord's Son* (2004), Richard Clarke's *The Scorpion's Gate* (2006), and Robert Baer's *Blow the House Down* (2006), portray the Orient as a *terra incognita* of adventure and exploration, a collective cultural space that is subject to spying and suspicion, replete with religious fanatics who succumb to the irrational lure of Islam. Though novels and short fictions, such as Philip Roth's *The Plot Against America* (2004), Jonathan Safran Foer's *Extremely Loud and Incredibly Close* (2005), Don DeLillo's *Falling Man* (2007), John Updike's *Terrorist* (2006), Joseph O'Neill's *Netherland* (2008), and Teddy Wayne's *Kapitoil* (2010), appear to be liberal modernist in outlook, their implied obsession with the event (9/11), the Twin Towers, the physical space of New York City, public grief, and national trauma implicate an external force (presumably the Oriental world) as the reasoning device for the tragedy that is thrust upon this innocent (Western) world. But it is perhaps Ian McEwan's *Saturday* (2005), Salman Rushdie's *Shalimar the Clown* (2005), Kiran Desai's *The Inheritance of Loss* (2006), Yasmina Khadra's *The Attack* (2006), and Mohsin Hamid's *The Reluctant Fundamentalist* (2007), which are among the most nuanced, yet sensible, critiques of Orientalism and imperialism to have appeared after 9/11. They challenge populist conceptions of terror as an irrational ideology of revenge and redemption by unmasking the legacies (as "inheritance") of colonialism, the systematic destruction of the political sphere as well as cultural institutions that fed into terrorist causes in the first place.

In the domain of images and imaging, however, the Internet, films, and video games have become more or less entrenched in the popular imagination as the simulated twins of the real war, while satellite images and manipulated video evidence were used to justify the wars in Afghanistan and Iraq. Although Orientalism is not new to Hollywood, feature films such as *United 93* (2006), *World Trade Center* (2006), *In the Valley of Elah* (2007), *Lions for Lambs* (2007), and *The Hurt Locker* (2008), have induced an entirely new set of technical sensibilities: by allocating minimum "screen time" to the enemy, the suffering of the self is melodramatized to a maximum effect. There are, however, a few notable exceptions to this media mirage of Orientalism both within and outside of mainstream cinema: *Green Zone* (2010) *Paradise Now* (2005), *The Road to Guantanamo* (2006), *The Messenger* (2009), and *My Name is Khan* (2010). The various typologies and mutations of Orientalism outlined in this chapter provide the genealogical foundation for the exposition of the complicity and collusion between Orientalism and terrorism in the following chapters.

2

Imagining the Terrorist:
A Post-Orientalist Inquiry*

Introduction

Although the Middle East has become practically synonymous with "terrorism" since 9/11, the US-led global "war on terror" has strategically demarcated all the Islamic-led political dissents throughout Asia as potentially "terrorist," replete with "irrationally religious people who threaten civilization with deadly chaos" (Ludden 2003: 1061). Today, a complex network of area studies, counterterrorism studies, and state-sponsored think tanks have unpacked a "new terrorism"[1] discourse that draws connections between Islamist groups in Bangladesh, Sri Lanka, Pakistan, Indonesia, India, Malaysia, Thailand, Mali, and the Al-Qaeda terrorist nexus. According to critics, while these developments have contributed to the spectralization of 9/11 as a "world-historical" event (Lazarus 2006), their ideological underpinnings have complex genealogical precedents. It is not, for instance, that the 9/11 attacks have resulted in an entirely new corpus of imperialist sensibilities, but merely strengthened the pre-existing anxieties about the Orient, adding fuel to the redemptive violence triggered by the counterterrorism campaign (Salaita 2005; Sivanandan 2006).

Here, if such pre-existing anxieties refer to an enduring episteme of Orientalism, then Hamid Dabashi's thesis on post-Orientalism (2009) holds particular relevance to the articulation of its temporal character that corresponds to, if not is reinforced by, a singular event (9/11).

* This chapter was previously published in *Kasarinlan: Philippine Journal of Third World Studies*, 2008. This text has been edited for typographical errors, stylistic consistency, and sequential organization in order to make it suitable for inclusion in this book.

For Dabashi (2009: 213), a salient aspect of post-Orientalism is its tenuous and disposable function in the absence of a linear epistemic trajectory or continuity, providing "instant gratification" for a given hegemonic discourse to uphold its legitimacy by way of contorting, mutating, and reapplying the master discourses of colonialism, imperialism, and post-9/11 militarism. For instance, although 18th- and 19th-century discourses on Orientalism encompassed a whole host of Oriental societies and cultures—from Mongolia to the Philippines, and to the Pacific Islands—the post-9/11 Orientalism is characterized by an urgency to conflate (and communicate) "threat" with "Otherness," wherein only its partial signifiers—skin color, specific phenotypes—become the objects of a renewed discourse.

Today, the list of suspect terrorist countries compiled by the US government consists of organizations and states across four continents—Cuba, Iran, North Korea, and Syria—although much of its "on ground" counterterrorism operations are carried out in select parts of South Asia, Southeast Asia, and the Middle East. Not only that such additive quality of "mapping terrorism" points to a constant realignment of Orientalism's geopolitical coordinates which can be disposed after use (Dabashi 2009: 213), but it entails complex constellations of biopolitical and necropolitical engineering[2] by means of which post-Orientalism seeps into populist imagination. An understanding of these discursive constellations requires a careful reading of the transgressive nature of Orientalist epistemologies from one era to another, from one discipline to the other, and in the context of this chapter, from the 18th-century Orientalist theses on Indian village communities to the 9/11 attacks. Accordingly, this chapter aims to foreground the mutations, alterations, and digressions within the Orientalist episteme from cultural and geographical mapping to criminalizing—its uses, abuses, and after-uses—through select examples from Indian history, anthropology, and area studies.

In developing my arguments on the cultural mapping of Orientalism, however, I will restrict my examples to the Indian case—not only because it is impossible to offer a consolidating cultural narrative of the Orient in the space available here, but just(ly) because India is touted as the heartland of all colonialisms and, for that reason, a social laboratory of control, governance, and other wild experimentations (Kapila 2007). Having said that, I shall not confine my analysis on the geopolitics of Orientalism to the Indian case, for the discourse on terrorism has a global and multinational character, albeit essentialist, in that sense Orientalist, implications (Godlewska and Smith 1994; Hardt and Negri 2000). It is, thus, important that a larger milieu of events and evidence is taken into consideration.

Anthropology and Indian Orientalism

Orientalist scholarship since the 18th century has constructed the caste system[3] as a unique social category, which had no parallel in the West. This almost alien perspective of Indian social structures has portrayed the caste system as a rigid, if not mystic, systemic pattern of social relation that is supported by religion, custom, and the collective nature of the "village communities" in the 18th and 19th centuries (Dumont 1966; Maine 1876; Wilks 1810). As Dumont (1966: 64–75) has argued, both the discursive and empirical precedents for the "village community" as a social institution were inspired by the revenue settlement interests of the colonial administration, which in turn helped reinforce the theories on caste hierarchies and their economic function in the administrative literature of the era. In the pseudo-ethnographic reports of the early 19th century (1806–57), the notion of village community is vaguely described as a community of brotherhood or an independent republic, which held the internal unity of Indian villages while practicing "communal production" (Maine 1876: 176–77). In the absence of private property or the very notion of private ownership, India at large is understood as a collection of villages that remained isolated from civilization and the outer world (Mukherjee 1996: 69). Yet, the communal spirit of the Indian village was celebrated as the epitome of Indian civilization that was presumably held by the "organic unity" of the caste and its constituent *jajmani* (caste-based division of occupations) system (Maine 1876: 57; Wiser 1936). These theories, as critics have suggested (Mukherjee 1996; Dumont 1966), were developed against the backdrop of pan-Orientalist desires of "Victorian life to be speculative" (Mukherjee 1996: 67) and "Victorian-evolutionary ideas and preoccupation," which sought to account for "the infancy of society" or the "remnants" of Europe's past (Dumont 1966: 11).[4]

Henry Sumner Maine, a British jurist and historian, played an instrumental role in drawing the theory of Indian village community into "the circle of world history" (ibid.). Maine, who spent a considerable amount of time in India in the 1860s, was a staunch advocate of Darwinism, and had admittedly less faith in the idea of ethnography and dealing with "ignorant puzzled peasants" than in the theories of "great European thinkers" on India and even the "most hurried generalizations by the great Indian administrators" (Maine cited in Mukherjee 1996: 71). Subsequently, his views on the Indian villages' organic unity led him to theorize that:

[a]s we move eastwards through the German and Slavonic countries this primitive social organism grows stronger and stronger. It is plainly discernible under the superficial crust of Mussulman institutions, until in India it emerges in its most ancient form as the village community, a brotherhood of self-styled kinsmen settled on a space of land. (Mukherjee 1996: 72)

While Maine's theories on the village communities in India provided the raw material for his subsequent pan-Orientalist theories (Maine 1861; Maine 1876)—which Edward Said equated with latent Orientalism's shared desire among European thinkers to conceive the Orient as a homogenous entity—for the British administrators of the era they had an immense practical use (Dirks 2001).

Here, my interest in the discussion on the Indian village community, caste, and agrarian structure is geared toward uncovering the morphing nature of the Orientalist discourse between its latent (Orient as desire), manifest (Orient as an object of knowledge), and institutional (Orient as a site of militant action) trajectories. In due course, my focus moves from the pan-Orientalist constructions of India to the biopolitical control of village communities, through to the criminalization of Indian castes and tribes in the aftermath of the 1857 Sepoy revolt.

Even before Maine's theories gained purchase in the "circles of world history," Mark Wilks's *Historical Sketches of South India* (1810) provided the necessary theoretical condiments to the colonial bureaucrats in Southern and Central India to (re)engineer Indian castes for practical use (Bates 1995).[5] The demarcation of caste as India's cultural and genetic boundary, and its transformation and categorization were carefully deployed to introduce new land-tenure systems, revenue collection, and privatization of property, while somehow "preserving" the spirit of the Indian organic unity. Mark Wilks, for instance, was in full agreement with the then governor of Madras, Thomas Munro, that the ryotwari system of revenue collection, which established direct link between the cultivator and the state, could be implemented without disrupting the communal spirit of the Indian village community. But the very notion of village community as a site of communal production or a miniature communist republic had little or no ethnographic merits. As Dumont's analysis (1966: 4–14) reveals, the vague description of 12 village specialists of the village community was first mentioned in a report by Munro in 1806, which was reproduced verbatim by Wilks in 1810. Both Munro's and Wilks's definitions and descriptions are adopted (with slight variations) in various administrative reports by W.K. Firminger in 1812, Mountstuart Elphinstone in 1819 and Karl Marx in 1853, Henry Maine in 1876, and William Wiser in 1936 (Dumont 1966). With the exception of Karl Marx's adaptation of the Indian village community, all the rest of the accounts were both directly and indirectly invoked to justify the implementation of the ryotwari system in Madras during Munro's tenure as a governor. Thus, for Dumont (1966: 3), the observations on village communities are not based on individual findings but as a reiteration of an ill-conceived theme in the colonial archive: "[W]e are dealing with something like a myth, a piece of belief widely shared among the administrators of the period."[6]

As Inden (1986; 1990) has argued, such reductionist and pseudo-scientific views of caste and Indian social structure have helped British colonialism to construct a powerful social science discourse on the grounds of religiosity, hierarchies, and the perceived disunity of Indian village communities to construct a coherent national community. In what Said calls the "synchronic essentialism" (2003 [1978]: 240) of Orientalism,[7] such discourses could not be conceived as passive instruments of knowledge, but were also pressed into institutional practice and service (Prakash 1995: 207–09). In line with both Inden's and Said's theses, in *Castes of Mind* (2001), Nicholas Dirks has argued that census reports, anthropological knowledge, and anthropometric theories in the 19th century have been effectively used to (re)invent castes where they did not exist. The ascription of caste status for the Thuggees (so-called "traveling thieves") in the 1830s is one such invention; once conceived to be redundant to the harmonious model of Indian village community, they were labeled as inherently criminal (Sleeman 2011 [1836]). These processes remained complicit with the institutionalization of caste hierarchies, such as the replacement of local kingships, biopolitical control of castes, and the recruitment of castes into colonial service in accordance with the perceived benefits of the Indian social hierarchy (Dirks 2001). For instance, throughout the 19th century, castes, such as Rajputs in North India and kshatriyas and other "military castes" in the South, were recruited into the provincial military regiments. Brahmins, the only English-educated class, were favored in bureaucracy. These efforts were strengthened by the production of caste- and tribe-based censuses for local-level administrators, army officers, land and plantation owners, as well as "others with the information they felt necessary to know and to manage the peasants, sepoys, clerks, and coolies who fell under their control" (McBratney 2005: 153). In an attempt to "reinstitute" the autonomy of the Indian village community and its agrarian structures, castes and tribes were labeled "criminal," and were prevented from disrupting the self-contained domain of the jajmani system.

But it is not until the 1857 Sepoy Revolt that the "criminalization" of Indian castes and tribes emerged as a full-fledged biopolitical project (Tickell 2012). While the Thuggees of North India already bore the tag of "hereditary" criminal castes who displayed occult symbolism, codes, and customs in 1859, the accounts of W.J. Hatch described Kuravers as "hereditary criminals" (Lal 1995). During the same era, railway robbers were identified in southern India, whose criminal vocation was often dubbed as a caste or tribal entitlement (Naidu 1915).

Following a circular issued by the Asiatic Society of Bengal in 1866, ethnologists C.J. Lyall and George Campbell embarked on a hunt for "inferior and helot" tribes, the "wandering tribes," or the "waifs and relics of aboriginal tribes" across India (Bates 1995: 18–19). These efforts yielded in a grand-scale physiological project by respective regional commissioners who were commissioned to gather data on Indian "specimens" by deploying anthropometric measures, including the measurements of height; size of nose, skull, arm, lower arm, thigh, and leg; diet; beard and mustache; and so forth (Bates 1995: 11–20; Freitag 1991: 246–48). Italian criminologist Lombroso's theories on "killer footprints" and creatures who barely escape their "bestial origins" have had a boundless influence on Indian ethnologists and police departments of that era.[8] Anthropometry became an active pursuit in policing the Indian body, and a whole range of castes or sub-castes, often interchangeable with tribes and gangs, have eventually been identified as being "congenitally" criminal. As Meena Radhakrishna states: "In the popular ethnographic literature of the period, a sketch was drawn of a criminal who possessed not just bizarre social customs, but a strange body and psyche as well 'which had criminality written all over'" (2001: 4).

Similarly, the earlier works of Kali Kumar Das, a British educated phrenologist, had set out to prove that criminal mental capacities were congenital and humanity by nature was unequal (Kapila 2007: 497). Das's theses were not only brought into anthropometric limelight, but were also used to "observe" heads of criminals in the Chandernagore jail (ibid.). Between 1889 and 1912, a wandering caste or tribe called Sansiahs became a major concern of the British administration (Freitag 1991: 244–46). In 1887, a local police officer from the Oudh wrote that Sansiahs could be found all over India, and they are believed to be not only "'ruthless in the destruction of human life', committing 'violence and even murder wantonly' but were also 'cowardly except when in overpowering numbers'" (ibid., 246). And by the 1870s, the administrators of the era instituted these forms of identities into criminal code (ibid., 247).

A few decades later (1901–10), Edger Thurston and H.H. Risely, both colonial ethnologists, became immersed in developing a scientific method of identifying criminal castes informed by anthropometry in South and Central India (Bates 1995: 21–23; Dirks 2001). Subsequent census and ethnological reports went on to identify the Maravars and Kallars (heriditary thieves and robberers) in Tamil Nadu as fierce groups "with great military prowess and, later on, for [their] considerable 'criminal' proclivities" (Dirks 1993 [1987]: 72). Such criminal proclivities bore testimony to the pre-existing notions of these groups as "[o]f strong limbs and hardy frames and fierce-looking as tigers … the blood-thirsty Maravar, armed with the bow bound with leather, … shoot their arrows at poor and defenseless travellers, from whom they can steal nothing, only to feast their eyes on the quivering limbs of their victims" (Kanakasabhai 1965: 42–43).

Instigated by the anthropometric evidence, the various civil and criminal codes adopted by the British Raj between 1859 and 1871 stipulated and then subjected the criminalized castes to a strict discipline. They were required to report to local police authorities, attend a daily roll call, and possess passes to enter other territories. As Lal (1995: xi) notes, "surveillance and monitoring of the habitually criminal classes" were further aided by "innovations such as photography and fingerprinting." In 1904, the Thuggee and Dacoity Department, which was originally set to annihilate "thugs," was altogether abolished, having been replaced by the Criminal Intelligence Department. Subsequently, following the amendments of the Criminal Tribes Act in 1911, which was extended to the Madras Presidency to control the Kallars in particular, some 237 tribes were identified as criminal and treated accordingly (Tolen 1991: 110). By controlling and criminalizing castes, it was believed that "the nefarious influence of the Brahmins and maulvis," which supposedly knit the caste system and the Indian despotism in general, could decisively be removed (Lal 1995: viii). As Raheja (1996: 495) states, "the colonial imagination had seized upon caste identities as a means of understanding and controlling the Indian population after the blow to administrative complacency occasioned in 1857."

It is against this very backdrop of criminal threats, espionage, and the dangers presented by unidentified, half-bred castes or even outcastes that Rudyard Kipling's *Kim* (1901) and Arthur Conan Doyle's *The Sign of Four* (1890) gained prominence. Not only did Kipling extend his support to Major General Frederick Roberts's, the Commander-in-Chief of the Indian Army, call for "a more robust defense of Empire" (Moran and Johnson 2010: 2), but he was granted unlimited access to the military and intelligence records of the Raj by virtue of his close relationship with the Major (Moran and Johnson 2010: 5). Although a better part of Kipling's novel deals with the external threats to the Raj, arising from the Muslim kingdoms and the so-called Great Game led by the Franco-Russian alliance, its espionage plot was equally motivated by the Indian Army's lack of faith in the police service and the author's deep distrust for, in the words of Lord Roberts, "[n]ative troops" (Roberts cited in Moran and Johnson 2010: 7). It, thus, comes as no surprise that in 1901, Frederick Roberts had asked Kipling to "write some stirring lines to bring home to the public the danger of allowing ourselves to a second time in the same risky position without any properly trained troops in the country" (ibid.). Although Doyle's involvement in the affairs of the Raj is less implicit, as John McBratney (2005: 155) argues, his depiction of Indian criminal and racial types closely espouses the ethnographic observations made in the 1881 *Imperial Gazetteer of India*, which in itself is modeled after the 1871 India-wide census. The dramatic setting of *The Sign of Four*, too,—the Andaman Islands—heavily draws upon the "scientific and pseudo-scientific" observations of the disciplines "such as physiognomy, pathognomy, phrenology, and criminal anthropology" (ibid.). Like Kipling, Doyle reassures the moral high ground of the colonial rule, while repeatedly criminalizing and racializing the insurgents as "murderers," "hello hounds," "fanatics," and "devil's worshippers" (ibid., 156–57). In sum, Doyle's text paints the rebels of the 1857 mutiny "not as opponents of a political order against which they might have a justifiable grievance but as disturbers of a social order that they regard with a motiveless malignity" (ibid., 157).

Taken together, the presumed lack of individuality, property ownership, and governance structure are taken as an adequate proxy for despotism. Caste, village communities, and religion were portrayed as social infirmities of the Indians who were effectively "lazy" and disengaged them from the capacity to rule or rebel politically, but only criminally. In fact, most political protests were immediately construed as criminal acts. The 1922 Chauri Chaura incident, the suppression of Naxalite minorities in Telangana and Tebaga, and Srikakulam tribal insurgents in the early 20th century were soundly informed by the colonial criminology (Tolen 1991; Ramanujam 1942). Thus, cultural engineering was meant to be a mere instrument in the grand project of rescuing the native subjects from the shackles of despotism and decadence.

Although not all colonial experiences and historical processes and transformations across societies and cultures were the same, the social engineering of India has been, by and large, the dominant trope of comparative colonialisms. For instance, the four-fold division of Indian castes influenced "the present-day taxonomy of seven racial/physical types" (McBratney 2005: 152). Anthropological, anthropometric, and comparative linguistics from Germany to Italy and to India exchanged the knowledge on the natives of all colonialisms (Driver and Gillian 1992). From Malabar's dacoits to Balinese "beasts," the social engineering of Indians was "an arrangement that, given the fundamental immutability of type posited by physical anthropology, would likely last for all time" (McBratney 2005: 152). The implications of such racial anthropology in the Orient gained support from the geographical and travel narratives of European travelers of the preceding centuries. William Hodges's works, for instance, painted India, the world of Pacific and Southeast Asia as a singular geocultural entity. The pet theories of H.H. Wilson, a prominent Orientalist, remained central to the "global comparisons between so-called races [that] became embedded with the increasing planetary expansion of the British Empire" (Kapila 2007: 481). And, perhaps, it would be a great disservice to Wilson's textual authority at length should we reduce his pan-Oriental paradigm into a single statement: "[T]he innate, savage-like character not only of Muslims, but inherent in the very nature and character of the 'Asiatic'" (ibid., 501).

Geography, Geopolitics, and Post-9/11 Orientalism

Although it was anthropology that contributed to the culturalist notions of Self and Other, its influence on geography and the spatial characterization of its determinants have not received scholarly attention during the colonial period. Its relationship with the implied geographic origins and cultural characteristics—often associated with landscapes, environments, and other ecological characteristics—became popular only in the first half of the 20th century. In line with the colonial anthropological vision, the imperialist mapping of social geography meant that race is seen:

> both to complement and to counter national formation and character. Those whose "racial origins" are considered geographically somehow to coincide with national territory (or its colonial extension) are deemed to belong to the nation. (Goldberg 2009: 7)

In other words, territorial bounds had to be attributed to, or derived from, the discursive genealogies of the race–culture nexus in anthropology. To that, it was in the last phase of European colonialism that a fruitful combination between anthropology and geography yielded pseudoscientific disciplines such as anthropometric cartography and "ethnoclimatology" (Driver and Gillian 1992; Livingstone 1991). These disciplines, with distinct colonial origins, sought to map "variations in human physiognomy," and the relationship between "climates and human anatomy" (Griffin 2013: 158).[9] The race, culture, and climate nexus, which are generally attributed to the scientific travel writings of Alexander Von Humboldt at the outset of the 19th century (Motyl 2001: 185) assumed new disciplinary forms and wider empirically currency "[a]t the hands of geographers," which "began with the leap from anthropoclimatology to anthropometric cartography" (ibid.). This leap entailed a scientific project, built on the existing racial typologies of anthropology, of establishing "not only boundaries between people, but allegedly casual relationships from the physical and natural world to the cultural" (ibid.). It is under the very scientific guise of "racial mapping of people according to the principle that climate determines races" (ibid.) that the modern census and modern survey techniques in the colonial world took shape. These developments played a decisive role in mapping national borders both in the metropolis and the colony, wherein the "very act of mapping cultural differences suggested the possibility of boundaries where none had existed before" (ibid., 186).

The institutional origins of quasi-academic disciplines, such as Geographical Information Systems (GIS) in the 1960s, and "geopolitics" in the 1970s, had only added "ammunition to the already well developed theoretical campaign to demote nation from a primordial manifestation of human society to, at best, a construction of the modern state or an imperative of capitalism" (ibid.). "Geopolitics" in particular, with its unique discursive constellations of culture and space, race and territory, anthropology and geography, emerged as an intuitional discourse: "an act of geographical violence through which space was explored, reconstructed, re-named and controlled" (Crush 1994: 337). In this sense, the emergence of new disciplinary conventions became chiefly responsible for: (a) the emergence of (geo)political fissures between the first world and the third world, (b) a discourse of international security, and (c) the geopolitical construction of the Orient as the terrorist homeland.

While the term "geopolitics" has been popularized by Henry Kissinger in the 1970s (Hepple 1986), its ideological underpinnings have a longer history. In Britain, the writings of imperial and military scholars, such as

Halford J. Mackinder, James Rennell, and Robert Orme, were used as geopolitical devices to controlling seas for martime trade and military expansion. But it was essentially the American geographers Isaiah Bowman and Nicholas Spykman who sought to place geography in service of a global democratic doctrine (Mamadouh 1998: 238).

After the formal end of colonialism, the rise of new nation-states challenged the pre-existing geographic order of the world. The new cartographic anxieties featured prominently in the debates on national security (Ludden 2003: 1067) as the rise and fall of World Wars instilled fear and instability in Europe; in the metropolis, both external and internal margins required protection from alien threats. Somehow or the other, geographical boundaries needed to be drawn as "those whose geo-phenotypes obviously place them originally (from) elsewhere are all too often considered to pollute or potentially to terrorize the national space, with debilitating and even deadly effect" (Goldberg 2009: 7). Once "all histories of all peoples have come to appear inside national maps" (Ludden 2003: 1058), grafting ethnic and racial affiliations to national identities posed an impossible challenge to geography.

With the end of the First World War, as most Empires ceased to exist, the geographers of the era believed that "[a]t no time in the history of Europe have political boundaries more closely expressed the lines of ethnic division" (Bowman cited in Smith 2003: 177). These post-war ethnic sensibilities, Bowman believed, presented an ideal opportunity for imperialist (and external) intervention. To bring order into disorder, Bowman believed that "[e]mpire builders must think in terms of space as well as time" (ibid., 458).

Between 1915 and 1935, Bowman spearheaded the production of the Millionth Map at the behest of the American Geographical Society. He took professional pride in its makers that they had "gone out into the unknown and vanquished and charted it" ... and the resulting map represents not only the "indomitable determination of men to know and to master the world," but also "the forces of civilization advancing in spite of high barriers" (ibid., 97). Subsequently, with the help of French and British geographers, Bowman went on to produce intelligence information for the American government and helped develop a geo-ideological strategy for drawing the coordinates of the "New World" (ibid., 98–100). As with the emergence of the New World, alongside Europe and its formal Empires as the epicenter of post-war geopolitics, socialist societies were labeled as the second world, while the former colonies were relegated to the "third world" category (Ludden 2003: 1057–78).

Although the security issue remained central to the creation of the three worlds, it became prominent only after the Cold War. However, during the heyday of the Soviet Union itself, the question of international security emerged, as evinced in the modernization propaganda by the Americans against the socialist forces from the Soviet Union (Baber 2001). After the collapse of the Soviet Union, the remnants of socialism and its militant psyche in the Asian region presented a great threat to Europe as well as to the New World. To map these threats, mostly during the 1980s and 1990s, many regional studies experts turned their attention to conflicts and border disputes. According to Mamadouh (1998), much-studied countries and regions in this regard were Turkey, Afghanistan, Iran, the Gulf States, the Persian Gulf, and regions that were directly or indirectly influenced by socialist politics, such as India, Central Asia, East Asia, South Asia, and Cuba in which the major security concerns were the Kurds, Kashmir, China-Taiwan conflict, and so forth (see also Hafeznia 1994; Martel 1991). The post-Cold War geopolitical strategy "reduced conflicts to an ideological struggle between Good and Evil," and the territorial disputes concerning resources and interethnic conflict that affected the integrity of national boundaries were neglected, thus geopolitical strategies silently fell into abeyance (Mamadouh 1998: 238).

Following this line of inquiry, Luttwak (1993)—another American geographer—proposed a "geostrategy" by combining economic and military interests in the third world. Still, more traditional geostrategic approaches combining scholarship, and security and military interests have been prevalent as late as the 1990s (Brzezinski 1997; Kemp and Harkavy 1997). It is about the same time that the emergence of area studies as a subdiscipline of geography, or just as a variant of geopolitics, began remapping continental boundaries in the interest of strategic imperialism. America drew maps of Asia by "lumping countries into regions that officially define East, Southeast, Central, and South Asia" (Ludden 2003: 1059). In Ahmed Rashid's assessment, the cartographies of Asian and Central Asian countries were drawn "not along geographic or ethnic lines but in ways that seemed likeliest to suppress dissent, dividing clans, villages, and ethnic groups" (2002: 36). Perhaps the most glaring example of this has been the mapping of the Tajik territories as part of Uzbekistan despite their historical and cultural attachment to Bukhara and Samarkhand (ibid.). The mobility of "problematic" and "politically marginalized" ethnic nationalities as a result of the Cold War, in a majority of cases, was deemed to be an imminent danger to both national and international security (Ludden 2003: 1060–62). The fear of the recalcitrant political Other, in fact, became the crux of the subsequent geopolitics in determining which culture belonged where and, more important, which culture should belong where.

But it is not until the Gulf War in the 1990s that the Arab world, as a collective cultural entity, became a prominent discourse. To this, the pretext was the Iran hostage crisis in 1979–80, which beamed the popular "Muslim" terrorist image across the world for the first time, and thus was merged, albeit intriguingly, into the Arab world (McAlister 2001: 200). For the same reason, the Arab world of the 1960s and 1970s became "the Islamic world" in the 1980s (Jacobson 2002: 312). Following the 9/11 terrorist attacks, Islam, Arabs, Iran, and terrorism became synonymous with the Middle East in populist terms, although more Muslims live in Africa, and South and Southeast Asia (Palat 2004b). Subsequently, Afghanistan and Pakistan have been suddenly relocated into the Middle East for its perceived cultural association with Islam.

The strategic cultivation of the Muslim world as a collective terrorist world by states and think tanks is clearly informed by contemporary geographers and area studies scholars, although the criminalization of the Orient has undoubtedly had adherents in the earlier Orientalist fantasies. In an attempt to trace the expansion of al-Qaeda into East Asian countries, a good deal of studies since 9/11 have been devoted to exploring terrorist organizations in Indonesia, Malaysia, Southern Thailand, Southern Philippines, including Singapore and Brunei (Veness 2001; Gunaratana 2005; Rodell 2005). Zachary Abuza's *Militant Islam in Southeast Asia: Crucible of Terror* (2003) and Paul Smith's *Terrorism and Violence in Southeast Asia* (2005) also fall under this category. By ignoring the ethnopolitical context of the militant organizations in Southeast Asia, many areas studies approaches remain complicit with select modes of re-Orientalism, while reinforcing the institutionalist discourses on counterterrorism (Connors 2006). In Barber's (2003) view, not only such studies connecting local struggles with the al-Qaeda network were supported by weak evidence, but they have most categorically undermined the historical contexts of internal and external colonialism in Southeast Asia, hence joining the ranks of the populist diatribe of "terror from the East." Drawing on this "outer hazard" thesis, Barber (2003: 117) argues that corruption, weak and undemocratic regimes, resulting from the failed promises of postcolonial nation building and a handful of marginalized states, affected by American policies are considered an adequate justification for terrorism and destruction. Posed in this way, poverty, violence, ecology, and irrationality become the dominant features of terrorism from the East, whereas in fact "the global spread of markets and democracy is a principal aggravating cause of group hatred and ethnic violence" (Chua 2003: 9).

The religious, racial, militant, and geographical factors notwithstanding, critics argue that the modernization and economic liberalization projects pursued by Southeast Asian states have, to a large extent, contributed to terrorism as well as aggravation of "the situation by undermining [older forms of horizontal community solidarity and hierarchical patriarchal sociality] traditional authority and socio-economic structures" (Chalk 2001: 242). Hence, the underdevelopment of the East Asian countries, struggles for communal life, religion, identity, and ethnic questions have been taken as a free pass to Islamic terrorism and political violence. Similarly, as Gilmartin and Berg (2007) note, most postcolonial critiques of imperialist geopolitics remained largely ineffective due to their preoccupation with deconstructing colonial discourses, rather than engaging with their continuity (see also Flint 2003; Cutter et al. 2003). In the Security Studies discourses, too, a decisive program for transforming geography into an arena of critical academic knowledge to understanding terrorism, security, and defense strategies tends to place, albeit inadvertently, Western lives at the heart of the issue, while simultaneously depicting terrorism as a hazard from outer space (Mustafa 2005; Beck 2003; Tirman 2004). Today, a rare blend of area studies, geopolitics, security studies, and anthropology (Sluka 2009) has resulted in the discourses on "new terrorism" and "counterterrorism studies." While conventional or "old forms" of terrorism are generally defined in terms of political aspirations which are rooted in a given national context, "new terrorism" is understood as a loose network of insurgents, who do not have a particular attachment to nationality or nation, and use of indiscriminate violence that far exceeds the motives of media or public attention (Burnett and Whyte 2003; Gearson 2002). However, as critics such as Jackson (2007: 245) have pointed out, the "theoretical and institutional origins" of "new terrorism" can be traced to orthodox counterinsurgency studies which are often masqueraded as social sciences. This has led to the creation of epistemic communities within the counterterrorism discourse, which are informed by "problem-solving" theories that conflate "the 'problem' of terrorism" with "other forms of subaltern violence," and thereby fail to acknowledge "the hierarchies and operation of power and the inequalities and injustices thus generated" (ibid.). According to Burnett and Whyte (2005: 7), these developments call for a redefinition of the entire discourse on new terrorism as one driven by "the rationale for a new counter-terror precautionary principle." Because "new terrorism" is considered "a ubiquitous threat," it "requires a ubiquitous response ... that legitimises the targeting of groups that are tangentially associated with terrorists, whether this is translated into criminalization, racial harassment, or violent victimization" (Burnett and Whyte 2005: 7). Sure enough, in today's counterterrorism studies, such "ubiquitous" threats are dealt with equally "ubiquitous" forms of surveillance and intelligence, which includes drones, satellite imagery, and forensic science. In other words, from the rudimentary anthropometric discourses on Oriental bodies to clandestine warfare, the biopolitical trajectories of colonial Orientalism have evolved into complex forms of "post-panoptical" (Baumann cited in Jabri 2013: 4) and post-Orientalist governance (Dabashi 2009). Though contemporary (post-)Orientalist discourses may find anthropometry or anthropology more or less outdated and even disposable, they are certainly built on the dichotomous impulses of the older disciplinary practices which are merely enhanced by the cosmetic value of new scientific discoveries and technologies, such as "Communication Logistics," "XG Radio Technologies," "ERSI GIS Systems," and so forth.[10]

Conclusion

From the colonial anthropometry to the American geopolitics, and to counterterrorism studies, the saga of mapping, farming, and criminalizing the Orient continues until today. Although the new Orientalism, in its varied mutable forms, has been at the crux of these developments, an understanding of post-9/11 Orientalism requires a careful consideration of post-Orientalism's *epistemic endosmosis* and "disposable" character. Having said that, however, it would be misleading to read post-9/11 Orientalism purely in ahistorical terms. As my genealogical analysis of the academic disciplines suggests, the new Orientalist project owes a great deal of gratitude to the colonial discourse, regardless of its dislocated subject (as object of study) from the conventional race-territory nexus in the course of its evolution. And given the magnitude of Orientalism's effects —from the invasion of Iraq to the occupation of the Okinawa islands—I am bound to agree with Dabashi's observation that "no amount of individual anecdotes about one Orientalist or another will have the slightest effect on the principle veracity of Said's argument" (2009: 274).

Notes

1. "New terrorism" is defined as a loose network of militants who operate transitionally and lack an organizational structure and a decentralized hierarchy that are generally associated with "old terrorism." New terrorism is also defined in terms of its indiscriminate and irrational use of violence that is not inspired by a specific political motive or function. See Morgan (2004: 30–34) for a discussion on various characteristics of new terrorism. See also Chapter 3 for a discussion on the limitations of "new terrorism" as a concept.

2. Mbembe (2003) defines necropolitics as the flip side of biopolitics. If biopolitics refers to the controlling of human populations (and biological life) through disciplinary mechanisms brought about by the discourses on knowledge, then necropolitics refers to the biopolitical control exerted by way of controlling, organizing, (re)ordering, and authorizing death.

3. An endogamous social unit tied with occupational guilds in which a person's identity, status, and occupation in a society are ascribed by birth. See Srinivas (1987) and Omvedt (1988) for a basic definition of caste.

4. My subsequent citations of Dumont's essay are based on a draft version of the original essay published in *Contributions to Indian Sociology* (1966: 67–89), available online at http//de.scribd.com/doc/61841968/Louis-Dumont-the-Village-Community-in-India (downloaded on February 1, 2015).

5. However, it was not until 1871 that an official nation-wide census on Indian castes and tribes was issued, largely inspired by the fears and anxieties of the Raj in the aftermath of the 1857 mutiny.

6. This critique forms the basis for Dumont's thesis (1970) of *homo hierarchicus*, which in itself suffers from a rather inverted Orientalist reading of the caste system, by suggesting that it is not the village community but the caste ideology, and its hierarchical collectivity that holds the Indian society together.

7. This corresponds to Said's notion that the Orient can be seen panoptically as a collective Other and is often discoursed in "essentialist" terms, but is always met with diachronic interruptions. Said implies that the colonializer's efforts to control these disruptions is what leads to the execution of Orientalism through institutional disciplines (Said 2003 [1978]: 240).

8. See Seth (2010: 219–22) for more on the relationship between criminology and Indian anthropometry.

9. These discourses, which helped to construct a bifurcated view of the world that naturalized the colonial world against the historicization of European races, were also applied to the marginalized and colonized societies in Europe (Ireland). See Lentin (2007: 612–13).

10. Basic information on these technologies can be accessed on the Internet. See Davis et al. (2014), for relevant details.

3

"Pulp Orientalism": Representations of Afghanistan and Pakistan in Popular Fiction*

Introduction

In the past two decades, pulp genres, such as crime thrillers, detective fiction, "Chicklit," "Cricklit," and graphic novels have gained a great deal of purchase in the postcolonial world. Internet blogs, literary forums, and social media circles are studded with the flashy covers of crime thrillers and the marketing videos of emerging pulp writers. In India, the jaded sight of the airport bookshop shelves stacked with the autobiographies of national heroes and cricket stars is gradually being replaced with the catchy titles of espionage thrillers, self-help books, and spiritual guides by new-age gurus. From Nigeria to India, writers, such as Nwokolo Chuma, Kishwar Desai, and Chetan Bhagat, have made careers in popular fiction with roaring commercial success. In India, Bollywood filmmakers have become increasingly dependent on popular novels for their creative anti-establishment plots and their local adaptations of terrorist and crime thrillers.[1] While it is true that popular fiction from India and other parts of the postcolonial world may bear potential for certain liberationist and revolutionary tendencies, in the Western world the genre itself has been shunned by literary critics for its poor literary quality and its ideological compliance with dominant political views, stereotypes, motifs of sexism,

* This chapter was previously published in *Journal of Postcolonial Writing*, 2012. This text has been edited for typographical errors, stylistic consistency, and sequential organization in order to make it suitable for inclusion in this book.

racism and xenophobia (Irwin 2011; Reddy 2002). However, Emma Dawson Varughese's recent works, *Beyond the Postcolonial* (2012) and *Reading New India* (2013), have sought to contextualize certain variants of popular fiction in the "post-millennial" turn of the world English literature, a phase that is less concerned with the legacies of colonialism or injustices of the past but with the representation of "current realities" (Varughese 2013: 9–30). Yet, given the tainted reputation of popular fiction genres at large, it remains to be seen how postcolonial novelists deal with its ideological compliance with dominance and high culture.[2] The focus of this chapter is not postcolonial pulp fiction per se, but given the unresolved tensions between Western pulp and its discursive nexus with Orientalism (Irwin 2011), racism and xenophobia (Reddy 2002), it sets out to examine what happens to popular fiction when it is transported into a postcolonial setting.

Dan Fesperman's novel, *The Warlord's Son* (2004), which is arguably a pulp incarnation of Joseph Conrad's *Heart of Darkness*, illustrates my analysis. Commissioned by his tabloid editor to "[h]elp us understand" why they "hate us" (ibid., 30), the American war journalist Stan Kelly (Skelly) embarks on a solitary voyage into the "dark labyrinth" of the Khyber Pass "a story" (ibid., 44, 222). With no destination in mind, Skelly moves from Islamabad to Peshawar, and then on to Jalalabad and Alzara where only "opium lords," "dead conquerors," and "dead explorers" (ibid., 159) reign, where even the one-legged amputees shoulder and fire weapons like "grizzled flamingo[s]" (ibid., 445). In this barren terrain of "snoops," "lurkers" (ibid., 51), "con artists" (ibid., 237), and "glorified ruffians" (ibid., 430) where there is no law and justice, "deceit" and "betrayal" are household names (ibid., 288), and death is the greatest badge of glory: the ultimate weapon of choice for every itinerant tribesman who can kill wantonly. At the outset, one may be tempted to read the sort of aggressive, frenzied, and even hostile Orientalism that runs through the pages of Fesperman's novel as simply an overdose of 19th-century European Orientalism. But its "pulp" origins become apparent once the generic complicity between populism and Orientalism is explored. This chapter attempts a conceptual exposition of pulp Orientalism through Dan Fesperman's novel. Drawing on the writings of Achille Mbembe and Hamid Dabashi, among others, I propose a three-fold conceptual framework—endosmotic banality, *terra necro*, and "splintered" subjects—through which pulp Orientalism can be articulated as a mutation of Euro-American Orientalism.

Orientalism in Popular Culture

Edward Said's *Orientalism* is often criticized for its excessive focus on 19th-century French Orientalism; its inability to distinguish between the Orientalisms of different historical periods, and the uneasy conflation of well-meaning Orientalists ("high-brow literati") with pulp writers. Robert Irwin (2011), for instance, questions Said's emphasis on canonical figures, such as "George Eliot or Joseph Conrad, while yet, neglecting the novels of Sax Rohmer and Dennis Wheatley." For Irwin, popular Orientalism thrives on its own epistemic turf "outside" of literary Orientalism's totalizing gaze that Edward Said's thesis originally accounted for. Echoing this, John MacKenzie (1995: 14) argues that "Said has [not only] failed to make any distinction between 'high art' and popular culture," but he made no mention of the "convergence" of Orientalism in "elite and popular culture" between different historical phases and periods, such as the "late Victorian and Edwardian times followed by an era of divergence in the inter-war years" within which various tenets of Orientalism may have evolved. Among other critics, Marwan Obeidat (1998: 23–25) and Abdulla Al-Dabbagh (2010: 3) argue that Said's absolutist and ahistorical treatment of the Orient as an abstract category fails to explain its transmutation into an aggressive and hostile Orientalism in popular, public, and policy spheres in the 20th century.

While most of these critiques are well justified, they are certainly overstated. To Said's own credit, he neither underplayed the power of popular Orientalism nor did he undermine the distinction between 18th-century Orientalism, and the late 19th- and 20th-century American Orientalism. Said wrote that his interest in Orientalism began with:

> the Arab-Israeli War of 1973, which had been preceded by a lot of images and discussions in the media in the popular press about how the Arabs are cowardly and they don't know how to fight and they are always going to be beaten because they are not modern. (Said 2005 [1998]: 2)

In *Covering Islam* (1997 [1981]), Said dedicated an entire chapter titled "Islam as News" to a discussion on the role of popular media in Orientalist discourse. Furthermore, Said lamented that almost 16 years since *Covering Islam* was published, "the situation got worse. And that what you had instead now was a much more threatening picture of Islam, represented for example by [a] television film called *Jihad in America*" (Said 2005 [1998]: 7–8). Singling out Hollywood as the main culprit, Said observed:

many films end up with huge numbers of bodies, Muslim bodies strewn all over the place, the result of Arnold Schwarzenegger or Chuck Norris, lot's of films about guerrillas going into kill Muslim terrorists. So the idea of Islam is something to be stamped out. (Said 2005 [1998]: 9)

Addressing his critics in his 1995 afterward to *Orientalism*, Said draws upon the internal consistency between classical and popular Orientalism:

> … many of the stereotypes of Islamic sensuality, sloth, fatalism, cruelty, degradation and splendor, to be found in writers from John Buchan to V.S. Naipaul, have also been presuppositions underlying the adjoining field of academic Orientalism. (Said 2003 [1978]: 345)

Notwithstanding Said's late engagement, popular Orientalism did not receive the same level of sustained attention in literature as it did in journalism and film studies. At best, Orientalism in pulp fiction is often dismissed as unworthy of literary criticism given its aesthetic poverty and limited shelf-life (Irwin 2011). Despite the fact that there is a long tradition of pulp literature in the West, one that is preoccupied with the task of "writing" and eventually "taming the other"—the criminal, anomic, anti-social, deviant other—it is somewhat puzzling that neither the critics nor the interlocutors of *Orientalism* have paid sufficient attention to its extension in the (post)colonial context.

Pulp Fiction and Orientalism

Pulp fiction is often "defined by what it is not: 'literature'" (Schneider-Mayerson 2010: 22). According to Clive Bloom, pulp is the opposite of the canon, and canonical forms are often reinforced by pulp:

> All *vernacular* literature was *ipso facto* popular (common, coarse—vulgate—vulgar), opposed to classicism's purity and aristocracy of descent. … Popular fiction predates serious fiction and serious fiction is cursed to act as popular fiction's antidote and nemesis. (Bloom 2008 [2002]: 19; emphasis in original)

Pulp fiction is not merely a form of publishing produced on poor quality paper, but it is also indicative "of popular publishing neglected through the overemphasis placed on canonic texts" (Bloom 1996: 3). Although the phenomenon of *Volksbücher* ("cheap," "mass" books) is a 17th-century development, it is not until the 1970s that pulp fiction began to attract serious literary attention.[3] Feminists, in particular, took a strong exception to the reaffirmation of patriarchal values and the "validation of difference and community in crime novels" (Schneider-Mayerson 2010: 26). Since then, a number of critics have attempted to bring various genres of popular fiction, such as hard-boiled, crime, vernacular, and romantic thrillers under the umbrella categories of cult, popular, or pulp fiction, with little consensus over the formal or the literary-aesthetic parameters of the genre at large. For some intemperate critics, however, pulp is nothing but "junk," "crap," or even "trash" literature,[4] a notch below detective fiction (Roberts 1990; Bloom 1996; Morgan 2002). Yet, for a handful of apologists, pulp is a literature of the "vernaculars" and "masses;" a corrosive and even a subversive form of resistance to bourgeois art and cultural aesthetics that almost borderlines with avant-garde (Bloom 1996: 16; Morgan 2002).

In terms of its literary and aesthetic merit, pulp is considered equally rudimentary: it succeeds by telling stories that espouse newspaper reality (Bloom 1996). With its excessive focus on formulaic plot structures and settings, characters are the biggest causality in pulp literature, which remain emotionally weak or underdeveloped. Instead, the fast-paced, action-charged narration of ordinary events or places turns "its language [into] *a form of lifestyle*, foregrounding objects and events rather than psychological characterisation" (Bloom 2008 [2002]: 21; emphasis in original). Pulp novels typically employ omniscient and third-person narrators for their "godlike ability" to delve into the motifs of the characters, their inner psyche, past and future alike. Accordingly, "there is no discernible distance between the narrator and the detective; in the absence of irony, the narrator might as well be the detective, so close are their language and attitudes" (Reddy 2002: 8)—a trait central to the narrator of *The Warlord's Son*—who is a veteran war journalist like the author himself.

According to Maureen Reddy (ibid., 18), "[h]ard-boiled fiction's rise, then, coincides neatly with widespread anxiety about race and about the difficulties of maintaining the whiteness of the United States." As the forbearer of pulp, Reddy observes that "hard-boiled ideology is an exaggerated version—but only a very slightly exaggerated version—of mainstream American ideology, particularly as that ideology was propounded in the years between the world wars" (ibid., 9). While detective fiction always enjoyed "imperial authority" over the colonized Other, the clue-puzzle stories of the 1920s, particularly Ronald Knox's tales, "continued to use foreign countries and colonial holdings both as sources of mystery and evil and as exotic backdrops for otherwise conventional mysteries of 'closed circle societies' […] of Englishmen" (Pearson and Singer 2009: 5). According to Julie Kim (2005: 1), the popular literature of the early 20th century was all about ferreting out culprits: "detective fiction cannot escape being about Others." "After all," Kim asks, "what is more "othering" than to be murdered?" (ibid.). For all its moral poverty, pulp "typically neglects to resolve social decay by casting it as a conflict between cultures and races" (McCann cited in Pearson and Singer 2009: 5). Such tensions between races and unknown Others of "outside" communities can be traced to early pulp Orientalist magazines, such as *Oriental Stories*, *The Spider*, *Wu Fang*, and *Dr Yen Sin* in the 1930s and 1940s, which were specifically devoted to Yellow Peril themes in the New World.

Although American Orientalism lacked direct contact with the colonial Other (Obeidat 1998: 23–25), it revealed an ideological complicity between late Victorian Orientalism ("cultural") and post-war American Orientalism ("geopolitical"). The complicity is marked, as it were, by an epistemic break (as in Edward Said's "style") in the way Orientalist ideology was transformed to fulfill the imperial ambitions of the Western world in the postcolony as well as in the post-war Europe (Ludden 2003). Unlike European Orientalism, American Orientalism primarily dealt with the territorial mapping of the (readily available) culturally demarcated Other.[5] The collusion between the two types of Orientalism can be traced to 19th-century Victorian and American literature. Arthur Conan Doyle's *The Sign of Four* (1890), Kipling's *Kim* (1901), and R.M. Ballantyne's *The Coral Island* (1858) not only reflected the geopolitical ambitions of expansion and exploration of the late Victorian era, but also expressed a deep concern for the anxieties that arose from the waning political control over the colonies. Correspondingly, Nathaniel Hawthorne's *Rappaccini's Daughter* (1844), James Fenimore Cooper's *The Last of the Mohicans* (1826), and Harriet Beecher Stowe's *Uncle Tom's Cabin* (1852) are clearly informed by the American perceptions of Otherness through the European lens (Obeidat 1998: 24–25); their shared passion for imperial exploration and expansion of the late Victorian era; and in the former, a latent desire to separate, preserve, and protect the new world's glamour from the threats presented by the outside the world.[6]

Against the backdrop of these external anxieties, in *Plotting Terror*, Margaret Scanlan (2001: 1) locates the rise of the new genre of the "terrorist novel" within the past five decades:

[t]his paradoxical affiliation between our violence and our *fictions* lies at the heart of those complex novels about terrorism sometimes called "literary thrillers", as vital to them as gore and mayhem are to the blockbuster.

For Scanlan, the terrorist novel prior to the 1970s was concerned with uncovering ("plotting") the motifs and causes of terror, while the new generation of writers, such as Doris Lessing and Don DeLillo, had to cope with the global electronic media and its propagation of distorted images of terror. If terrorism can be defined as "both actual killing and a fictional construct" (Scanlan 2001: 2), Scanlan cautions that the terrorist novel (and the novelist) may fall prey to the same "fictional" ideologies that it seeks to challenge: "the usual story of sinister Islamic terrorists preying on the West" (ibid., 15). In the popular novel, then, the representation of terror always connotes "an imputation of violence or underhandedness" (ibid., 6), a trait central to the emerging genre of "international thrillers" set in the former colonies. Pulp Orientalism is, thus, fundamentally geared toward "apprehending" and "taming" the "deviant" Other who is not found at home, but in the "estranged" sphere outside of society, while broadening out its quest "from individual criminal acts to implicate larger social ills" (Pearson and Singer 2009: 6).

Pulp Orientalism in *The Warlord's Son*

Besides the cheap paper, the covers are a defining feature of pulp fiction, illustrating a flamboyant display of guns, terrorists, and villains, among other impending signs of doom and danger. The cover of *The Warlord's Son* features a shaded imprint of a turbaned male triumphantly raising an AK-47 over his head, surrounded by six or so other turbaned males. Only the AK-47 and rising fists are reprinted on the back cover, with the face and the turban hidden under the bar code scan. The marketing blurb on the top of the back cover reads "shortlisted for the CWA steel dagger of thriller of the year"—a fitting reminder of pulp's penchant for self-congratulatory gestures and mass marketing. The central plot of *The Warlord's Son* revolves around the expedition led by the protagonist Skelly and his "fixer" Najeeb Azam, an American-educated banished son of a Pashtun warlord. The subplot introduces Daliya Qadeer, daughter of the Pakistani deputy minister for commerce, who escapes Islamabad in a bid to reunite with her ever-eluding lover—Najeeb. The narrative moves through a failed attempt to enter Afghanistan at Torkham near the Khyber Pass, and then to a successful one at Parachinar, where they join the forces of Mahmood Razaq, another warlord stationed in Hayatabad, who is moving toward the North to remobilize his forces against the Taliban. The ill-fated voyage comes to an abrupt end with the capture of Razaq and his allies by the Taliban. Aided by his uncle Aziz, Najeeb escapes the Taliban's capture near Jalalabad along with Skelly, finding refuge at his father Malik's *hujera* in Bagwali. Meanwhile, with the help of the Islamabad-based Professor Bhatti, Daliya reaches Afghanistan masquerading as a man to rescue Najeeb. Stranded at Malik's *hujera* (men's guest house), Skelly manages to break free, eventually rejoining Najeeb and Daliya en route to Peshawar. Their safe return to Pakistan is endangered by Arlen Pierce and Sam Hartley, two dubious Americans who separate Skelly from Najeeb and Daliya at gunpoint, leading him to a death trap laid out by Haji Kudrat, a close ally of Bin Laden.

In an almost tautological relay, every minor halt in the novel's plot and subplot feeds into the ravenous Orientalist appetite of its narrator. Although Skelly is betrayed by his own countrymen, his brutal slaying at the hands of a Taliban agent not only reaffirms the "predatory" nature of Talibani Afghanistan, but it lends all the more legitimacy to the exceptionist logic that American lives "must be" sacrificed for the greater good of fighting evil. The slow and senseless movement of the main plot; the protagonists' blind determination "to go to Afghanistan" without a plan or purpose; his failed attempt to get the "right fixer"; another failed attempt to cross the Afghani border—all provide the narrator with ample time and space to absorb, abstract, and ingest every microscopic detail of the Oriental life from a meta-cultural vantage point.

The subplot of the novel casts a rather inverted Orientalist gaze by pitting native against native. Despite her "upper class" urbanity, Daliya's blind voyage into Afghanistan where "[e]ven two women dressed properly can't get very far unless a man is with them" (Fesperman 2004: 335) serves no other purpose than providing the narrator with a new pair of native eyes to scan the Oriental landscape in even more intimate detail, hence rendering the protagonist's Orientalist account all the more authentic and legitimate. For both Skelly and Daliya, then, Afghanistan represented a collection of warlords, while the inherently "war-mongering" traits of its subjects were presented as "primal" and "congenital" features of a society, rather than socio-historical or hermeneutical exegeses. And given that such "knee-jerk" Orientalism is easier to consume than conceptualize, my reading of

The Warlord's Son employs three distinctive analytical categories, namely, endosmotic banality, *terra necro*, and "splintered" subjects.

My formulation of "endosmotic banality" stems from two separate conceptual expositions: Dabashi's "endosmosis" and Mbembe's "banality." For Dabashi (2009: 222), endosmosis refers to "a mode of knowledge," which is found in the "cellular labyrinth of dissemination or cavities of transmutation—toward the public domain at large and there mutated into a greater concentration." Applied to the post-Orientalist context, such mutated forms of knowledge "resist categorization" by "operating on a cacophonous modulation" (ibid.). Much the same way, Mbembe's notion of "banality" refers to the everyday context of power relations that are in excess of their functional purpose—"with a surplus of meanings" (Mbembe 2001: 103)—often expressed in the most extreme and grotesque forms.[7] For instance, if the imperial domination in Africa was exerted by reducing its subject to a colonial "animal" or a thing that is "nothing," Mbembe asks, "what does it mean to do violence to what is nothing?" (ibid., 174, 187, 193). For the purpose of this chapter, a synthesis between "endosmosis" and "banality" helps conceptualize (a) the dissemination of Orientalist knowledge into all aspects of Oriental life ("biopower") and (b) the "excess" of its discursive function against which the notions of the European sublime are constantly rehashed, reified, and reasserted.

My use of the term "terra necro" is based on the Latin terms "terra" (land) and "necro" (death). By "terra necro," I refer to the necropolitical manifestation of sovereign (imperium) power, which falls beyond the regulatory ambit of biopower. For example, as Stephen Morton (2007b: 39) argues, following the French Revolution, European philosophers construed terror as an aesthetic and sublime category, one that is to be contemplated from a safe distance. These views, according to Mbembe (2003: 22), were at the forefront of the Enlightenment project, which favored biopower to necropower in governing the European populations. As a result, necropower was relegated to the non-European domain of the postcolony. By using maximum force of destruction, necropower retains sovereignty by conceiving its subjects as dead while they are alive—"a form of death-in-life" (ibid., 21). "Terra necro," in this sense, alludes to the Orientalist rendition of this principle where territories, such as Afghanistan and Iraq, are reduced to the lands of the "living dead."

My understanding of the term "splintered" subject[8] is based on Mbembe's conception of "homo ludens." For Mbembe, "homo ludens" is a condition, an expectant subject-position that results from an uneasy constellation between the colonial commandment (a form of endosmotic banality) and the colonial subject's deployment of "a sense of fun" or a "talent for play" (Mbembe 2001: 104) that are presented as latent forms of political resistance. This situation, Mbembe argues, leads "subjects to splinter their identities and to represent themselves as always changing their persona; they are constantly undergoing mitosis, whether in "official" spaces or not" (ibid.). Thus, for Mbembe, "splintered" subjectivity is not something that is imposed upon the colonized subject; instead, it is a form of agency developed as a result of sharing the same space with the colonizer. In that sense, Mbembe's reading of "homo ludens" sharply contrasts with Said's notion of "synchronic essentialism" in Orientalist discourse. For Said, the discursive imagination of the Oriental subject as static, mute, and unchanging ("essentialist") remains more or less complicit ("synchronic") with the actualization of the discourse through discipline, violence, and militant action. This has led critics, such as Homi Bhabha (2004 [1994]: 102–03), to question Said's reluctance to account for the "diachronic" aspects of Orientalism,[9] that is, the "instabilities" produced by the colonized subjects to the normative, normalizing, and homogenizing discourses of the colonizer. Having said that, however, it is reasonable to assume that both the dominant discourse ("synchronic essentialism") and its resistant forces ("homo ludens," "diachronic instability") have coexisted in various forms at various stages of colonialism and imperialism. If, then, the Orientalism of canonical literature reproduced a certain preconceived Oriental subject as static and immutable, I contend that the Orientalism of popular literature reproduces just another kind of preconceived Oriental subject as "splintered" and mutable. In pulp Orientalism, this strategy proves effective not only because it strips off the agential challenge(s) posed by the "splintered" subject to any given homogenizing discourse of power (such as Orientalism or terrorism), but also, in doing so, it naturalizes the "splintered" character as inherently Oriental and primitive, one that is devoid of any political and practical purpose. Constructed in this manner, the terrorist figure represented in *The Warlord's Son* is a "splintered" subject par excellence who, as it were, is not only naïve, religious, loyal, and devoted to his cause, but also dangerous, cunning, opportunistic, and destructive to the lives of others as well as his own kind.

"Endosmotic Banality"

Throughout Skelly's expedition, every minuscule detail of the Oriental biosphere, including the phenotypes, appearances, smells, sounds, sights, landscapes, and everyday objects of use are presented as gross anomalies to any normative conception of civilization at large. And it is not by chance that in the popular novel "[w]hite bonding generally takes place "on a" less than fully conscious level, in an exchange of glances, laughter at racist jokes, and sharing of assumptions about people of color" (Reddy 2002: 10). "Hell, give 'em another month and they'll be tired of reading about bearded fanatics ...'" (Fesperman 2004: 83), exclaims Sam Hartley, addressing Skelly. In line with pulp's penchant for creative use of serial, adjectivized nouns (Irwin 2011), Skelly frequently refers to natives as "white-turbans," "bushy heads," "rheumy eyes," "pests," "elves," and "dwarves" (ibid., 118–426). Positive virtues of the local characters are acknowledged only when they conform to Western cultural standards. Babar, the first fixer Skelly hires from a hotel lobby, is reduced to an animal-like creature with odd demeanor: "Babar, same name as the elephant. Just look at him, Skelly thought. The man's wide eyes and strangled look of panic bespoke his lack of qualifications far more eloquently than his broken English" (ibid., 24). By contrast, Najeeb is qualified as an "[i]nteresting fellow, and his English was perfect" (ibid., 48), owing largely to the four years he had spent in America. Yet, Skelly finds it irresistible to poke about Najeeb's native demeanors: Pashtun "[s]tony expression," "Najeeb the Inscrutable," and "the stone-faced sage" (ibid., 45), implying that he had the right combination of Western and oriental temperament to give Skelly a sneak peek "inside Pakistan's tribal aristocracy" (ibid., 49). During his first encounter with Mahmood Razaq in Hayatabad, Skelly qualifies his English as "polished, almost formal, probably because he'd been educated in Europe" (ibid., 123). If Najeeb and Razaq were blessed with a gentle stroke of Western habitus, Professor Bhatti is an embodiment of the Western sublime; she is one of the "most worldly professors" (ibid., 181–82) by virtue of "spending two months every few summers in Boston, among American colleagues at Harvard, and after each such trip she returned with another increment in hustle and determination" (ibid., 182). Yet their native traits are immediately relegated to the innate Oriental character: Razaq sat "as plump as a Buddha, rarely stirring from the embroidered cushions of his parlour, more attuned to his interest rates and import quotas" (ibid., 53), and "Professor Bhatti was short, another handicap to overcome" (ibid., 181). Like a page from Mark Twain's *The Innocents Abroad*, Skelly's "scrap notes" paint an equally sorry sight of the native landscape: "*Small stream in muddy ravine w/tent pitched next to goat herd. 3 water buffaloes knee-deep in irrig ditch & one grazing in tall grass. ... Tall mud chimney belching heavy black smoke, terrible smell*" (ibid., 36;

emphasis in original). The inhabited territory of "people" is then described as "caves," "ocean of beards" and even more dismissively as "a few dozen mud homes shoved against each other at the edge of the dry valley as if swept aside by a broom" (Irwin 2011: 61, 93–94, 264). Anything that does not resemble the sound of English is either a "raspy burst of Pashto," or a voice shouting "maniacally in some foreign tongue" (ibid., 464, 312). To Skelly's terror, "here even the old fellows carried guns. It was apparently part of their wardrobe—*kameez*, sandals, blanket, turban, and Kalashnikov" (ibid., 415). Even "hills were not engineered for graceful ageing, nor was the lifestyle" (ibid., 417). As the entire local topography becomes an eyesore to Skelly, a soothing sense of familiarity returns when he spots Sam Hartley in his "khaki trousers and a blue work shirt, the top buttons undone and the shirttail out" (ibid., 448). "It was a jarring sight," reckons Skelly, "after days of seeing nothing but *kameez*" (ibid.).

And for one reason or another, people are always accompanied by animals: "endless streams of people and herds of sheep," "barefoot children and bony dogs," and "a dozen men ... shooing goats" (ibid., 119, 264, 308). The odd deposition of the native bodies, and their misfit outfits themselves speak for a supposedly Orientalist anarchy: "For all its medieval character," Malik's territory "was a knighthood of *kameez* and bandoleer, not ermine and armour, of turbans not tiaras; Kalashnikovs, not lances" (ibid., 165). Like a scene from a Hollywood blockbuster, a mule carrying a satellite phone triggers the most striking anomaly:

> imagine what it must have been like piloting tanks down the narrow road—the big green craft beetling along the alien creatures, turrets swiveling .... Then some barefoot mujahid in a turban rising up form a boulder to fire a tube from his shoulder, a shell whooshing into the treads as warriors swarmed suddenly from the rocks, darting flares of blue and white gowns. (ibid., 311)

"Our" war is rational and "their" war is irrational (Porter 2009): anything that is not colored by Western habitus is part and parcel of nature or "within" nature. A description of wayside landscape at the Afghan–Pakistan border reads:

> there were children everywhere, running barefoot through the dust. ... it would never occur to most children here to do anything other than gawk at a foreigner, as if some exotic bird had been blown in on a zephyr. ... a legless beggar moving past, swinging his arms like crutches and scraping

along on his knuckles, which had turned the colour of the soil. (Fesperman 2004: 202–06)

Never mind how the beggar lost his leg, Skelly's endosmotic obsession reaches paranoiac proportions when he finds every passing Afghani with onion smell in his breath, or sometimes onions "but no hashish" (ibid., 196) or a combination of "sweat and onions and tobacco issuing from them" (ibid., 351). Such an endosmosis is not unique to Skelly; it seeps into the local characters themselves on account of the narrator: after "sampling the bounty of bright new places" (ibid., 16) in America, Najeeb finds his home "small, plain and crude" (ibid.). He, thus, becomes acutely aware of "all these tribesmen with their Stone Age amenities and their warriors on horseback, living by firelight on bread cooked in clay pits then cast upon the floor" (ibid., 277). And "[p]erhaps, he [Najeeb], too," Skelly reckons, "needed ... a refresher course now that he was back in the hills" (ibid., 289). As if the Orientalism of the narrator is not enough to achieve the desired dramatic effect, the Oriental subjects themselves become the "objects" of self-Orientalism.

"Terra Necro"

If endosmotic banality rests on principally anomalous civilizations where difference is fetishized ("synchronic essentialism") without recourse to diachronic interruptions, the creation of death worlds—"terra necro"— serves as an ideological proxy for popular Orientalism's presumed lack of intellectual oeuvre.

"Fuck him," a reporter shouts when the caravan driver Fawad leaves a hoard of Western journalists at the Afghani border. "'If he can't even deal with a bunch of paper-pushers they'll eat him alive over there'. 'Good', someone answered. 'It'll strengthen the Pashtun gene pool'" (ibid., 195), implying that Fawad would be killed by Talibani henchmen. In what Ludden calls the "maps in the mind," the Orient as a collection of "fearsome people and demons [who] lurk in the dreaded forest, wild steppe, fierce desert, mysterious mountains, and endless untamed darkness of the sea" (2003: 1061) is common to post-9/11 populist discourse. To be sure, Najeeb "was respectful of its mysterious cloaking powers, because things had a way of disappearing in Peshawar" (Fesperman 2004: 13). If, for outsiders, the Oriental space represents a "terra necro," it then follows that the people who live "inside" this space, as Mbembe puts it, are the embodiment of the "living dead" (2003: 11–40). If the words "No Return" (Fesperman 2004: 131) engraved on Razaq's sword are merely symbolic of the "cloaking powers" of the land itself, the mysterious note found in Najeeb's apartment with a passage from the Koran is like a death warrant issued by prophet Mohammad himself: "4:78. *Wherever you be, death will overtake you; though you put yourselves in the lofty towers*" (ibid., 144; emphasis in original). Though the allusion to "lofty towers" may be a pure coincidence, death is still worth the gamble if it is to unlock the secrets of those who "cohabited" it:

> Yet, there was something rather noble about it as well, as if the man were laying claim to his small niche in history, like every other foreigner who had made a name in these hills – spies and soldiers ..., monarchs and ministers – all had traipsed naively into the dust. And now here was Skelly, scribe of the West, trying to make sense of these imponderable rustics for the enlightenment of the plainfolk back home. (ibid., 305)

Throughout Skelly's expedition, both Pakistan and Afghanistan are conceived as places that not only invite, inspire, and cultivate death, but are "cohabited" by it in every speck of dust and every grain of sand in their entire landscapes. On Skelly's account, the local terrain reveals nothing of its people and their lives: "There was no one but them in the valley, it seemed, them and the big clean sky where only a hawk was on patrol, spiralling on an updraught as it disappeared over the ridge" (ibid., 311). So treacherous and dark the land is that Skelly is unable to resist "imagining that tribal warriors were concealed there, training their gun barrels on the intruders as they had done for centuries" (ibid., 155). The Katchagarhi camp in particular, Skelly recounts, "was like a scene of biblical plague" (ibid., 120). While contrasting it with a less chaotic refugee camp in Hayatabad, Skelly remarks: "It's a wonder the people from Katchagarhi don't just cross the highway and kill everyone in their sleep" (ibid.). Pakistan, in particular, reminds him of "every other capital of world misery he'd visited—Managua, Baghdad, and the deserts of Kuwait" (ibid., 27–28), and even "the anarchy of Liberia—the very kingdom of random death" where "[m]alice and cunning had grinned from thin faces and deep-socketed eyes ... of twelve-year-olds, vacant-eyed boys who had lost all sense of fear, order and limits" (ibid., 28).

In the "dark labyrinth of Katchagarhi" (ibid., 222) and beyond, "killing," "slaughter," and "slaying" are the primal, if not primate, instincts of people who not only "conceal thoughts and dreams," but also in doing so, sheath "emotions ... like a weapon" (Fesperman 2004: 16). Barely in his teens, Najeeb was fascinated by the lammergeier because it hunted alone and knew "how to unlock the hidden treasures of the marrow" (ibid., 167). When Najeeb is forced to handle a rifle during his expedition, he explains to a surprised Skelly: "Where I grew up you don't make it to your tenth birthday without firing one of these...." (ibid., 329).

Necropower is no less endosmotic than biopower. By means of its "splintering occupation"—an occupation "dictated by the very nature of the terrain and its topographical variations (hilltops and valleys, mountains and bodies of water)"—it retains a "vertical-sovereignty" as opposed to horizontal hegemony (Mbembe 2003: 28). In *The Warlord's Son*, each and every crawling being represents a weapon, a parasitic killer, a periodic reminder of impending death and decay, including the "dirty carpet" in Skelly's hotel that was a "host to a caravan of ants, winding their way to a sprinkling of crumbs by a crumpled crisps packet in the corner" (Fesperman 2004: 236). Dramatic, cunning ploys of death and danger are the congenital traits of the Afghani; catching fish with homespun explosives was "the greatest entertainment the children might witness for weeks as stunned fish bobbled to the surface, dead eyes turned to the sky" (ibid., 165–66). Faith, superstitions, rituals, too, are fuelled by diabolical instincts; the prayers of the prostrating men "looked as though they were speaking into the ground, casting spells on the land itself" (ibid., 254). Save the accursed prayers, deranged amputees can be as deadly as a hungry predator:

> one of them missing a leg yet travelling at surprising speed with the aid of a crutch – a ragtag foursome, but well armed, and Skelly watched with amazed horror as the amputee dropped the crutch and shouldered his weapon while balancing on one leg like a grizzled flamingo. (ibid., 445)

If, as in Bataille (cited in Mbembe 2003: 38), "death reveals the human subject's animal side" as their natural state of being, Skelly's naturalization of the Afghani subject is complicit with the necropower that enables the conqueror to "*savage life* [as] just another form of *animal life*" (Mbembe 2003: 24; emphasis in original): "The boys he'd seen earlier ducked in and out of doorways, reminding him of prairie dogs at the zoo.... bobbing prairie dogs, poking heads form their dusty caves" (Fesperman 2004: 265). Wilder still, as the men who were lynched by the Taliban "produced trailing gobs of brown liquid, from the hash and tobacco they'd been chewing,"

Skelly notes, "[o]ther men leaped forward in ones and twos to slap at the victims' heads and kick at their calves" (Fesperman 2004: 354). Notwithstanding this "savage" spectacle unfolding before him, Skelly cannot resist being amused: "Free gift to the first fifty customers. Free hanging to the first fifty Pashtuns" (ibid., 351)… "[s]houldn't someone be selling popcorn [here]?" (ibid., 353).

For Mbembe, necropolitics operate when the living subjects confront death while they are (kept) alive. Echoing Mbembe, Skelly describes one of his "casual" sightings on his way to Bagwali: "Old men leaned towards the windows with grizzled faces and missing teeth," while "[u]nderfed curs snarled and barked" (ibid., 397), as though the latter were preying on the former.

The "Splintered" Subject

Typical of pulp literature, in *The Warlord's Son* minor characters are the chief victims of its formulaic narration, which necessitates constant splintering, morphing, and transforming of their subjectivity in order to highlight the normative virtues of the protagonist. In pulp Orientalism, this formulaic deployment spills beyond the regular characters into landscapes, objects, and tropes of cultural expression, thereby "subjectifying" humans and nonhumans alike.

Islamabad, for instance, is portrayed as a highly Westernized, non-Oriental, and most un-Pakistani space: "you could hardly tell you were in Pakistan at all…. Thus, the longstanding joke about Islamabad's convenient location: 'only ten miles from Pakistan'" (ibid., 95). This internal rift not only serves to portray Pakistan's inherent anachronism, but it leaves Daliya—a Westernized Islamabadi—to contend with the archaic tradition that is banished to the "other Pakistan." The curious, otherwise impossible love saga between Daliya, the daughter of a Pakistani minister, and Najeeb, the son of a tribal warlord, serves a double purpose: to split Najeeb's subject position into one who is "native" enough for Daliya to rekindle her own hidden nativity, and one who is "Western" enough for Skelly to re-Orientalize his own native roots. "Yet here they were now," the narrator exclaims, "ever deeper in the world that had produced him, in a valley where the power grid was smashed and water was still hauled from the ground by buckets" (ibid., 277), sharply contrasting Najeeb's

American experience that still rings in his head like "a thrilling symphony that had roared up out of stream grates" (Fesperman 2004).

It is no surprise, then, that Daliya's Westernized, Islamabad upbringing "had to be" tenuous, as the impending threat of an arranged marriage would drive her out of Islamabad in pursuit of a warlord's son with a "fifteenth century" (ibid., 94) heritage. And if not for the four years Najeeb had not spent in America,

> he never would have been open to the possibilities of their first brief encounter; would never have been able to read that look in Daliya's eyes that spoke so eloquently of loneliness and need. Such signals never appeared on the male-female radar screens of the Tribal Areas, where a virtual communications blackout was imposed once girls reached ten. (ibid., 100–01)

Yet, it is impossible to conceive how a land that produced only raving fundamentalists could produce someone like Najeeb, "with no taste for combat," who could turn, however incongruently, "defeat into a sort of automatic victory" (ibid., 101). Like a freak accident, there he is, the 150-dollars-a-day henchman, created solely for the purpose of providing Skelly a sneak peek inside of "tribal aristocracy" (ibid., 49). On his native turf, Najeeb repeatedly "employed the old Pashtun stoniness, working to keep his face unreadable" (ibid., 220), but, when in America, the same stoniness would serve an exotic purpose: "I bet you were a big hit. The Omar Sharif look. You must have been fighting them off with a stick." (ibid., 277), quizzes Skelly, alluding to his affairs with American women.

After an overnight ordeal of fornication, a curious exchange unfolds between the lovers:

> "Another blow against the extremists," she said, smiling. "Doing our part for a more secular tomorrow." ... "You think that's what this is? A political act?" "I think it has been all along," she said ... "At some level, anyway. We're spitting in the face of everything we grew up with." (ibid., 105)

If the mere after-euphoria of sex between two individuals can be dubbed as a political statement against anti-secularism, then the very act of sex in the Oriental culture inundates an unnatural, anti-god-like perversion:

> a morning in Chapel Hill when he [Najeeb] had first experienced the pleasure of awakening next to a women ... he had wondered how such a deep feeling of calm and well-being could possibly result from an act of sin, an act against God. (ibid., 113)

Here, doing one's "part for a secular tomorrow" no longer alludes to the tolerance or acceptance of all gods alike, but the preference for an unsinned-against god over the sinned. Najeeb's retrospection of waking up with an American is perhaps less unwitting than naïve, for he admittedly feels less sinful waking with a woman whose god approves "a deep feeling of calm and well-being," than waking up with one whose god forbids it.

Echoing the late 20th-century theories that Oriental societies are "status-"and "honor"-based, the narrator recounts:

> Such was the lifestyle of these hills, where every division of power had its subdivision, and every line of demarcation was a zone of struggle and torment. There were four major tribes in the Khyber Agency alone, with each divided in *khels*, and every *khel* into clans, every clan into subclans, and so on, down to the rival gangs of begrimed boys, tangling dawn to dusk for the last remaining scraps of pride and conquest. (Fesperman 2004: 164; emphasis in original)

Despite their clan, creed and other customary obsessions, all that Afghanis valued apparently were Western commodities: Marlboro, Surf detergents, television sets (ibid., 163) and pens, which "were always one of the first things children begged for in Third World countries [whose] shortage was probably one of those odd things that had bigger repercussions than any dictator ever imagined" (ibid., 117). Never mind how a society can embrace tribal honor, pride, conquest and Western modernity all at the same time, since it is all the more befitting to the popular Orientalist subject who is congenitally split. Like the Indian Thuggees who are portrayed as masters of backstabbing with a smile on their face: "'Betrayal is a skill here,' Najeeb said finally. "An art. Even an honourable one, in its way. Maybe because it is always expected of an adversary" (ibid., 288). "You speak of betrayal as if it is something dishonourable, Mr. Kelly" (ibid., 287), exclaims Razaq. "It is dishonourable only in the sense that a Westerner might understand it" (ibid.). And "... it was perfectly acceptable to receive two guests with courtesy and generosity" exclaims the narrator, "... yet still have them tracked down and killed the moment they left your territory ..." (ibid., 288). In this pious land of "wild-eyed holy men" (ibid., 333) who believe in nothing but the word of god and scraps of pride, it is indeed a wonder how "[d]eceit here took shapes he [Skelly] never would have dreamed of" (ibid., 288). Yet, Razaq affirms Skelly that Haji Kudrat is "[a] friend of the Taliban. Who tomorrow will no longer be a friend of the Taliban, if that is what suits him" (ibid., 297). It is as if all

Afghanis "ought to be" honorable by birth, almost congenitally, but are dishonorable because they are "not" what they "ought to be"—"splintered" subjects *par excellence*.

Conclusion

As Patrick Porter (2009: 2) argues, war is a potent site of Orientalism: "in, and through war people formulate what it means to be Western and non-Western." As I have tried to demonstrate in this chapter, pulp literature provides an ideal platform for such formulations about the self and the Orient in the most aggressive, unapologetic fashion. In *The Warlord's Son*, the endosmotic nature of Orientalism courses through an "excess" of banality (Mbembe 1992: 3) that lacks a decisive form and function, yet "creates" and "institutes" a "master code" (ibid.) with a governing logic of the discourse. This logic succeeds in making Orientalism more palpable than, say, canonical fiction, because of pulp's complicity with other outlets of popular culture at large—Hollywood, TV, and mass media (Scanlan 2001; Reddy 2002). Unlike the serious (Orientalist) fiction that invests in certain moralization and rationalization of the Other that the reader may be unfamiliar with, pulp feeds into the banalities of difference that the reader has *already* acquired by virtue of their endosmotic presence. Furthermore, as in Kim's exhortation that othering by "murder" (Kim 2005, 1) is an endemic trait of domestic popular fiction, the trope of "murder" is (in)organically translated into "terra necro" when the action is set against an Oriental backdrop in international pulp thrillers. Indeed, the ideological precedents for relegating the Oriental hemisphere to a place of death and destruction, already set in the Victorian detective novels, continue the same legacy of imperial ambitions in which the fantasies of taming, apprehending, and "ferreting out" the recalcitrant Other could be played out with a profuse sense of impunity and domination. Nonetheless, such desired fantasies require an ideological conditioning by which Oriental subjects could be demonized in the first place. In pulp fiction, it is the white detective hero who stands as the normative self—an embodiment of urbanity, modernity and morality, one who always knows "what truth is" (Reddy 2002: 8)—against which the native subjects are posited as splintered and nonnormative. This strategy works more persuasively because, unlike "serious" fiction where the Oriental subjects are represented in their static and unchanging mode (Said 2003 [1978]), the lack of irony, weak emotional space, and limited shelf life (Bloom 1996; 2002) of pulp fiction constantly demands variety and melodramatic fantasy.

And, given the magnitude of its Orientalism, I fully agree with Irwin that pulp literature deserves closer scrutiny than it currently receives in literary studies. However, I find his claim that "all" Orientalism is pulp; in that literary Orientalism never existed in the way Said argued it did, an overstatement. After all, what other forms of Orientalist knowledge supplied the ideological condiments necessary for pulp fiction than literature and travel accounts when the written word was the only source of all Orientalisms? Pulp Orientalists may be the proud owners of their cheap paper, but the ink they use has always belonged to the canonical scribes. If European Orientalism is the source of its ideology and American Orientalism is the skin, then pulp Orientalism is its flashy cover.

Notes

1. One of the all-time highest grossing films *3 Idiots* (2009), for instance, is based on Chetan Bhagat's novel *Five Point Someone: What Not to Do at IIT!* (2004).
2. I am fully aware of the fact that not all writers discussed in Varughese's work can be classified as pulp or popular fiction authors.
3. It is often argued that since pulp fiction has a limited shelf life and is more easily accessible in airports, sports loungers, and railway stations than, say, academic libraries, it did not merit the attention of literary critics (Irwin 2011).
4. Hard-boiled "detective fiction," on the other hand, is often spared from such "low-brow" classification as "junk" or "crap," given the canonical status of its predecessors, such as Conan Doyle, Agatha Christie, Wilkie Collins, and Edgar Allan Poe, among others. See Morgan (2012: 11–12) for a detailed account on these typological distinctions.
5. This encompasses the "domesticating" trait of American Orientalism, as inflected in fears and anxieties over foreign immigration in the early American pulp.
6. Applied to the post-war context, Little (2002: 314) argues that the historical antecedents of such imperialist ambitions can be found in the American Orientalism practiced today: "a tendency to underestimate the peoples of the [Arab] region and to overestimate America's ability to make a bad situation better."
7. Although for Mbembe (2001: 102) banality is something that is produced as a routine, he is concerned with the "elements of the obscene and the grotesque" that exceed such a routine. These elements are generally attributed to "nonofficial" cultures but in Mbembe's view, they "are intrinsic to all systems of domination and to the means by which those systems are confirmed or deconstructed."
8. The term "splintered subjects" is my own coinage, based on Mbembe's notion of "splintered" occupation in the postcolony (discussed later in this chapter). My preference for the term "splintered subjects" over "splintered occupation" or "homo ludens"

is largely cautionary. For instance, Mbembe's deployment of the terms is based on the sociological and anthropological observations from Africa and Eastern Europe (Mbembe 2003: 5, 30), which may not entirely be applicable to the context of Afghanistan or Pakistan. However, the conceptual implications of Mbembe's terms are not distorted by my alteration as my reading is thoroughly supported by the literary exposition of splintered subjectivity throughout this chapter.

9. Although Said acknowledges the pressures of diachrony both in *Orientalism* (2003 [1978]: 240) and in *Culture and Imperialism* (1994a [1993]: 106–08), his critics, such as Warraq (2007) and Varisco (2007), have pointed out that Said's theses barely address the question of agency, the sites of resistance to the actualization of the Orientalist discourse.

SECTION 2

Disjunctures: Humanism and Interdisciplinarity

4

After Orientalism: Difference and Disjuncture in Postcolonial Theory*

Introduction

In "Postcolonialism Now: Autonomy, Cosmopolitanism, and Diaspora," Brydon (2004: 691) argues that postcolonial theory needs to rearticulate its "starting points, its shifting terminologies, and its limits" in order to contextualize its theoretical commitment to globalization and cosmopolitanism. Correspondingly, in *Postcolonial Cosmopolitanism*, Rao (2007: ii) asserts that any normative postulations of postcolonial theory "must grapple simultaneously with both a hostile 'outside' and 'inside'" and "must speak in mixed registers of universalism and particularity." According to some critics, however, these mixed registers contain certain "unyielding" textual compositions that draw "uneasy" parallels between ethnocentric politics and the cosmopolitan alternatives (Chowdhury 2006; Leonard 2005). While the discussion on postcolonial theory's integration into cosmopolitanism and globalization studies is fairly recent, it is certainly not without a precedent. In fact, the "uneasiness" concerning the local/ universal binarisms can be traced, by a large measure, to the conventional antinomies of foundationalism and relativism, humanism and nativism, secularism and culturalism within postcolonial discourse. This chapter is an attempt to uncover the differential (and disjunctured) tropes of some of these antinomies in general, but humanism and nativism in particular. Covering a wide range of arguments, this chapter provides a

---

* This chapter was previously published in *Distinktion: Scandinavian Journal of Social Theory*, 2009. This text has been edited for typographical errors, stylistic consistency, and sequential organization in order to make it suitable for inclusion in this book.

reading of three distinct ideological strands in postcolonial discourse: the foundational aspects of Edward Said's postcolonial theory, including his humanist project; the essentialist politics of the subaltern studies group and its allies—Dipesh Chakrabarty and Ranajit Guha; and the post-essentialist strategies of Gayatri Spivak and Homi Bhabha. Against all normative and totalizing readings of postcolonial theory, this chapter suggests that the disjuncture between humanism and nativism is rooted in the diverse theoretical orientations of the postcolonial project at large.

Postcolonial Theory and the Humanist Challenge

Since its inception in the 1970s, postcolonial theory's major concern has been to forge a specific understanding of European reason and its ideological depredations, including the effects of colonialism (Spivak 1999). In this respect, postcolonial theorists argue that the European constructions of the(ir) former colonies are corrupted by a compulsion to claim a suspicious universality with a sublatory effect (De Oto 2003). In the latter, the rational human is defined as a "normative category" against which "excess" (monsters) or "lack" (slaves) forms an inorganic background (Melas 1999: 15). In the colonial context, this "norm is generalized into the universal (the European)" and "set off against the particular" (ibid., 15). As the "humanist self was fundamental to the practice of European Enlightenment ... colonialism as a 'civilizing' mission" operated on the principles of "pacification (and passivication) of both savage cultures and savage nature" (Armstrong 2002: 414). Within this, the humanist discourse further consolidates "[t]he colonial space [as] the terra incognita or the *terra nulla*, the empty or wasted land whose history has to be begun, whose archives must be filled out, whose future progress must be secured in modernity" (Bhabha 1991: 205). This is a discourse which, in its progressive and teleological trajectory, further disfigures native subjects as a mass of objects to be studied, sorted out, and eventually drawn into the singular narrative of universal history, as in Said's reading of Orientalist discourse. In this respect, although postcolonial theory's major concern has been to rearticulate marginalized knowledge that has been disfigured by the humanist curriculum (Gandhi 1998), the ideological and political orientations of the postcolonial project are neither homogenous nor formulaic (Moore-Gilbert 1997).

In fact, in a shift from rescuing the native subject from the crimes of colonialism to crafting "postcolonial cosmopolitanisms," arguments range from portraying contrapuntality and hybridity as liberating alternatives to ethnic and "nativist chauvinism" to uneasily drawing parallels between oppression and emancipation (Bhabha 2004 [1994]; Rao 2007; Said 1994a [1993]). Yet, the tacit move in postcolonial theory's emphasis from the critique of European humanism from a nativist standpoint to resorting to contrapuntality[1] and other cosmopolitan consolidations does not lend itself to an easy categorization or conceptual ornamentation. Although postcolonial theory's ambiguous position on humanism has been documented by a number of studies (Apter 2004; De Gennaro 2003; Huggan 2005; Melas 1999), it is certainly not discussed in the genealogical context of postcolonial discourse.

Edward Said and the Antinomies of Universal Humanism

In Said's *Orientalism*, "humanism is rarely directly indicted, but as the ballast of philological Euro-nationalism, and as the purveyor of Orientalist tropes and archetypes, its complicity with Orientalism becomes evident" (Apter 2004: 37). The reason for the omission of humanism is, as Prakash (1995: 207) points out, that *Orientalism* is characterized by a "conflictual representation" of discourse and its function, which is also expressed in "the opposition between the stability of synchronicity and the instability of diachrony." While Orientalism as a Western discourse operates "as a set of self-contained representations" (ibid., 206) of the Orient, Said emphasizes that the discursive form transforms into an "instrument of power" (ibid., 207).

Although Said terms the question of representation as "synchronic essentialism," implying that the Orient as a place and its reception in the discourse of Orientalism becomes a fixed object, he contends that his "critique was premised on the flawed nature of all representations .... This required saying explicitly that my work was not intended as a defense of the real Orient or that it even made the case that a real Orient existed" (Said 2004a: 48–49). Therefore, in Said's intention, Orientalism did not function as a mere representational discourse without relating to its subjects, which it surely did, but it was also pressed into a discipline "to prod the Orient into active life, to press the Orient into service, to turn the Orient from unchanging 'Oriental' passivity into militant modern life" (Said cited in Prakash 1995: 207). As discursive imagination is transformed into discipline, "the 'synchronic essentialism' of Orientalism is subjected to the pressure of diachrony" (ibid.).

By enabling Orientalism's transition from synchronic essentialism to diachronic instability,[2] "Said removes the possibility of placing the dominant in the same field of discourse and power as the dominated" (ibid., 207–08). In this sense, "the critique of the discourse cannot arise in its own functioning but must emerge from the outside" (ibid., 208), of both the dominant (the Orientalist discourse) and the dominated (the victim of the actualized discourse). This situation, Prakash (1995) argues, "creates space for Said's appeal to humanism" because by refusing to place the representativeness of the "real Orient" against the Orientalist production of knowledge, Said denounces the very notion of divisive human reality: "Can one divide human reality ... into clearly different cultures, histories, traditions, societies, even races, and survive the consequences humanly?" (Said 2003 [1978]: 45).

Correspondingly, by challenging the "realities" of the differential Orient, Said states (2004b: 874) that his "intellectual approach has been to use humanistic critique to open up the fields of struggle, to introduce a longer sequence of thought and analysis to replace the short bursts of polemical, thought-stopping fury that so imprison us." Therefore, Said's association with humanism can be traced to "the critique[s] of dichotomies and essentialisms" (Prakash 1995: 208) that are outlined in *Orientalism* (Apter 2004). Furthermore, contrary to Aijaz Ahmad's (1992) charge that Said's humanism falls into the same Eurocentric elitism that it rejects, Said locates three principle abuses of Western humanism in his later work.

The first one is "associated with very selective elites, be they religious, aristocratic, or educational": T.S. Eliot, F.R. Leavis, the Southern Agrarians, and the New Critics (Said 2004a: 16). The second abuse, which Said calls "reductive" and "didactic humanism," is originally found in the writings of Paul Elmer More, Irving Babbitt, among other the New Humanists of the 1920s and 1930s (see Payne 2005: 88–91). In particular, Said identifies Harold Bloom's claim that "[o]nly in the Western nations, i.e. those influenced by Greek philosophy, is there some willingness to doubt the identification of the good with one's own way" (Bloom cited in Payne 2005: 90) as the hallmark of didactic humanism. Said terms the third abuse as "chauvinistic humanism" (ibid.) as exemplified in the conservative and the neoliberal humanism of Saul Bellow and Samuel Huntington.

Counterpoising the abuses of Western humanism, Said reinstates his commitment to a rather universal humanism by reinstating that "there can be no true humanism whose scope is limited to extolling patriotically the virtues of our culture, our language, our monuments" (Said 2004a: 28). This perspective also corresponds to Said's original interest in humanism as staked-out in *Orientalism*, where he questions the division of human reality by exposing the gap between the desire and discipline of the Orientalist imagination (Prakash 1995: 207).

On the other hand, while responding to James Clifford's (1988: 271) critique that *Orientalism* "relapses into the essentializing modes it attacks" as it is "ambivalently enmeshed in the totalizing habits of Western human-ism," Said broaches the problem of totalistic-humanism (as antihuman-ism) with the belief that "it is possible to be critical of humanism in the name of humanism and that, schooled in its abuses by the experience of Eurocentrism and Empire, one could fashion a different kind of human-ism that was cosmopolitan" (Said 2004a: 10–11). In this respect, in spite of its human-centrality, "traditional humanism" becomes "all too easily assimilated to the political export of hegemonic models of democracy," as it "repeats and reinforces old Orientalist binarisms that have acquired new currency in Samuel Huntington's 'clash of civilizations' paradigm" (Apter 2004: 46). Critical humanism, by contrast, is a universal humanism that transcends conventional binarisms by rescuing the humanist concern from its ideological abuses.

However, critics have repeatedly faulted Said's affiliation with universal humanism for its weak epistemological foundations (Clifford 1988). In Mufti's (1998: 111) argument, albeit the "troubled" epistemological status of *Orientalism* and Said's relationship to empiricism, "[t]he relationship of Said's critical practice to Enlightenment and humanism is dialectical—as expressed in his account of the dialectic of filiation and affiliation in modern consciousness." In this sense, Said's appeal for universal human-ism is driven by an "interest, and *from the perspective*, of all those who would be minoritized in the name of a uniform 'national' culture ... this is a cosmopolitanism of 'stepchildren', and not of the 'ruling kind'" (ibid., 112; emphasis in original).

Said's argument that all minoritized and marginalized cultures should be evaluated on the basis of "noncoercive" universality is introduced in his later writings as contrapuntal analysis (Niyogi De 2004: 43). In *Reflections on Exile*, Said offers a decisive critique of "identity politics that pervade our world, stemming at once from a nativist defense of monolithic cultures and an imperialist 'pit[ting]' of local cultures 'against (or on top of) another'" (Said 2000: xxv; Niyogi De 2004). Against this, by telling stories of those who have common grounds, in *Culture and Imperialism* (1993), Said undertakes the arduous task of a universal, in that sense a "contrapuntal", reading of humanism.

The essence of contrapuntality lies in defining as well as articulating the Self in terms of the Other(s). In so doing, Said argues that all cultures render "a hybrid, radically impure" perspective "that belongs equally to the history of culture and the historical experience of overseas domination" (Said 1994a [1993]: 137). For example, if we consider Verdi's *Aida*, it is neither representative of the Italian opera nor the 19th-century European civilization (ibid.). As such, *Aida* is an extension of the Egyptian culture to which Verdi had little or no inclination as his connections were more to France, Germany, and the general fulfillment of the aesthetic dreams of the imperialists (ibid., 100–20). Given the populist status of metropolitan literature, Said considers Rudyard Kipling's *Kim* a unique text of contrapuntal analysis. In *Kim*, in spite of its irreducible political judgment, it is as if Kipling is saying that "India is ours and therefore we can see it in this mostly uncontested, meandering, and fulfilling way," while at the same time suggesting that "India is 'other' and, importantly, for all its wonderful size and variety, it is safely held by Britain" (ibid., 194). Regardless of their imperialist ambitions, Kipling's narratives open up to a vast corpus of cultural sensibilities that render a contrapuntal reading of the colonizer's journey to the Self-same (Britain) through Otherness (India).

Said argues that such contrapuntal reading of texts and their contexts enshrines "a simultaneous awareness both of the metropolitan history that is narrated and of those other histories against which (and together with which) the dominating discourse acts" (ibid., 59). "Rather than focus on deeply entrenched and viciously ideologized 'us and them' differences" (Robbins et al. 1994: 16), Said turns to geographical imaginary space to acknowledge intertwined histories of divided nations and differentiated cultures. In Said's view, the rejection of humanism by poststructuralist interlocutors has only advocated the non-consolidation of difference as ever-contingent, as if "unknowability" (to the Self) is a prerequisite for the ontological reality of the Other (ibid., 17). In order to refute the politics of ontological difference, Said goes to the core of postcolonial theory; rereading the ambiguity of Fanon's nativist essentialism and his view of humanity as contrapuntally interconnected: "Fanon wants somehow to bind the European as well as the native together in a new nonadversarial community of awareness and anti-imperialism" (Said 1994a [1993]: 331).

Said's commitment to humanism remained unfazed until his death: his posthumously published work, *Humanism and Democratic Criticism* (2004), is deeply immersed in the Auerbachian homage to universalism, laying grounds for a more consolidating theory of "Welt-humanism."

Subaltern Studies and Nativist Essentialism

In his justly famous essay, "Tradition and the West Indian Novel," Wilson Harris (2005 [1999]: 135) writes that "we [the natives] have to put aside at this moment for the purpose of our discussion" the very claustrophobic notion of sameness, by which Harris refers to the rhetorical sameness inscribed by the tropes of universal humanism. Postcolonial theorists became familiar with the politics of redemption and exclusion by virtue of Fanon's appeal to "the restoration of some authentically human condition distorted by European colonialism's inhumanity" (Melas 1999: 16).

In this regard, the arrival of subaltern studies (1982–2002) in postcolonial theory marks the most defining movement in the field. Like Said's theoretical influences from Foucault, musicology, and American literary theory, the theoretical foundations of Subaltern Studies are multiple and varied, stemming from Gramscian Marxism to Foucault, and to the Indo-British historiographic tradition (Ludden 2001). Furthermore, subaltern studies have drawn on "antihumanist structuralist and poststructuralist theory" (Prakash 1994a: 1480).

Covering a wide range of issues and spanning over eleven volumes, Ranajit Guha's *Elementary Aspects of Peasant Insurgency in Colonial India* (1983) is widely regarded as the stepping-stone for the subaltern studies project. In this seminal work, Guha argues that the statistic historiography (of India) is marked by a cognitive failure that prevents from seeing subalterns as the conscious subjects of their own history. Statist history, written from the colonizer's secular point of view, inimically pathologizes peasant rebel-consciousness as effectively "pre-political," if not recalcitrant and criminal. Guha's critique therefore goes to the core of Western secular humanism, which is "[u]nable to grasp religiosity as the central modality of peasant consciousness in colonial India" and, hence, fails "to conceptualize insurgent mentality except in terms of an unadulterated secularism" (Guha 1988: 81).

Following the examples set by Guha, rescuing "authentic" subaltern voices from the ruins of elite or state histories, as well as colonial forms of secular humanism became the most celebrated themes of the subaltern studies project. In addition to this, addressing the historical, ethnological, and the psychological aspects of subaltern consciousness are some of the common subthemes that run through the subaltern studies essays. Correspondingly, Dipesh Chakrabarty's *Provincializing Europe* (2000) features a provisionally post-Eurocentric differential method to the recognition of subaltern voices. Chakrabarty's starting point is Western historicism, which depicts native time as dead-time in the empty chronological time of progress. Universalistic historicism, in this sense, Chakrabarty suggests, is common to Marxist, liberal, and similar histories of capitalism, industrialization, and nationalism and all other secular institutional forces of the West.

In the history of modes of production, historicist accounts portray capital as a teleological world-historical process that will eventually sublate differences in keeping with the universalization of the history of capital. But Chakrabarty contends that the histories of capital's "'life-processes' are always in excess of 'abstract labour', because the disciplinary processes of the factory" (Mishra and Hodge 2005: 396) (central unit of capitalism) cannot sublate the master–slave relationship. Since the history of capital is founded upon the universalistic norm that all human phenomena could be reduced and abstracted into labor unit(s), it fails to register "expressive forms of being human" (ibid., 396) outside of the logic of capital (Chakrabarty 2008 [2000]: 60–66). As an alternative to this global history of capital, Chakrabarty writes that real labor "belongs to a world of heterogeneity whose various temporalities cannot be enclosed in the sign 'history'" (ibid., 92–93). In the colonial–historical convention, however, the only history that achieves recognition is the history of "the becoming of capital"—the so-called History 1.

Against Marx's enunciation of universal capital and the tutelage of abstract labor, Chakrabarty locates the possibility of multiple ways of being human in History 2, which are "'vanished social formations' ... 'partly still unconquered'" (ibid., 65). In this sense, the anachronistic past of the native history that did not have a chance to live in its vanished social formation, nonetheless returns to History 2 as the teleological future of the past of History 1. Accordingly, *Provincializing Europe* invariably becomes a reading of History 2—the native ways of being human that are "alive in Sanskrit or Persian or Arabic are now only matters of historical research for most" (ibid., 5–6). Thus, Chakrabarty's attempt to provincialize Europe goes a long way in uncovering the historical sites of being human in the non-European world.

However, the modes of exchange alone cannot provincialize Europe since History 1 sets the European subject as the ideal human figure against which to judge all other subject histories. In this respect, Chakrabarty proposes that History 2 must be understood in terms of its own historicism, reason, and philosophical tradition. Chakrabarty's call for native historicism against the vigilances of European humanism, universalism, and secularism are soundly informed by earlier and subsequent writings of Guha (1997), Chatterjee (1997), and volume XI of *Subaltern Studies* (Chatterjee and Jeganathan 2000).

Spivak and Bhabha: Post-essentialist Strategies

In the past two decades, however, the critical reception of nativism in social theory has inspired prominent members of the subaltern studies group to re-examine the political orientation of their project. Spivak (1988b: 284–85) for one reconciles that, although Guha's call for the historian to gauge the "*specific* nature and degree of the *deviation* of" (emphasis in original) the discourse on subalternity and identity "from the ideal and situate it historically" might seem essentialist, as subalternity itself "is defined as a difference from the elite," Guha avoids the tag of essentialism.

In spite of her pronounced reservations for essentialism(s), Spivak is not entirely averse to essentialist, in the sense of nativist, politics. As popularly exemplified in her earlier writings on strategic essentialism, Spivak's essentialism derives from the "ambiguous superimposition of global and local productive frames in the postcolonial cultural field" (Chew 2001: 613–14). Since the disparities in global power structures allow little or no "attention space" (ibid.) for non-Western societies, nativist essentialism is touted as the most effective political tool of negotiation.

Complicit with her own views on differential politics, Spivak's original thesis on postcolonial theory—*A Critique of the Postcolonial Reason* (1999)—locates the native figure on the margins of European Enlightenment and critiques its humanist legacy as the edifice of difference. Spivak embarks on an in-depth postcolonial reading of Kantian humanism, which leads her to isolate an important anthropological constant ("what is man?" vs. "raw man") in the Enlightenment project (Mishra and Hodge 2005: 386). The "examples of absolute rawness, the irredeemable native Others," are then "presented as figures who cannot be the subject of speech or judgment in

[Kant's] third *Critique*" (Mishra and Hodge 2005). Rejecting "the bourgeois male subject of instrumental reason" (ibid., 385), Spivak advances the "subaltern woman subject" as the native figure who remains outside of discourses on feminism, secularism, modernism, and even Subaltern Studies.

Notwithstanding her guard against the regulative use of essentialist categories such as humanism, nationalism, and feminism, Spivak (1993: 3) calls for strategic negotiations through "a persistent (de)constructive critique of the theoretical" from subalternized essentialist positions. In that sense, strategic essentialism not only operates as a political force, but also as an intellectual artifice, which serves as the "conscious adoption of an essentialist mode of enunciation in order to precisely reveal the non-essentialist character of the histories of difference" (De Oto 2003: 92). In other words, as Maeda (1997: 125–26) remarks, "rather than seeking to reverse or escape oppositions through the use of essence," Spivak challenges colonial discourse from a provisionally subaltern position.

Although Spivak's selective deployment of anti-essentialisms comes close to espousing Saidian contrapuntality, Spivak clearly differentiates from the former in her critiques of humanism and colonialism. Unlike Said's meta-narratives of discursive difference, Spivak appeals to the heterogeneity of all colonial experiences. These experiences include the subaltern woman and the variances in the course of colonial experience by historical, spatial, textual, and even vernacular contexts—"multiple others" (Spivak 1999). Unlike the subaltern studies scholars, who position both discursive and political agency outside of the Western text and context, Spivak views postcolonial agency as something that is situated within the master discourse—"a situation that Spivak describes as saying an 'impossible 'no' to a structure, which one critiques, yet inhabits intimately'" (Spivak cited in Kapoor 2008: 8). Spivak's suggestion that there is an "unavoidable collusion and complicity between the colonizer and the colonized" (ibid.) is further configured as a post-Eurocentric move in Homi Bhabha's writings.

Bhabha seizes upon the discursive instability evident in the colonial (and Orientalist) discourse and its practice, claiming that structures of power need not be homogenous in order to be hegemonic (Kapoor 2003: 570–76). Drawing on Derrida, Lacan, and Fanon, Bhabha contends that colonial power was preconditioned by a psychic process of ambivalence by which the colonizer exerts both recognition (as master) and separation from the Other. In "Signs Taken for Wonders," Bhabha shows how Indian villagers contest the conversion into Christianity by arguing that the word of god cannot come from the mouth of a meat-eater (Bhabha 2004 [1994]: 167–68). The alterations of colonial impositions such as "vegetarian god" and "vegetarian Bible" not only produce a supplemental position for the native, but pose an impossible cognitive challenge to the colonizer's discourse in the guise of a third space (ibid., 32–37). In the essay "Of Mimicry and Man," Bhabha traces the colonizer's failed attempts at forging a civilizing mission by making "mimic men" as the recognizable others to "the dream of post-Enlightenment civility [which] alienates its own language and liberty and produces another knowledge" (ibid., 123). Hence, as if denouncing all the meta-narratives of the human and the humanist, Bhabha issues the ethical dictum that "the techniques and technologies of politics need not be *humanizing* at all, in no way endorsing of what we understand to be the human—humanist?—predicament" (ibid., 93; emphasis in original). Bhabha further contends that the very premise of the humanistic discourse of "accounting for ourselves," or the autonomy for all, is fallacious and illusory, which remains complicit only with "textual or narrative subjections—be they governmental, judicial or artistic" (ibid., 92). Against the structural impositions of this false self-autonomy in the humanist discourse, Bhabha's alternative is to "constitute a postcolonial, critical discourse," which can contest "modernity through the establishment of other historical sites, other forms of enunciation" (ibid., 365).

Yet, Bhabha's critique of humanism in the colonial discourse and its suggested contentions are not as explicit as other postcolonial theorists. For instance, Bhabha's stance that colonial power was never fully operative in its intended form or content—other than its "hybrid" mode—takes recourse to somewhat curious agential capacities of the native subjects. For Bhabha there is no agency without subjection to power (Kapoor 2003: 571–74). In other words, as in Foucault's notion that there is no power without resistance, agency is possible only when the colonized is operating within the discursive ambit of the colonizer's power (ibid.). It is thus no surprise that Bhabha's conditioning of agency to the colonizer's discursive subjection is at odds with those postcolonialists who advocate the revival of "authentic" or "indigenous" cultural forms as the departure point of postcolonial theory (Chatterjee and Jeganathan 2000; Guha 1988).

Nevertheless, the question of humanism under the regulatory guise of the European master narratives often takes center stage in Bhabha's work. It could even be argued that Bhabha's consolidatory position between the Self and Other emerges from the very encounter of the European humanist ethos with the colonized, and the search for native agency within the discursive subjection of this epic encounter. That said, Bhabha's rejection of all essentialisms—both European and non-European, including nativism and nationalism—assumes a different (even extreme) form in his later writings on diaspora, nomadism, globalization, and cosmopolitanism (Breckenridge et al. 2002).

Conclusion

From the various strands of postcolonial theory outlined in this chapter, it can be argued that the specific attempts to forge an articulation of difference no longer operate on the conventional rules of postcolonial theory, which critiques the Western construction of the Orient/native while purporting to offer an alternative representation of the latter. Conversely, the concern with difference and differential politics has developed into an overt disjuncture between humanism and nativism. The disjuncture, which is far more pronounced between Said's contrapuntal humanism and subaltern studies nativism than the others, has been the frequent source of "uneasiness" for those concerned with the "starting points" and other normative postulations of postcolonial theory.

Yet, the linking of Said's work with subaltern studies in postcolonial theory by "the advocates of the field or by journalists in the popular media seeking to account for its origins is somewhat less caricatured than that of the conservative public intellectuals" (Brennan 2000: 579). In fact, it could be argued that Said himself has contributed to this ambiguity in postcolonial theory by praising the subaltern studies scholarship ad infinitum. As a case in point, in response to the perils of nativism that *Orientalism* has mistakenly advocated, Said wrote an appreciative foreword to the *Selected Subaltern Studies* against essentialist and nativist politics:

> [I]f subaltern is construed to be only a separatist enterprise … [i]t is also likely to be as exclusivist, as limited, provincial, and discriminatory in its suppressions and repressions as the master discourses of colonialism and elitism. In fact, as Guha shows, the subaltern alternative is an integrative knowledge, for all the gaps, the lapses and ignorances of which it is so conscious. (Said 1988: viii)

Notwithstanding Said's stance against nativism and identity politics, there have been persistent attempts to draw Said's work into the subaltern studies project: "Edward Said's *Orientalism* provide[d] the grounds for Partha Chatterjee's critique of Indian nationalism, Said also wrote an appreciative foreword to a collection of Subaltern Studies essays" (Prakash 1994a: 1483).

Although Spivak's and Bhabha's post-Orientalist and post-essentialist conceptual strategies offer somewhat consolidating positions, their vexed relationship to the debate cleverly underwrites the antinomies of humanism and nativism as a matter of identity in difference. Thus, as Miyoshi (1995: 81) aptly remarks, what we find in the works of Spivak, Bhabha, and other post-Orientalist strategies in postcolonial theory is that "[b]inarism is out, blurriness is in." The blurriness of Bhabha's and Spivak's writings often translates into the unyielding synthesis of postcolonial theory with cosmopolitanism and globalization studies, in which the question of nativism is promptly dismissed as "differential nationalism" and "national identity as cosmopolitan difference" (Leonard 2005: 150–56). In this regard, this chapter echoes the concerns of prominent critics that postcolonial theory needs to fully rearticulate its old conceptual fissures before it can embark on a new cosmopolitan voyage (Brennan 2000; Brydon 2004; Chowdhury 2006).

Notes

1. Contrapuntality refers to the geographical and spatial imagination of locating interwoven histories between the Self and Other; see Said (1994a [1993]). Hybridity refers to the ambivalence marked in the colonial discourse through the disruptions and interventions produced by the native subjects in the actualization of colonial power structures; see Bhabha (2004 [1994]).
2. Said's use of the term "instability" refers to the interruptions produced in the Oriental societies in the process of "pressing" the discourse into action; see Prakash (1995).

5

Postcolonialism: Interdisciplinary or Interdiscursive?*

Introduction

The spectacular arrival of cultural studies in the 1970s was bound to unleash social theory from the clutches of disciplinary hegemony. Although the odds of a twin emerging from the backwaters of commonwealth literatures were no less remote, postcolonial theory's affiliation with interdisciplinarity is more vexed than the euphemistic challenge it poses to disciplinarity. While contesting its premature celebrations as a "counter-discourse" to Western hegemony, Dhillon (1999: 191) argues that postcolonial studies is part and parcel of "the cultural production of the intellectual institutions of the very Western liberal–democratic state whose position of global privilege" it "seeks to question." Dhillon's unashamedly candid position reveals the paradoxical (dis)location of postcolonial theory in interdisciplinarity: rejecting the very disciplinarity as a trope of Eurocentric (and hegemonic) knowledge production about non-European societies, on the one hand, and invoking interdisciplinarity—one that "proliferates" disciplinarity—as a methodological validation for its presumed lack of disciplinarity on the other.

The many "state-of-the-art" books to have appeared in the field since the 1990s, as Huggan (2008: 5–7) observes, are assumed to be interdisciplinary by definition, with definitions being "few and far between." For instance, in *Postcolonial Theory and Autobiography*, David Huddart writes

---

* This chapter was previously published in *Third World Quarterly Journal of Emerging Areas*, 2011. This text has been edited for typographical errors, stylistic consistency, and sequential organization in order to make it suitable for inclusion in this book.

that "postcolonialism has to be interdisciplinary (or at least it usually is assumed that it must be)" (2008: 155; parenthesis original) … "to remain true to its unfaithfully creative, piratical and performative tendencies" (2004: 24). In *Beginning Postcolonialism*, John McLeod claims that the very shift in nomenclature, from "commonwealth literatures" to "postcolonial," signals "a new generation of critics" repudiation of older attitudes in preference of the newer, more interdisciplinary approaches (2000: 25). Not only just "that it is interdisciplinary," Quayson and Goldberg (2002: xvi) declare, but also that "anything that serves its purposes, whether originally thought of as postcolonial or not, is pressed into the service of postcolonial analysis." Echoing this all-embracing view, Rasiah S. Sugirtharajah claims that postcolonialism is "interdisciplinary in nature and pluralistic in its outlook …, and it is attracted to all kinds of tools and disciplinary fields, as long as they probe injustices, produce new knowledge, which problematizes well-entrenched positions and enhance the lives of the marginalized" (2006: 538).

Thus, a mere "cultural turn" from literary criticism, "heterogeneity," "pluralism," or a concern for "oppression and marginalization" is taken as a free pass for interdisciplinarity. Very few studies, if any, demonstrate or engage with the diverse conceptual underpinnings accompanying such a "cultural turn" in the individual disciplines. This has led to what Huggan (2002: 246) calls "the perceived inability" of postcolonial studies "to locate its object, or even horizon of enquiry," which is "linked to broader conceptual and methodological inadequacies surrounding the shift from literary to cultural studies." Yet the lack of a definable approach to interdisciplinarity being one problem, the naming of the individual disciplines in such a non-normative interdisciplinary campaign is another. Consider, for example, Neil Lazarus's introductory passages to *The Cambridge Companion to Postcolonial Literary Studies*: "[T]he study of 'postcolonialism' might be said to implicate most of the humanities and social sciences—from anthropology and political science to philosophy, musicology, economics, and geography" (2004a: 15). Lazarus then goes on to situate his collection in "history, sociology, philosophy" that "abut and influence postcolonial literary studies" (ibid.). If "implicating most" of the humanities and social sciences in the span of, say, less than three decades is not an overstatement, the mere implication of variously named disciplines (as being involved) in postcolonial studies is certainly evasive of any normative conception of interdisciplinarity.

Nevertheless, the attribution of interdisciplinarity to an inconsistent, even an arbitrary list of disciplines, theoretical movements, area studies, and emerging concepts is common to postcolonial scholarship. Keown's (2005: 10) view of postcolonial interdisciplinarity crosscuts fields, such as "anthropology, psychoanalysis, philosophy, history, and medicine." For Sebastian (2000: 213), postcolonialism is "an interdisciplinary field sometimes encroaching upon ... anthropology, history or culture studies." According to Zeleza (2006: 13–14), if postcolonial theory "rescued" anthropology from its negative image, it elevated literature into the "queen" of the humanities. "Drawing on," "encroaching," "combining," "implicating," or "rescuing" aside, Cherland and Harper (2007: 90) assert that post-colonialism "responds to" European discourses in disciplines, such as "philosophy, history, anthropology, literature, and linguistics." For others, a "more open-ended search beckons" (Venn 2006: 39–40), one that enables the field to trespass the traditional disciplinary boundaries, into "the massive literature already established in postcolonial studies," including development studies, diaspora studies, and even "cognate fields" such as "third world studies" (ibid., 40).

Such nit-picking of the disciplinary tags and the conjugative verbs used to describe the nature of interdisciplinarity may well be less appreciative of the quality of scholarship that courses through the pages of these texts, but it certainly calls our attention to the callously non-normative perception of disciplinarity and interdisciplinarity in postcolonial studies— callous, I contend, because the oft-cited involvement of "sociology" in postcolonial studies, either through "implication" or "encroachment," is largely unfounded. There are very few, if any, postcolonial critics who seriously engage with classical or modern sociological thinkers or the disciplinary epistemologies that are preoccupied with several modes of structure-agency debate.[1] It is equally incorrect to say that postcolonial theory "draws upon" anthropology (worse, is "rescued" by it), although anthropology was affected and influenced by postcolonial theory and shared similar concerns long before its inception. I use the term "non-normative" because the existing claims for postcolonial interdisciplinarity hold no conceptual merit. At best, they invoke individual disciplines as having been assimilated or implicated (or both) by the field without accounting for their theoretical and methodological underpinnings. This approach not only confounds the ways select disciplines have shaped, and are shaped by, the field of postcolonial studies, but it also forges an irresponsible license to disciplinary crossing in the name of interdisciplinarity.[2]

This chapter, thus, undertakes a double task: to locate the disciplinary bases of postcolonial studies proper to its inception and influence; and to examine whether the convergence of relevant disciplines can sustain postcolonial studies' claims for interdisciplinarity. By "inception," I refer to what I identify as the foundational disciplines of postcolonial studies— literature, history, and philosophy. By "influence," I refer to the disciplines, sub-disciplines, and theoretical movements that are affected, influenced, or transformed by postcolonial studies—the supplemental disciplines. For reasons of economy, however, I will restrict my case to three supplemental disciplines: anthropology, geography, and development studies.[3]

Interdisciplinarity in Perspective

The definition of interdisciplinarity is often traced to the Organisation for Economic Co-operation and Development's (OECD) document, "Interdisciplinarity": "the interaction among two or more different disciplines" that "may range from simple communication of ideas to the mutual integration of organising concepts, methodology, procedures, epistemology, terminology, [and] data" (Apostel et al. 1972: 25–26). Following this, Julie Klein and William Newell (1997: 393–94) surveyed the various practices of interdisciplinarity throughout the 1970s and 1980s, yielding a more concise definition:

> a process of answering a question, solving a problem, or addressing a topic that is too broad and complex to be dealt with adequately by a single discipline or profession … [which] draws on disciplinary perspectives and integrates their insights through construction of a more comprehensive perspective.

In 1985, the OECD issued an updated report entitled "Interdisciplinarity Revisited," concluding that its earlier document had little impact on traditional disciplines or the changing forms of knowledge production (Levin and Lind 1985). Reflecting on the new developments in the 1980s and 1990s, Klein proposed two revised models of interdisciplinarity: instrumental and critical. Instrumental interdisciplinarity refers to collaborative teamwork initiated by independent disciplines to address "real-world" problems outside the academy, while critical interdisciplinarity is concerned with "the question of transformation" to "interrogate the existing structure of knowledge and education, raising questions of value and purpose" (Klein 2005: 57) and "dismantle the boundary between the literary and the political, treat cultural objects relationally, [and] be inclusive of low culture" (ibid., 58).[4]

Correspondingly, Leeuwen (2005: 5–10) proposed a threefold model of interdisciplinarity: centralist, pluralist, and integrationist. The centralist model unfolds between two autonomous disciplines on overlapping subject matters (for example, implications of neurology to psychology and linguistics). The pluralist model aims to bring disciplines together, as equal partners, to resolve problems that affect all the disciplines involved (for example, the impact of urban migration on ecology and economics). The integrationist model holds that no single discipline is equipped to solve a given problem. Various disciplinary approaches are required to forge a conceptual synthesis (for example, cultural studies).

Complementing this, Lattuca's (2001: 81–91, 114) fourfold taxonomy adds another conceptual variant. Lattuca's "informed disciplinarity" refers to borrowing theories and methods from other disciplinary components in the service of a host discipline (for example, sociology and ethnography). Synthetic interdisciplinarity pertains to issues that do not belong to a single discipline, but are found in the intersections of two or more disciplines (for example, biological and psychological aspects of "human communication"). Transdisciplinarity, Lattuca's third variant, asserts that individual disciplines do not contribute their components to understand an issue, but provide analytical settings for a concept or theory that moves across disciplines (for example, Marxism, structuralism). Lastly, Lattuca's "conceptual interdisciplinarity" asserts that conventional disciplines are inadequate to understand certain social phenomena, and a free-floating conceptual fusion is required (2001: 117–18).

Not only do these various models signal a decisive transition from the traditional "two-disciplinary" model, but they reflect new practices of an increasingly commonplace perception of interdisciplinarity. Based on their shared traits and features, I propose three reclassified models for the purpose of my discussion: problem-based interdisciplinarity, transitional interdisciplinarity, and normative interdisciplinarity. Problem-based interdisciplinarity combines Klein's instrumental interdisciplinarity, Lattuca's synthetic interdisciplinarity, and Van Leeuwen's pluralist model. A defining feature of this model is problem solving through teamwork and/or by bringing various disciplinary approaches together to confront a prescribed issue. The second model, transitional interdisciplinarity, is representative of Van Leeuwen's centralist model and Lattuca's informed disciplinarity and transdisciplinarity. This model, which collates the features of "trans-," "multi-," "cross-," or "plural" interdisciplinarity, has the widest purchase in the humanities and social sciences today—albeit wrongly—as interdisciplinarity. The third proposed model, normative interdisciplinarity, combines Van Leeuwen's integrationalist model, Klein's critical interdisciplinarity, and Lattuca's conceptual interdisciplinarity. This model holds that disciplinary knowledge is inadequate to solve certain problems; therefore, theoretical interventions that do not belong to an individual discipline may forge the means of an interdisciplinary synthesis.

The normative model, however, has been labeled as "weak" or "instrumentally misguided" for its latent antidisciplinarity. As Klein (1990: 88) points out, "weak" models can lead to "distortion and misunderstanding of borrowed material … use of data, methods, concepts, and theories out of context." This is certainly the case with postcolonial theory, which stands accused of irresponsible "poking about" in established disciplines. How, then, can postcolonial studies be placed in the maze of such seemingly non-regulative models that deny clear "procedural rules" or "any codified definition of 'interdisciplinarity?'" (Weingart 2000: 35). Quayson (2000), for one, compares postcolonial studies with "synoptic interdisciplinarity"—a collection of ideas and concepts from the established disciplines that results in a synoptic overview of the real world problems in the postcolony. For Khair (2004: 101–10), however, postcolonial theory is transdisciplinary at best, as it leaves the academic walls of the established disciplines basically intact. While others make a case for postcolonial "cross-disciplinarity," "counter-disciplinarity," and "antidisciplinarity," Huggan's coinage of "interdiscursivity" has particular relevance to the way the subsequent sections examine the disciplinary relationship to postcolonial studies.[5]

Disciplinary Foundations of Postcolonial Studies

English Literature

If, as most postcolonial scholars regard it, Said's *Orientalism* is the founding text, English literature(s) is arguably the founding discipline of postcolonial studies. Two distinct, yet interrelated, influences characterize this foundation: Said's critique of Orientalism, which exposed the ideological infirmities of the Western literary canon; and, by extension, the trenchant critiques of textual realism that predicated literary (mis)representation of the colonized societies. These concerns were originally acknowledged—albeit somewhat uneasily—in the commonwealth literatures movement during the late 1960s. Combining ideology with the crisis of representation, the task of the new-found postcolonial studies (1980s) was then to expose the underlying structures of Eurocentrism, including "imperialism, passivism, utopianism, historicism, Darwinism, racism, Freudianism, Marxism, Spenglerism" (Said 2003 [1978]: 43).[6] For postcolonial English literature(s), however, this meant recasting an "authentic" native representation as an oppositional critique. Largely confined to English and comparative literature departments, some of the key oppositional methodologies to have emerged since the 1980s include, but are not limited to: (1) repudiating the Western literary canon; (2) nationalism; (3) *Négritude* and *creolization*; and (4) "catachresizing" English.

As Marx (2004: 83) observes, postcolonialism "is held to *repudiate*" (emphasis in original) the Western literary canon by revisiting and rewriting it. Among other notable examples, some of the most rigorously debated texts are Shakespeare's *The Tempest* (1623), Charlotte Brontë's *Jane Eyre* (1847), and Daniel Defoe's *Robinson Crusoe* (1719). George Lemming's reworking of Shakespeare's *The Tempest* in *The Pleasures of Exile* (1960) and Aimé Césaire's *A Tempest* (1969) provide an oppositional reading of Caliban's character. Jean Rhys's *Wide Sargasso Sea* (1966) rewrites the imperial spatial tropes in *Jane Eyre* by allegorically reversing Bertha Mason's character from a woman who is locked up in the attic of a British mansion to a native island(er) nurturing a multi-ethnic society and identity. In much the same way, J.M. Coetzee's *Foe* (1986) countervails Defoe's character of Robinson Crusoe. Told through the first-person account of a female character, Coetzee's narrative erases the binary structures of colonizer/colonized by invoking marginalization and resistance from multiple subject positions (women, natives, place).[7]

Repudiating the canon, however, is no substitute for self-representation. As most narratives on colonial societies are produced by "gentrified settlers," "travelers," "sightseers," or bureaucrats, postcolonial literatures are perceived as counter-narratives of self-representation articulated through struggles of displacement and migration, slavery, transportation, or struggle for identity and authenticity (Ashcroft et al. 2002 [1989]: 5–9). Correspondingly, the quest for identity through rebuilding the (destroyed) nation has been a central motif of English literature(s) emerging from the colonized world. If Mumbi, the mother figure in Ngũgĩ wa Thiong'o's *A Grain of Wheat* (1967 [Kenya]) represents an iconic figure of a promised nation, the narration of a lost nation and the desire for national reconstruction are the common themes in Chinua Achebe's *Things Fall Apart* (1958 [Nigeria]), V.S. Naipaul's *A House of Mr Biswas* (Trinidad [1961]), and George Lamming's *In the Castle of My Skin* (Barbados [1953]). Although later writings portrayed "nationalism" as a failed project—Salman Rushdie's *Midnight's Children* (1980 [India]) and Ben Okri's *The Famished Road* (1991 [Nigeria])—carried over from commonwealth literatures, it has been a quintessential theme of early postcolonial literatures (Ashcroft et al. 2002 [1989]: 27; McLeod 2000: 67–129).

Despite its roots in the French colonial resistance, the concept of *Négritude* (introduced by Césaire and further developed by Léopold Sédar Senghoar and Léon Damas) enjoyed a unique status in (early) postcolonial English literature(s). As a pan-African paradigm as well as an antithesis to European universalism, *Négritude* appeals to the unique aesthetic, cosmic, and metaphysical essence rooted in Black cultures. Like *Négritude*, "creolization" has been a prominent postcolonial theme emerging from Caribbean diasporic literatures. Originally introduced in the writings of Brathwaite (1977: 41–62), creolization articulates the process of "interculturation" through cultural inheritance, and the absorption of newfound cultures. The concepts of "creolization" and hybridity have significant purchase in diasporic literatures today. Although specific to South American and New World culture, "creolization" is complemented by Homi Bhabha's later writings on hybridity—a discursive space and cultural state generated by the interruptions produced in the colonizer's dominant discourse.

"Catachresizing" the English language is a widely observed narrative technique in postcolonial English writing, and abrogation and appropriation are its piquant qualities. If abrogation denies the privileged English expression of metropolitan English (Narayan 1988 [1958]; Achebe 1994 [1959]), appropriation involves "the reconstitution of the language of the center, the process of capturing and remoulding the language to new usages" (Ashcroft et al. 2002 [1989]: 38). Joseph Furphy's *Such is Life* (1903), G.V. Desani's *All About H. Hatterr* (1948), and Wilson Harris's *Jonestown* (1996) are exemplary cases of abrogation and appropriation— all of which disrupt the teleological, chronological, and even progressive tendencies and techniques of European languages by tampering with, rewriting, and realigning received narratives from the victim's point of view (ibid., 33, 40–44). Furthering this view, Ponzanesi (2004: 37–48) asserts that postcolonial literature should be viewed as "minor literature" (as in Kafka's abrogation of the German language), that expresses distinct national and minority consciousness, an extra-linguistic cultural space within the major (that is, the colonizer's) language.

History

Historicist scholarship entered postcolonial studies through a subset of thematic, including subaltern studies, anticolonial nationalism, and post-foundationalist and post-Orientalist methodologies during the 1980s and 1990s.

Ranajit Guha's *Elementary Aspects of Peasant Insurgency in Colonial India* (1983) argued that the conventional historiographies proper to European, nationalist, and Marxist orientation have failed to represent the collective consciousness of peasant insurgencies in colonial India. Guha's (1983; 1997) critique of Eurocentric historiography goes to the core of two dominant schools of thought: Cambridge nationalists (Anil Seal and John Gallagher) and British Marxist historiographers (Christopher Hill, E.J. Hobsbawm, and E.P. Thompson). If Cambridge historians praised the Indian freedom movement orchestrated by the national bourgeoisie (Nehru and the Gandhian legacy) as both liberating and emancipating, British Marxist historians, on the other hand, perceived the Indian society as a by-product of uneven distribution of global (colonial) capital to a semi-feudal society, which is "pre-political" at its best (Chakrabarty 2000: 12–15). Not only is the peasant consciousness depicted as devoid of a political will in such historiographies (for example, Hobsbawm's *Bandits*), but, since, for the most part, historical documents are produced by the colonial elite, peasant consciousness is relegated to an absent archive or the "prose of counter-insurgency" (Guha 1983: 76–88; Guha 1988). Against this, Guha argues that the task of subaltern historiography is to read against the prose of counter-insurgency, which appropriates peasant rebellions into what he calls "primary," "secondary," and "tertiary" discourses, those that fail to register the insurgent thinking of the subaltern agent (Guha 1988: 45–49).[8]

Guha's argument laid the groundwork for the rise of subaltern studies (1982–2002), which opposed "… much of the prevailing academic practice in historiography … for its failure to acknowledge the subaltern as the maker of his own destiny" (Guha cited in Chakrabarty 2002: 7). Subsequently, the task undertaken by the essays of the subaltern studies project has had far reaching objectives, namely to: (1) reorient the subaltern as the subject of history; (2) in doing so, attend to a heteroglossia of subaltern resistances (peasant movements, women's movements, urban labor organizations, etc.); and (3) unveil the subaltern consciousness (its constitutive "grammar") that is acted out in the "horizontal" relationships and alliances of caste, gender, kinship, and religion.

The revisionist historiography of subaltern studies, however, did not enter postcolonial studies until the late 1980s. In Spivak's "Can the Subaltern Speak?" (1988a), Said's "Foreword" to *Selected Subaltern Studies* (1988), Chakrabarty's "Postcoloniality and the Artifice of History Who Speaks for "Indian" Pasts" (1992), and Prakash's *After-Colonialism: Imperial Histories and Postcolonial Displacements* (1994b) played a vital role. In particular, Prakash's coinage of "post-Orientalist histories" argued that, by positing class struggle, anticolonial nationalism, or anti-imperialism as emancipatory alternatives to colonial oppression, both Marxist and liberal historiographies accepted the essentialist binaries of modern/pre-modern, self/other, capitalist/semi-feudal endemic to European (Orientalist) historiographies. To write post-Orientalist histories, however, is not to reinvent a "real" Orient that might have existed outside of these essentialisms, but to refuse any sort of fixed categories that would undermine the view of third world identities "as relational rather than essential; and to view the third world's histories of resistance as having organized along horizontal lines (linguistic, economic, social, cultural, and "multiplicity of changing positions"), rather than vertical ones (class, capital, and political and teleological narratives; Prakash 1990: 399–401).

In other words, rejecting the essentialist image of the Orient painted by post-Orientalist historiographies also means writing post-foundationalist histories. Influenced by Bhabha's critique of Eurocentric binaries of self/ other, colonizer/colonized ("Signs Taken for Wonders") and Spivak's caution that the subaltern cannot be reduced to a (fixed) representable figure ("Can the Subaltern Speak?"), Prakash (1990: 394) argues for the abandonment of all foundational politics that: (1) thrive on essentialisms and (2) represent for the subaltern (class struggle, nationalism, anti-colonialism). In this way, Prakash's post-foundationalist histories propose a historiography that refutes the post-Enlightenment ideals of reason and progress by understanding third world histories as inherently modern, ceaselessly resisting and colliding with the colonizer's dominance even in their semi-feudal, communal, and underdeveloped forms, however discursive they may be (Prakash 1990; 1994b: 3–20). Further supported by Chatterjee's (1993) critique that nationalism based on anticolonial sentiments relapses into Western secular ideologies, both post-Orientalist and post-Foundationalist histories have been instrumental to subaltern studies since the late 1980s.

Philosophy

Like literature and history, postcolonial studies' engagement with philosophy unfolds as a radical oppositional discourse to Eurocentrism, hosted by two prominent figures in the field: Gayatri Spivak and Homi Bhabha. Spivak's essay "Can the Subaltern Speak?" marks the arrival of a post-structuralist critique of representation, humanism, and Derridian deconstruction in postcolonial theory. Spivak's departure point is the problem of representation within the Western political discourse. In particular, Spivak singles out Deleuze and Foucault's notion of "theory is a relay of practice," and practice is representable because "the oppressed can know and [can] speak for themselves" (Spivak 1988b: 275–79). Spivak problematizes this view, suggesting that it conflates the political interests of the oppressed with the desires of the radical intellectual, and further reduces the oppressed subject into a fixed (knowable) position. The problem, however, is not merely the unknowability of the oppressed person's political interest, but the complex conditions of power, language, and structural privileges conditioned by the intellectual's benevolent radicalism. To this, Spivak locates a two-layered problematic of representation: in speaking "for" (political representation) or speaking "of" (textual, aesthetic re-presentation) the subaltern, the voices of the marginalized become secondary to all forms of representation. Spivak further situates this representational failure in the context of the "international division of labour" (1988b: 272–74). By "international," Spivak alludes to the imperial domination exerted over the postcolony; by "division of labor" she refers to class disparities in general wherein, especially in the metropolis, Deleuze and Foucault claim to speak for the marginalized (prisoners, patients, etc.). To illustrate the axiom of domination and privilege, Spivak turns to the doubly marginalized tribal societies in India. For Spivak, the oft-liberating narratives produced by the colonizer's attempts to save Indian women from sati (widow-burning) deny subaltern women's representation at two levels: first, by obfuscating their subjecthood to their immediate other (that is, the Indian patriarchal system) and then by ignoring the subjecthood to their indirect other, the colonizer. In this way, as Al-Kassim (2002: 170) puts it, "[T]he western liberal and radical efforts to represent the interests of Third World women have the unwitting effect of reinscribing a global class system precisely through the unexamined politics of speech."

If, as in Spivak, the subaltern is configured as a "heterogeneous" phenomenon, speaking for the subaltern presupposes a fixed representation of political desire and one mode of representation over many. In this sense, Spivak's critique goes to the crux of Western humanism: structuralist humanism, which sees the universal grammar of human societies as principally undifferentiated; classical Marxism, which supersedes self-representation through ideology; and Enlightenment humanism whose sublime is set against the foreclosure of the not-yet-human (native). In *A Critique of Postcolonial Reason*, Spivak (1999: 13, 34, 88) refers to foreclosure as a hidden site of the native figure in the Western philosophical canon, against whom the entire Enlightenment rationality is set as a heteronomical quest. In Kant, the native figure is the "raw man" as opposed to the rational human. In Hegel, the native figure is an antiquated, unconscious spirit. In Marx, the native becomes a despotic figure, left behind by the evolution of the modes of production. The various disfigurations of the native as a pre-modern, raw, and despotic subject have served the European sublime as an object of self-reflection. Against this, Spivak's *A Critique* positions the author as a transnational feminist, while cautiously distancing from the role of "a native informant" in mainstream postcolonial theory.

Like Spivak's conflation of philosophy and theory, Bhabha's thought stems from a synthesis of deconstruction, psychoanalysis, and philosophy of history. Reiterating Derrida's notion that "there was nothing outside of text," Bhabha declares that there is no knowledge "outside representation" (2004 [1994]: 33). Complicit with Derrida's assertion that "outside the text" does not refer to what is present and what is absent (in text), but the simultaneous representation of both presence and absence, Bhabha argues that if all representations are embedded in text, including (non) misrepresentations (colonial archive), then text becomes the locus of reversing and reinscribing any given representation of its meaning and signification (Gikandi 2004: 114–17). Based on this assumption, Bhabha rejects the logocentric binaries of Self/Other, White/Black and East/West in that the actualization of colonial discourse is not a one-way process, but a hybrid one. Bhabha turns to the (colonial) historical archive to test his argument that colonial power did not operate in its intended form, as it was constantly (and consciously) interrupted by native subjects. This discursive encounter of power and interruption—what Bhabha calls hybridity or "third space of enunciation"—opens up supplemental political positions to native subjects. As a result, the colonizer's discourse is further unsettled by way of an induced (yet unconscious) ambivalence toward native subjects as *"almost the same, but not quite"* (Bhabha 2004 [1994]: 122; emphasis in original). Hence, as Gikandi (2004: 116) observes, Bhabha's deployment of poststructuralism can be seen as a philosophical response to "imprisoned" theories of Eurohumanism and universalism, such as "subjects as transcendental and unified, and forms of representation tied to realism and a consensual moral community."

Postcolonial Studies and Supplemental Disciplines

Anthropology

Anthropology was originally implicated in postcolonial debates at the American Anthropological Association's annual meeting in 1987, entitled "Anthropology's Interlocutors: Edward Said and Representations of the Colonized." If in Said's view (1989: 210–15) anthropology's interlocutors are essentially the suppressed colonial subjects, ethnography as a methodology authorized the constitutive role of the observer "I" against the geographical disposition of its immediate other—the interlocutor. In its collective invocation of the geographical other, ethnography then departs from the preconditioned axiom that the other must be different—not the sort of difference implied between cultures, but a totalizing and exoticizing difference distinguished from the self. Exoticism, however, is not the greatest of Said's concerns; it is the lack of self-reflexivity in the anthropological practice that denies its own role as a direct agent of political dominance, as a representative of outside power in relation to its interlocutors.[9] As a latent Orientalist project, Said's critique had much to do with the way anthropology conflated and authorized the personal encounters of missionaries, translators, evangelists, and philologists with the Orient, whose continuity remains complicit with the authority exercised by the ethnographic method today.

Said, however, was not the first one to question the hegemonic role of anthropology and its method. Drawing upon British and French colonialisms, Asad (1974) and Leclerc (1972) explored the relationship between European philosophy (universalism) and the practice of anthropology as a marker of Western access to colonial knowledge. During the 1980s and 1990s, the poststructuralist turn in anthropology challenged the practice of ethnographic authority, textual representation of cultural description, and the geographical essentialism implied in the very concept of "culture."

The ensuing *Writing Culture* debate called for new ways of authorizing the knowledge of others, a more generalized ethnography that is representative of multiple voices and plural authorship as opposed to "interlocution" (Clifford and Marcus 1986; Marcus and Fisher 1986). While Said was appreciative of these developments, his held that by ceaselessly reworking methods of representation, ethnography continued to "subordinate" and appropriate the lives of the represented "to the purposes of metropolitan rhetoric" (Thomas 1991b: 7). Thus, Said's *Orientalism* merely added to the anthropological wounds of autocriticism, yielding a limited but fruitful body of works in the 1990s.

Johannes Fabian's *Time and Other* (1983) argued that anthropological practice creates its ethnographic object in another domain—a domain necessary for anthropology's own existence. Fabian's genealogical study demonstrates how anthropology invokes a linear concept of time and a visual representation of text to make the "Other" an object whose time (verbal–aural) is naturalized, and whose culture (graphic–visual) is textualized in an alien domain (Fabian 1983; 1990: 767). Against this, Fabian proposes that anthropologists should be allowed to "do" ethnography but cautions against "writing" as the ultimate method for describing, classifying, comparing, and indexing cultures. This, in Fabian's (1983; 1990) view, opens up space for a dialogistical reflection of ethnographic experience to produce not another ethnography, but poetics of anthropology.

Among other notable critiques, Peter Pels and Oscar Salemink's *Colonial Subjects* (1999) responds to Said's concerns by positively situating the production of colonial texts in the contexts they served, discussing the role of the pseudo-anthropometric measures, bureaucratic gazetteers, and manuals in policing, criminalizing, and gentrifying the colonial subjects. In a similar vein, Nicholas Dirks's *Caste of Mind* (2001) locates the production of anthropology in the service of colonialism. Equally responsive to Said's critique of exoticism, Nicolas Thomas's "Against Ethnography" contends that anthropological fieldwork "should be drawn into other kinds of writing that move into the space between the theoretical and universal and the local and ethnographic, and that are energized by forms of difference not contained within the us/them fiction" (1991a: 315). Correspondingly, Jean and John Comaroff's (2003: 146) coinage of "postcolonial anthropology" argues for an ethnographic method that is "empirical and imaginative," an ethnography of "multiple dimensions, that seeks to explain the manner in which the local and the translocal construct each other, producing at once difference and sameness, conjuncture and disjuncture" (ibid., 172).

Geography

Geography's foray into postcolonial studies was well anticipated by Said's critique of imaginary otherness in both *Orientalism*, and *Culture and Imperialism*. For the colonial project, while anthropology drew the cultural boundaries of the "native Other," geography placed cartographic coordinates over the latter (Driver 2000). Evidently, early schools of social geography in the West defined themselves, just like anthropology, as systematic studies of "non-modern" and "rural" societies. Among other preoccupations, conventional human geography (consisting of social and cultural geographies) aimed to understand how societies come to be situated, functioned, and governed themselves in relation to space, and, inversely, how space influenced the development of cultures, languages, customs, and material and economic organization. The latter, however, became the most effective tool for the racialization of the colonial world which, as in the evocative terms Fanon's (1968 [1961]: 51), is often portrayed as a collection of "torpid creatures, wasted by fevers, obsessed by ancestral customs."

The call for "postcolonial geographies" is, thus, an attempt to rescue geography from the perils of Eurocentrism. In 1992, influenced by Said's critique of "imagined geographies," Alisdair Rogers argued that the notion of bounded territorial cultures as a perceived tradition of geography must give way to a more critical, normative reading of the Self/Other distinction as a global category. Rogers's concerns were echoed by a number of early geographers who contextualized the discipline in the service of the colonial institutions and the politics of (under)development, although the term "postcolonial geography" appeared only during the mid-1990s (Rogers 1992: 511–26).[10] Crush (1994: 336–37) defines the task of postcolonial geography as:

> the unveiling of geographical complicity in colonial dominion over space; the character of geographical representation in colonial discourse; the de-linking of local geographical enterprise from metropolitan theory and its totalizing systems of representation; and the recovery of those hidden spaces occupied, and invested with their own meaning, by the colonial underclasses.

The theme of decentering metropolitan geography from the local narratives of space implied that local geographies must be viewed as active sites of producing geographies, beyond the normative recognition allowed by the "geometries and cartographies of Enlightenment thought, private property regimes, democracy, individual rights, and the national state" (Pickles 2005: 358). Rejecting the regulative conceptions of space and ownership, postcolonial geographers draw upon indigenous knowledge that see place as an embodiment of culture as opposed to the nature/culture binary on which much of the Eurocentric geography is based (Nash 2002; Radcliffe 2005; Sharp 2010). In the latter, as geography is essentially tied to the spatial imageries of "civilization" and "development", McEwan (2003) appeals for a postcolonial intervention that recognizes local knowledge that was silenced, provincialized, or erased, but still central to the construction of imperial geographies. And, as the current practices in postcolonial studies are primarily concerned with textual and discursive strategies of representation, the proponents of postcolonial development geography (Cook and Harrison 2003; Raghuram and Madge 2006) invite an instrumentally guided development paradigm, one that responds to the North–South inequalities produced by neoliberal geopolitics: "material and political implications of different modes of belonging, place and identity ... shaped by the long and continued processes of migration, displacement, settlement, dispossession and the growing recognition of the rights of indigenous people ..." (Nash 2002: 224).

Development Studies

Unlike anthropology and geography, development studies emerged during the colonial aftermath; entering postcolonial studies during the late 1990s. Deriving from economics, Baber (2001) traces the emergence of development studies to the postwar and Cold War research context instigated by an aggressive modernization project through the establishment of anthropology, South Asian Studies, and other regional studies departments in third world universities. A modernist project at its best, by the 1980s mainstream development models ("heterodox models of human development") recognized that state-centered economic development theories on "poverty alleviation," "economic independence," and "food security" had little or no impact on former colonies (Sharpe and Briggs 2006). In a move from macro-models of mainstream development to "human development", "alternative development" models promoted nongovernmental organizations (NGOs), civil society, and community participation as agents of change, primed to address the "basic human needs" in third world countries (Srinivasan 1994). This was followed by a post-development movement, heightened by the failures of the alternative development, contending that both mainstream and alternative development models are inherently Eurocentric, and that it is not the alternatives "within," but the alternatives "to" development that are needed (Escobar 1992). Development studies came to embrace postcolonial studies at this very critical juncture, the looming "cultural turn" that threatened the very existence of the discipline, especially when postcolonialism appeared to be too large to ignore.

In 1999, Christine Sylvester took concerned issues to task by appealing to both disciplines to converge upon what she considered a "mutual" interest—in the well-being of the subaltern. For Sylvester, postcolonial theorists should consider whether the subalterns have enough to eat before they know enough to speak. Nevertheless, since postcolonial studies are preoccupied with the historical and textual examination of Self/Other oppositions, Sylvester believes that it could complement development studies' concerns with ground realities, particularly the power imbalances between the global North and South. In the spirit of "postcolonial hybridity," Sylvester's argument received considerable support from scholars within development studies, geography, and political sciences (Power et al. 2006; Simon 2006). Since both fields are concerned about the conditions of societies affected by Western hegemony, McFarlane and Legg (2008: 10) envisioned that "postcolonial theory [can] create a productive crisis, which can enliven each discipline." In particular, they argue that development studies needs to embrace more definitive notions of power and agency, while postcolonial theory needs a constructive approach to resources, institutions, and networks (McFarlane and Legg 2008; McFarlane 2006). Echoing this view, Radcliffe (2005: 297) anoints the post-development turn as a positive sign insofar as it overcomes antidevelopment populism and the over-celebration of indigenous agency by engaging with "the everyday enactments of development in the varied landscapes of the North and South [that] rest upon (post) colonial relations" and social, political, and economic ties between regions. Thus, heterogeneous, hybrid, and "locally negotiated syncretic practices that constitute people's lived realities and aspirations" are seen as "emblematic of the coming together of (post)development and postcolonialism" (Simon 2006: 18). More recent attempts by Kapoor (2008), Biccum (2010), and McEwan (2009) call for a radical postcolonization of the development paradigm through the democratization of powerful development institutions and non-national forms of dependency (aid) from the Western world.

As the aforementioned analysis reveals, development studies, along-side anthropology and geography, merely integrated postcolonial theory into the existing critiques of Eurocentrism, Orientalism, and universalism in their respective disciplines. Contrary to the tendentious claims, postcolonial studies did not originate or borrow from the supplemental disciplines for it only implicated and influenced them in the course of its development. Taken together, then, the foundational disciplines—literature, history, and philosophy—operate as a cultivating ground to postcolonial studies by way of their own representational failures: in literature, the problems of textual realism and the Western literary canon; in history, Marxist and nationalist historiographies; in philosophy, logocentric binaries, foreclosure, and universalist historicism.

Interdisciplinarity, Counter-discourse, and Interdiscursivity

It goes without saying that postcolonial theory is not concerned with a unified "problem." Even though Eurocentrism comes close to one, there is no guided or "team-based" approach to the litany of its conceptual correlates: Orientalism, humanism, textual-realism, foreclosure, and subaltern representation. Admittedly, each discipline has its own tradition of receiving, instituting, and repudiating Eurocentrism. Hence, as an instrumentally guided approach, "problem-based interdisciplinarity" is not suited to postcolonial studies. As Quayson (2000: 42–45) observes, whereas postcolonial theory fails instrumentally, that is, to provide solutions to the practical problems it claims to represent, it succeeds only as a synoptic interdisciplinarity—as a synoptic overview of real world problems represented in the academic texts.

Like the "synoptic" model, "transitional" interdisciplinarity requires the integration of concepts and theories drawn from other disciplines in the service of a host discipline. This is certainly the case with the supplemental disciplines, which borrow and integrate the conceptual critiques of Eurocentrism developed elsewhere—the foundational disciplines. This, however, does not justify a wholesale application of transitional interdisciplinarity to postcolonial studies. For the supplemental disciplines are mere consumers of postcolonial theory, they are not its productive partners. And, whereas the transitional model requires a home discipline, postcolonial theory does not have a home. The problem is not, as it is for some, postcolonial theory's lack of disciplinarity, but the very model of transitional interdisciplinarity—a seemingly deductive, self-serving category with no prescribed conceptual validity. During the late 1990s, the various models of transitional (multi-, trans-, plural) interdisciplinarity emerged as necessarily self-defining gestures for the onset of classifying and categorizing cultural studies, area studies, and other cross-disciplinary fields in the social sciences. As a result, Quayson (2000: 46–47) is highly skeptical of the entire interdisciplinary discourse:

> [I]t is by no means possible or even desirable to legislate what modes of interdisciplinary configurations should be deployed in postcolonial studies … there is often a sense, sometimes produced quite in spite of the good intentions of the critics deploying interdisciplinary models, of a frantic celebration of theory in and for itself.

Perhaps, then, postcolonial theory is best suited to normative interdisciplinarity for its implied antidisciplinary stance, that is, no single discipline is better equipped to engage select social issues. Without exception, both the foundational and supplemental categories acknowledge that their own disciplines are inadequate or ill-equipped to overcome Eurocentrism. Yet, the normative interdisciplinarity practiced by postcolonial theory circumvents its own rhetorical facet: it rejects disciplinarity on the one hand, and embraces disciplinary methodologies on the other. Thus, for Khair (2004: 108–09), postcolonial studies can best be described as a form of transdisciplinarity, a flexible and free borrowing approach which cannot claim to be interdisciplinary if it is to transcend Eurocentrism. For Mitchell (1995a: 541–43), however, this "flexible" and "free borrowing" interdisciplinarity is an "indisciplined" or "anarchistic" movement, a site of "convergence" and "turbulence." Indeed, for many commentators, postcolonial theory thrives on counteractive suppositions. Invoking Said's *Orientalism* as an exemplary case of "interdisciplinary project", Behdad (1993: 44) conflates interdisciplinarity, discursive criticism, and antidisciplinarity at once: "the aim of postcolonial antidisciplinarity is to expose [the fact that] somehow seemingly specialized discourses are in fact linked in ways that allow for the complexities of Western cultural hegemony." In a similar vein, Zein-Elabdin (2004: 34) turns Spivak's catachresis into a "counter-disciplinary" tool, which "force[s] disciplines to lose their current autonomy and authority." Conceivably, Eurocentrism and its hegemonic discourses are not produced by a single discipline, but a constellation of disciplines. Hence, any anti- or counter-hegemonic practice requires not a disciplinary opposition or response, but a discursive one.

Discursive euphemisms, such as "writing back to the center", "postcolonial revenge", and "minority discourses" depict postcolonialism as counter-hegemonic in the sense of counter-discursive resistance to cultural identities authored by Western domination (Ashcroft et al. 2002 [1989]; Gandhi 1998). According to Tiffin (1987: 17–18), the operation of postcolonial counter-discourse is to "evolve textual strategies" in order for the dominant discourses to "consume their own biases." On the other hand, writers such as Janet Frame, Dennis Lee, and Wole Soyinka hold that any counter-strategies or concepts (such as *Négritude*) rallying for an "authentic" representation of some radically impure cultures are mis-guided because they tend to reinforce the very essentialist binaries of the colonizer's discourse (Ashcroft et al. 2002 [1989]: 40). If not for Ngũgĩ's unabated radicalism, an authentic critique of Eurocentrism cannot come from the language of the dominant discourse English. Consider, then, Deleuze and Foucault's generous concession: when the oppressed (such as prisoners), who are generally spoken for by others, "begin to speak for themselves, they begin to produce a counter-discourse" (Deleuze and Foucault 1977: 209; Moussa 1996: 89). Thus, a genuine counter-discourse can be produced only by those who are usually spoken for, that is, the subalterns, not by those who (claim to) speak for them—the postcolonial intellectuals.

Spivak, however, is quick to embrace the representational impasse, while distancing herself from all sorts of "counter-discursive" politics in her critique of the "elite postcolonialism" of subaltern studies. In *A Critique of Postcolonial Reason*, as Al-Kassim (2002: 172) points out, Spivak carves out "an imaginative and ethical openness to difference ... 'rather than remain[ing] caught in some identity forever.'" Spivak further contends that there is no more pure "indigenous theory" uncontaminated by 19th-century colonialism (Morton 2007a: 7). Based on this view, Spivak argues that "postcoloniality" no longer refers to the "'... colonization-decolonization reversal' in which nation was posited as the opposite of empire" (Spivak in Gikandi 2004: 118), but to a space that is displaced from (the "excess of") both essentialisms. Having said that, Spivak embarks on an inter-discursive reading between the rights-based societies in the North, and the responsibilities-based societies in the South: "[t]he former need supplementation for entry into democratic reflexes just as the latter need supplementation into the call of the other" (Spivak 2005: 131).

Like Spivak, Chakrabarty cautions that there can be no "wholesale rejection of the [European] tradition of rational argumentation or of ration-alism itself" (Chakrabarty 2002: 21). Chakrabarty asserts that, although

European thought is inadequate to understand the non-European cultures, it is even more indispensable by virtue of an imposed inheritance. It is the task of the (native) postcolonial critic to revise and renew rationalist thought "from and for the margins" (Chakrabarty 2008 [2000]: 16). For Bhabha, too, European and indigenous thought cannot be separated in the first place, since the very notion of Western civility (and modernity) derives from what Bhabha calls "the double moment" in the colonial institution: the ceaseless disruptions produced by the natives to "the Word of God or Man—Christianity and the English language" (2004 [1994]: 48). Even a less imposing notion of Said's "contrapuntality" argues for a trans-cultural reading of the European and non-European subject positions.

So far I have dealt with how the normative model of interdisciplinarity evokes antidisciplinarity as a counter-discourse, which further collapses into a mediating discourse between the European and the postcolonial thought—interdiscursivity. As Huggan demonstrates through a careful reading of Said's critique of "disciplinary fossilization", Spivak's "catachresis," and Harris's "transcultural humanities," postcolonial studies "is interdiscursive rather than interdisciplinary" (Huggan 2008: 5): "the collocation of disparate sources confirmed both the impulse towards high-cultural intellectual mastery and a paradoxical will to break down the hierarchies that sanction traditional (disciplinary) lineages of Western thought" (ibid., 10).

In my own reading of the disciplinary relationship to postcolonial studies, the relevance of interdiscursivity is twofold. First, the foundational disciplines can be seen as the mediating ground between European and third world discourses, whereby they reject, receive, and revise select strands of European thought for the onset of postcolonial theory. Second, the various conceptual tenets developed by the foundational disciplines are then received and reapplied by the supplemental disciplines as discursive critiques of Eurocentrism. In the latter, the interdiscursive effects are by no means restricted to the supplementary disciplines I have discussed in this chapter. Consider, for instance, some recent works in the postcolonial field: Joanne Sharp's *Geographies of Postcolonialism* (2010), Nalini Persram's *Postcolonialism and Political Theory* (2007), Mrinalini Greedharry's *Postcolonial Theory and Psychoanalysis* (2008), Michael Syrotinsky's *Deconstruction and the Postcolonial* (2007), and Sankaran Krishna's *Globalization and Postcolonialism* (2008). As the very titles indicate, "postcolonialism" stands as an indispensable (yet independent) body of discursive thought ("-ism" turned into "theory" on occasions), which must be sought after, imported, integrated, or added into disciplines, fields, paradigms, etc., by means of overt conjunctive gestures ("of," "and," "meets"). A traveling discourse at its best, postcolonialism is thus an incomplete, but an interdiscursively evolving field.

Conclusion

In this chapter, I have tried to demonstrate that a wholesale implication of the entire social sciences or a list of randomly selected disciplines in postcolonial studies is incorrect to say the least. On the contrary, postcolonial studies' relation to disciplinarity is highly selective, tactful, contriving, and by no means uniform across the spectrum. Both the foundational and supplemental disciplines have distinct roots, roles, and influences on the postcolonial field at large. This multidisciplinary character, however, does not automatically guarantee an interdisciplinary status. Even in the least normative sense, postcolonial studies fail to meet the taxonomical criteria required for the various interdisciplinary models discussed in this chapter. However, it is not my intention to suggest that the sort of postcolonial interdisciplinarity practiced today does not have any merit. It had certainly influenced a wide range of disciplines and "encroached" upon paradigms, having caused considerable damage to their Eurocentric underpinnings.

Nevertheless, contrary to Huddart's (2008: 155) contention that postcolonialism "has to be interdisciplinary," given the very European location of both disciplinarity and interdisciplinarity, and their quest for methodological synthesis through persistent drawing and re-drawing of knowledge boundaries, I wonder if postcolonial studies should desire to be interdisciplinary at all—should it remain faithful to the representations of the once colonized? For most indigenous societies, knowledge is perceived as a holistic pursuit, as part of one's own natural environment, livelihood, customs, religions, and cultural practices which, however, must be disciplined in order to be interdisciplined (Battiste 2000). In a sense, a neo-assimilatory process is already underway as most mainstream disciplines (sociology, psychology) list postcolonialism as just another methodology in their respective disciplinary traditions.

Notes

1. Although a few exceptions exist, their approach to postcolonialism is restricted to historical periodization following colonialism (Bhambra 2007; Goldthorpe 1996).
2. This has led to a spate of angry exchanges between anthropologists, historians, and postcolonial critics (Moore-Gilbert 2002). On anthropology's role in the debate, see Lewis (2007).
3. This selection is based on certain shared traits of "Othering:" anthropology in cultural mapping, geography in spatial mapping, and development studies in economic mapping (see also Chapters 1 and 2).
4. The late 1980s signaled a new era in the way knowledge was perceived, produced, and practiced in the context of a postmodern (Lyotard's thesis) and postnormal science (anticipated by Kuhn, Touraine).
5. For interdiscursivity, see Huggan (2008); for "synoptic interdisciplinarity," see Quayson (2000); for "anti-", "counter-", and "cross-disciplinarity" see Zein-Elabdin (2004), Khair (2004), and Behdad (1993). For a recent discussion on postcolonial cross-disciplinarity, see Brydon (2013).
6. Although the discourses of colonialism and imperialist pedagogies can be traced to the writings of Frantz Fanon, Albert Memmi, and Aimé Césaire (produced as political speeches and memoirs), these lacked the methodological coherence that Said's *Orientalism* had. See Moore-Gilbert (1997), and Chapters 2 and 3.
7. For an elaborate list of postcolonial readings of canonical texts, see Marx (2004) and Ashcroft et al. (2002 [1989]: 22–40).
8. See also Guha's "On Some Aspects of the Historiography of Colonial India" (1982).
9. Said (1989: 210–13) provides a disputed account of the term "interlocutor" arguing that is a laboratory term which suppresses the direct representation of the colonial subjects.
10. For a detailed genealogy of geography's foray into postcolonialism, see Gilmartin and Berg (2007).

Indigenism(s): Cosmopolitanism, Rights, and Cultural Politics

6

Cosmopolitanism Within: The Case of R.K. Narayan's Fictional Malgudi*

Introduction

> This is truly the age when the joota is Japani, the patloon Englistani, the topi Roosi. But the dil—the dil is and always will remain Hindustani.
> —Mahasweta Devi[1]

These words, first immortalized by the Indian film legend Raj Kapoor, and poignantly recaptured by Mahasweta Devi, are a glaring reminder of postcolonialism's paradoxical (dis)location between nationalism and cosmopolitanism. The *dil* (heart) is there, apparently masked by foreign accessories, which are neither undesirable nor particularly unavoidable, but it is there, and it beats for a Hindustani drum even if the dance features Russian *topis* (hats) and British *patloons* (trousers). Consider, then, the average Malgudi man who often "preferred to dress like a permanent tourist" (Narayan 2006 [1958]: 7): a striped business blazer over a draping *kurta*; a South Indian dhoti or Singaporean (ready-) made *lungi* over a pair of slip-on shoes; a plastic wrist-watch on his left hand (Narayan 2010 [1961]: 181) and a gaudy umbrella in the right, with the round-rimmed Gandhi glasses resting peacefully on his nose tip. Of course, if the striped blazer and Singapore *lungi* reveal the deceptively foreign/hybrid facet of the average Malgudian, not to mention the leisurely air and the bourgeois gait with which he wandered like a permanent tourist, the slip-on shoes,

---

* This chapter was previously published in *Journal of Postcolonial Writing*, 2011. This text has been edited for typographical errors, stylistic consistency, and sequential organization in order to make it suitable for inclusion in this book.

the draping *kurta*, the South Indian *dhoti* and the round-rimmed Gandhi glasses are in fact more deceptive than the simple-minded localism they countervail. The dhoti is symbolic of the neighboring Kannada and Andhra cultures; the *kurta* is distinctly North Indian, of Afghan/Muslim origin; the slip-on shoes are as *nawabi* (Hyderabadi) as they are a mismatch for a *dhoti*; the symbolism of round-rim glasses may be an oversight, but Gandhi is perhaps more foreign to Malgudi than Sir Frederick Lawley who stands mortified on the market road. It is only the *lungi* which seems to be distinctly Tamil (when it is not Singapore made).[2] Despite this vernacular diversity, and the (proto)cosmopolitan[3] quality with which Malgudi's central characters are tinctured, the image of Malgudi remains more or less complicit with ethnocentrism, nativism, agrarianism, Hinduism, or nationalism, among other essentialist readings of R.K. Narayan at large (Ramteke 2008; Walsh 1972).

A prominent figure within the Indian English literary circles, Narayan was inducted to the postcolonial pantheon of nationalist writers who inspired the Commonwealth Literatures Movement in the 1960s (Riemenschneider 2005). Accordingly, Narayan's work came to be associated with traditional, rural/agrarian tropes, as with the other leading Indian novelists of the time who featured village India as the locus of nation and nationalist politics: Kamala Markandaya's *Nectar in a Sieve* (1954), Raja Rao's *Kanthapura* (1938), and Mulk Raj Anand's *The Village* (1939) (Sethi 1999). Yet, the perceived images of Malgudi as an Indian "metaphor"—a macrocosm and microcosm (Walsh 1972: 166–67)—India as a collection of village communities, and the village as its "organic unit" where caste represents its genetic/generic boundary, have had their ideological adherents in the early Orientalist scholarship from Maine to Marx, and from Munro to Dumont. Within this, the notion of "microcosm" not only falls prey to essentialist readings of both Malgudi and India, but to the depiction of the Orient in general as an "organic community," an overwhelmingly agrarian, rural, pastoral space—a living museum of the West's past—one that was central to the earlier fostering of colonial relations as expressed in the metonymical binary of metropolis and colony (Dirks 2001). Conceivably, as the economic and cultural dominance of the European metropolis became central to the ensuing cosmopolitan imagination, Euro-humanist discourses further relegated the (post)colony to local geographies that are yet to be modernized, urbanized, and even metropolitanized if they are to breed cosmopolitan imagination at all (Said 2004a [2003]: 3–15, 62–80). A number of critics have challenged this view by uncovering the hidden sites of "alternative," "our," and "provincialized" modernities within the postcolony (Chakrabarty 2008 [2000]: 1–21; Gaonkar 1999: 1–18), paving the way for postcolonial critiques of metropolitan-centrism in cosmopolitan theory in the late 1990s.[4]

While rejecting the liberal cosmopolitan doctrine that each person is "a citizen of the world" (Nussbaum 1996: 15) who needs to "transcend parochial interests for the collective good" (Grovogui 2005: 104), the post-colonial view asserts that "cosmopolitanism might paradoxically emerge through an embrace of domesticity and kinship" and that it "should be less invested in a traditional idea of feeling 'at home' in the world and more committed to recognizing 'the world' through the home" (Black 2006: 45). Postcolonial cosmopolitanism, thus, entails the recognition that local cultures are active producers of place and geography rather than mere extensions of the metropolis; what constitutes the local serves as the site of cosmopolitan imagination by virtue of the colonial encounter: that is, resistance and inheritance (Said 2004a [2003]: 62–80; Pollock, Bhabha, Breckenridge and Chakrabarty 2000: 577–90). As Mike Featherstone (2002: 2) observes:

> While cosmopolitanism may well be a Western project and projection, how far have varieties of cosmopolitanism *avant la lettre* been present outside the west? What equivalent forms of cosmopolitan experiences, practices, representations and carrier groups developed, for example, in China, Japan, India and the Islamic world? What were the characteristic forms of civility and civic virtues, urbanity and urbane conduct, and how were notions of travel, exploration and cultural innovation valued? (emphasis in original)

Despite the validity of these assumptions, or for the very reason(s) they remain assumptions, cosmopolitanism in general "lacks empirical currency in its failure to impose restrictions upon the political sovereignty of individual nations [which] ironically provides the very conceptual basis for the development of a cosmopolitan vision" (Garratt and Piper 2010: 50). If the weak presence of "local" (as national/regional) in the global is taken as a free pass for the existence of a cosmopolitan condition, it then accounts for the unclaimed failures of the postcolonial critic in delineating the "local" from the "global" and the "transnational," including the "liberal" humanist facade(s) of cosmopolitan theory. By and large, the existing approaches to cosmopolitanism emphasize "tastes," "openness," "adaptation," "flexibility," and "acceptance" as the consumption of "world music genre," "Bollywood films," "tourism," or "Spanish pop-rock," which are routinely dubbed as the signifiers of cosmopolitan lifestyles (Regev 2011: 558–73; Turner and Edmunds 2001: 88–90; Peterson 1997: 75–87).

Accordingly, "exiles," "migrant minorities," "illegal workers," "refugees," "travelers," and "postcolonial writers" are depicted as active producers (and consumers) of this cosmopolitan experience (Nyers 2003: 1069–75; Werbner 2006: 496–98).[5] For critics, however, this is an "elite" and "boastful" cosmopolitanism of "Third World metropolitan celebrities" which is often celebrated at the expense of "the domestic or indigenous artist" (Brennan 1988: 134–35). In an attempt to refute both the normative and the "elitist" (mis)conception that metropolitan culture is a "prerequisite" for cosmopolitan imagination, this chapter turns to the "domestic" creations of an "indigenous artist"—R.K. Narayan's Malgudi. By virtue of its own fabulist localism, its unique physical and cultural topography, the encounters of foreignness "within" home,[6] and an ethno-humanist idealism cultivated by the local constellation of difference(s), Narayan's Malgudi, I argue, makes a compelling case for postcolonial cosmopolitanism.

Cosmopolitanism(s) in Perspective

A semi-agrarian, semi-urban settlement set in South India, Malgudi features in most of Narayan's writings (14 novels and over 100 short stories). Introduced as a small fictional town in his first novel *Swami and Friends*, it has been transformed into an unusual blend of town, country, and city, spanning over five decades of Narayan's literary career. Although the spatial and cultural coordinates of Malgudi are said to be inspired by Mysore, Coimbatore and Chennai, Narayan refused to compare it to any Indian city or town: "[I]t isn't the industrial city of Coimbatore, or tiny Lalgudi, and yet, it is all of those places. It is where we all belong and where we wish we lived" (Narayan cited in Gopal 2011). This elusive nature of Malgudi, as Narayan would argue, is typical of the very characters it breeds. In an attempt to demarcate Malgudi's physical and geographical coordinates, in 1981 Narayan wrote a calculated preface to *Malgudi Days*:

> I can detect Malgudi characters even in New York: for instance: West Twenty-third Street ... possesses every element of Malgudi with its landmarks and humanity remaining unchanged – the drunk lolling on the steps of the synagogue, the shop sign announcing in blazing letters ... FIFTY PER CENT OFF ON ALL ITEMS, the barber, the dentist, the lawyer and the specialist in fishing hooks, tackle and rods, the five-and-ten and the delicatessen ... – all are there as they were, with an air of unshaken permanence and familiarity.[7] (emphasis in original)

In his preamble to Shankar Nag's televised series of *Malgudi Days* (1986), Narayan adds: "[W]e can detect its [Malgudi] characters in any part of the world, in far-flung place like New York, Chicago, Warsaw or even Paris. Malgudi has spoken a universal language, it has spoken to so many."

The universality of human roles in their functional setting notwithstanding, Narayan's curious translocation of Malgudian characters to places, such as New York, Chicago, Paris, and Warsaw invokes, albeit inadvertently, the metropolitan genesis of cosmopolitanism in social theory. "Cosmopolitan dispositions," Featherstone contends, "are closely associated with cities" (2002: 2), more importantly with Euro-American cities. Accordingly, if the Greek term "kosmopolis" translates to "city of the world," the operational terms "polis" (city) and "poli-tes" (citi-zens) are essentially linked to its semantic correlate—metropolis; "mētēr" (mother) and "polis" (city) (Agamben 2010). Therefore, given its isonomic political character, "polis" as polity of economy, politics and colonial governance, the notion of cosmopolitanism itself carries the burden of "the liberal political thought that … descended from European enlightenment writings" (Gilroy 2001: 47). If, then, "metropolis" is a structurally demarcated geopolitical entity, cosmopolitanism is seen as its unstructured extension: not an existing state or city, "but a state of mind" (Hannerz 1990: 238). If the metropolis is the locale of "freedom," for Georg Simmel (2010 [1950]: 108), "[i]t is rather in transcending this visible expanse that any given city becomes the seat of cosmopolitanism."

Postcolonial critics reject both the geocentrism and Eurocentrism imparted by normative cosmopolitanism. For Homi Bhabha, migrant minorities in the West who preserve their "language, food, festivals, [and] religious customs" also inherit a certain "shared sense of civic virtue" (Bhabha cited in Knowles 2007: 7) that belong to the majoritarian cultures and its state. This makes them vernacularly cosmopolitan, as their assertion of "locality" becomes a "right to difference-in-equality" (Bhabha 2004 [1994]: xvii). Bhabha further extends this minority/immigrant perspective to the colonial context: "[p]eople living under colonial oppression had to deal with a number of values, mores and symbols as an act of survival in a culture over which they did not have power—this was the same for migrants in England and slaves in the South" (Bhabha cited in Makos 1995). To fully articulate these encounters both in colonial and postcolonial minority discourses, Bhabha asserts that "we need a sort of regional, or vernacular, cosmopolitanism, to question the division between central, canonical cultures and everyday cultures. And we can do this by understanding the unique way colonial cultures were themselves cosmopolitan" (ibid.).

Since not all colonial experiences are identical, one may concede that "cosmopolitanism be considered in the plural, as *cosmopolitanisms*" (Pollock et al. 2000: 584; emphasis in original).

Anthony Appiah's (1997) "patriotic" and "rooted" cosmopolitanisms draw upon the (post)colony as a site of diasporic and pan-ethnic expressions. Here, "patriotism" and "rootedness" refer to the individual's "membership in morally and emotionally significant communities" (Werbner 2006: 497), which includes families, local culture, and loyalty to ethnic groups. A "cosmopolitan patriot" is someone who remains loyal to the democratic institutions of the state within which one lives. This, for Appiah (1997: 621), cannot be conflated with nationalism for the same reason that humanism cannot be conflated with cosmopolitanism: "[f]or the cosmopolitan also celebrates the fact that there are different local human ways of being." James Clifford's "discrepant cosmopolitanisms" (1992: 108; emphasis in original) rejects this differential humanism/cosmopolitanism, while contending that "the project of comparing and translating different traveling cultures need not be class- or ethno-centric." For Clifford, the notions of "travels" or "traveling cultures" can no longer be confined to the "gentlemanly Occidental" (ibid., 105) traveler. Instead, people of color including servants, interlocutors, and indentured workers who accompany or encounter the Western travelers, are those who produce (often violent) discrepancies within the homological discourse of elite cosmopolitanism.

Timothy Brennan, too, rejects the "boastful" (1988: 134) cosmopolitan dilemma of being "at home in the world" as an alibi for expansionist or suffocating forms of power. Not only is the desire for "being at home" (pre)conditioned by a certain structural privilege (diasporic, class, cultural capital), but for Brennan (2001: 81), the cosmopolitan idea(l) itself of "being in the world" is based on an ideological fallacy that denies its local ground: "[C]osmopolitanism is a discourse of the universal that is inherently local—a locality that is always surreptitiously imperial." As in Brennan's inverted emphasis on the negation of "indigenous" and "national," Lazarus (2011b: 133) argues for a "local cosmopolitanism" set in "a certain *local* socio-natural order (a physical world, a mode of production, a specific set of social relationships, forms of belonging, customs and obligations) [which] is encountered, experienced, lived" (emphasis in original). Supported by literary examples, Lazarus goes on to contend that "there is no necessary contradiction between the ideas of the 'universal' and the 'local' or the 'national', but that, on the contrary, there are *only* local universalisms (and, for that matter, only 'local cosmopolitanisms')" (Lazarus 2011b: 134; emphasis in original).

Lazarus's notion that all cosmopolitanisms are "local," as in Brennan's subversive claim that even the global itself is the imperial local, holds that the binaries of "home" vs. "world" are irrelevant so long as all cosmopolitanisms (even the liberal, imperial variants) can be traced to their origins. This, for David Harvey (2000: 560), consists of a geographical articulation of the production of places themselves: "[t]he way life gets lived in spaces, places, and environments." Since "the production of space is as much a political and moral as a physical fact," Harvey contends, "[t]he geographical point is not to reject cosmopolitanism but to ground it in a dynamics of historical-geographical transformations" (ibid.). These approaches, despite their wide-ranging conceptual exponents—"vernacular," "local," "rooted," "geographically grounded"[8]—have far reaching implications for the way Narayan's Malgudi makes a case for postcolonial cosmopolitanism: a lived space of local/rooted/grounded/vernacular/discrepant cultures and characters; a town, a village, a city; a mere cultural topography studded with fictional streets with the remains of a colonial past.

Malgudi: A Case for Postcolonial Cosmopolitanism

A hand-drawn map of Malgudi, which first appeared in Narayan's collection *Malgudi Days* in 1943, looks at first glance like a huge camping ground. It reveals nothing of its character; an unusual blend of a town, city, and country: a paddy field in the Southwest, a heavy-loaded bus trundling along the Market Road, a taxi, surrounding hills, a handful of colonial structures, a locomotive on the tracks, temples, and shrines. There are neither any coordinates nor signs of residential streets having been scaled or mapped. The only orderly thing in this cartography is the New Extension and the North Extension; with their cone-roofed houses in neatly drawn columns and rows. Though the paddy field near Sampath's house and the untouchable village to the west fall within Malgudi's topography, it is no village. It is surrounded by villages—Tayu and Sokkur—but there are no signs of agrarian life. The huge market area opening up to Fountain Circle may be mistaken for a cattle or grain bazaar, but it sits next to the Modern Indian Lodge and the Welcome Restaurant. The Palace Talkies, the Sunrise

Picture Studio, the bus terminal, the medical center of Dr Krishnamurthy, and the board-less hotel and restaurant may bear the signs of a small-sized Indian town, but there are other discrepancies: the Animal Hospital, the Englandia Insurance Company, Dr Paul's Tourist Bureau, the Old East India Co, the Co-Op Bank, the Grand Malgudi Circus, and everything else that is a caricatured sign of the metropolitan raj—Madras, Delhi, Calcutta, and Bombay. In fact, the statue of Sir Frederick Lawley on the market road bears a greater resemblance to Sir Thomas Munro's in Madras or that of Sir James Outram in Calcutta than the statue of a hunched-over Gandhi in a typical Indian town. Furthermore, the Race Track, the Malgudi Cricket Club (MCC—an acronym for Marylebone Cricket Club at Lords), and the (Malgudi) Zoo are direct imports of leisurely metropolitan culture, carried over straight from St John's Wood to Bombay Gymkhana. True to its fictional character, Narayan continued to plant new structures and symbols with the passing of time: the Malgudi Film Studio, the Malgudi Archaeological Society, the Trade Union, the *Malgudi Times*, an optician, a dentist, and so forth.

And it is through this disorderly convergence of the agrarian and the urban that Malgudi's topography defies every normative conception of the European metropolis. Indeed, as Narayan's stories and characters course through Malgudi's landscapes, the ceaseless collusion between the two domains opens up to what Lazarus (2011b: 134) would call the "local ground" of "discrepant and discontinuous aspects of reality where 'cosmopolitan' is taken to describe a particular way of registering selfhood in a particular time and place." In Malgudi, the "discrepant and discontinuous aspects" are not simply a matter of fictional or fabulist interjection, but part of a (post)colonial legacy where both the resurrection and rejection of the agrarian trope becomes the inhabited "structures of feeling or fields of vision" (ibid., 133) that revives and rearticulates the contaminated (colonial) past. In *The Financial Expert*, Narayan writes that "[o]ne of the proudest buildings in Malgudi was the Central Cooperative Land Mortgage Bank, which was built in the year of 1914" (1981b [1952]: 1), around which the story of the protagonist Margayya's greed-filled schemes of peasant exploitation take place. In the face of an unfamiliar urban boom, Malgudians turn to their agrarian roots, local spirit, and mythic tradition, for it was "jungle" to begin with, as Lord Ram "may" have passed through it, or Buddha "may" have walked on its soil (Khatri 2006: 168). Mr Sampath, The Printer of Malgudi, begins his career in agriculture; Krishna, in *The English Teacher*, laments the loss of his "large, sprawling home in the village" (1980b [1945]: 28) with "coconut garden, harvest,

[and] revenue demand" (Krishna 1980b [1945]: 19). Raju in *The Guide* is haunted by the cherished memories of the tamarind tree "where village cartmen unyoked their bullocks for the night, [which] is now full of trucks and lorries-for there is brisk activities because of the laying of the railway tracks" (Iyer 2002: 43). Like Appiah's "patriotic cosmopolitan," in *A Tiger for Malgudi*, Jaggu grows violent at the tyrannies of urban life: "Let me go back to my village. I'll display my strength and make my living." (1984d [1982]: 93). Here, "going back" to the village becomes not only a source of "strength" but, as in Appiah, it reveals the "loyalty" for one's own inheritance of a morally significant community.

The conflict between agrarian purism and urban dynamism is a driving force of Malgudi's cultural character. In *The Painter of Signs*, an irritated Narayan writes:

> This is a jungle where other beasts are constantly on the prowl to attack and bite off a mouthful, if one is not careful. As if this were New York and I blocked the traffic on Broadway. He [Raman] would not recognize it, but Malgudi was changing in 1972. (1982 [1976]: 13)

It is through this very tension between the static and the dynamic—what Harvey (1982) would call the geographies of fixity and flow—that Malgudi's cosmopolitanism as a "lived geography" comes to the fore. For over seven decades, Malgudi represented a unique imaginary space in the slow but magnanimous transformation from rural-to-urban life, which many Indians of the postcolonial era witnessed. As Rosemary George (2013: 69) observes, "[f]or urban Indians, Malgudi bridged the gap between their own experience and what was everywhere (or at least in upper-caste narratives) promoted as the spiritual core, the rural heart of India." Yet "Malgudi the small town, with its villages, forests, and hills on hand, becomes the flexible space between rural and urban" (ibid.).

Nevertheless, a mismatch looms between the remnants of rural life and an incoming tide of urbanity. In *Swami and Friends*, Malgudi is said to be "one of the most detested towns in South India" in summers when "[e]ven donkeys and dogs, the most vagrant of animals, preferred to move to the edge of the street" (1978 [1935]: 78). In *Mr. Sampath: The Printer of Malgudi*, this rural infestation reaches paranoiac proportions:

> The labour gangs, brought in from other districts, spread themselves out in the open spaces. Babies sleeping in hammocks made of odd pieces of cloth, looped over tree branches, women cooking food on the roadside, men sleeping on pavements—these became a common sight in all parts

of Malgudi. The place was beginning to look more and more like a gipsy camp. (Narayan 1981a [1949]: 26)

As the village life threatens to taint the urban fabric, it is again in the village ideal that Malgudi's lost urban souls, having "wallow[ed] in isolation" (Narayan 1982 [1976]: 29), seek solace. Jagan in *The Vendor of Sweets* attains "enlightenment" at a pond near the villages of Tayu and Sokkur; Raju in *The Guide* finds a refuge in a nameless village near the Sarayu River; Chandran in *The Bachelor of Arts* "discovers his true self" (Narayan 1984a [1937]) at Koopal village.[9] As Ben Highmore (2002: 61) observes, it is the same hunt for a lost tradition, which led Walter Benjamin to characterize the Western city as "a paucity of communicable experience," which is "experienced as a perpetual assault on both tradition and the human sensorium alike." For Simmel (2010 [1950]: 107–08), then, the very notion of metropolis gains prominence against a "less fluid," smooth flowing rhythm of a sleepy small town or a dormant village. Contrary to this heteronomical recognition of anonymity/community and modernity/tradition, however, Malgudi bridges the gap between what Simmel would distinguish as the intellectualistic character of the city and the emotional character of the country "which rests more on feelings and emotional relationships" (ibid., 104). In that sense, transcending the gated walls of the (old) European metropolis, Malgudi is built upon a porous topography where the city and the agrarian pour in and pour out at will.

And perhaps, it is no coincidence that the idea of Malgudi is said to have "hurl[ed] into view" (Iyer 2002: 39) with the image of a railway station. This image, which was later made popular by a drawing by Narayan's brother R.K. Laxman, consists of a wooden fence, a small tiled-roofed passenger shelter, a banyan tree, a water tank, an electric pole, and two large narrow-gauge railway tracks, each for an "incoming" and an "outgoing" train. Subsequently, it is this porous image of "incoming" and "outgoing," not just that of trains, but also characters, symbols, objects, dreams, and desires, which characterizes much of Malgudi's cosmopolitan fabric. As Narayan himself admitted, he wanted "to be able to put in [Malgudi] whatever I liked and wherever I liked" (Narayan cited in Sen 2004: 142); and, as with the passing in and out of each train over the tracks, Narayan brings in as many new characters as he deports them to the outer world.

The flux of inside and outside worlds becomes all the more salient to Malgudi's imagined cultural fabric, which "necessitates" the interruptions brought about by the constant arrival and departure of characters in order to sustain its social (re)conditioning. Otherwise, the upper-caste elitism, Hindu orthodoxy, domesticity, repetition, family ties, boredom, and monotony of urban life threaten to break up the very fabric of Malgudi that it is made to transcend (Prasad 2006: 83–85; Khatri 2006: 148–62). In *Talkative Man*, Narayan introduces a mysterious green-eyed, blonde-haired character called Dr Rann, who arrives in Malgudi (by an "incoming" train) in his "three-piece suit" and "shining shoes" (2002 [1999]: 265, 311). Without much ado, he befriends the Talkative Man of Malgudi, having enchanted him with a United Nations passport and with his impressive résumé of travels from Rhodesia to Timbuktoo. The Talkative Man, a self-effacing figure akin to Clifford's "discrepant cosmopolitan," becomes a passive enactor of Dr Rann's philandering schemes, while cleverly appropriating his "European tastes" and "high culture" to advance his career as a journalist. Eventually, Dr Rann's attempts to elope with a local girl are brought to an unsavory end by his "once true" wife from "Delhi" (ibid., 352). While the likes of Dr Rann flee their own "tethered domesticity" (ibid., 367), the likes of Raju and Rosy flee from Malgudi "to all corners of South India, with Cape Comorin at one end and the border of Bombay at the other, and from coast to coast" (Narayan 1988 [1958]: 169). Then there is Chandran, "the Bachelor of Arts," who is caught between his unrequited love for a young girl, loyalty to his father, and his vague desires to go to England:

> If he was going to England how was he to dress himself? He had better get used to tie and shoes and coat and hat and knife and fork. He would get a first-class degree in England and come back and marry. (1980a [1937]: 96)

Malgudian "domesticity" is insatiable, and it takes extreme characters to test the limits. Mali, the son of Jagan in *The Vendor Sweets*, returns to Malgudi with a Korean-American girl from Michigan who "looks like a Chinese" (1983a [1967]: 43). Once the father learns that the couple were never married but were living under the same roof,

> [h]e stood looking at the girl. … he had relied on her so much and yet here she was living in sin and talking casually about it all. "What breed of creatures are these?" he wondered. They had tainted his ancient home. (ibid., 102)

Raman in *The Painter of Signs* had every reason to despise "this conservative town unused to modern life" (1982 [1976]: 115), for it never approved his love for a Delhi girl who leaves Malgudi as swiftly as she arrives. In "A Horse and Two Goats," an unlikely encounter between a Malgudian peasant (Kritam village) and a New York tourist ends in a pleasant business transaction as the peasant's two goats "get their first ride" (1987c [1975]: 29) in the New Yorker's motor car. In "The Roman Image" (1987d [1985]), an archeologist, like a Saidian contrapuntal philologist, becomes obsessed with discovering the secret link between Malgudi and ancient Rome. In "God and the Cobbler," a mere encounter between a Malgudian Cobbler and a hippie "from Berkeley or Outer Mongolia or anywhere" (1984c [1943]: 224) unfolds into a metaphysical confrontation: "[n]o need to explain the hippie was, the whole basis of hippieness being the shedding of identity and all geographical associations" (ibid.).

As Malgudi's characters themselves reveal the conflictual nature of its traditions, their desire to open up to new encounters arises from their own role-abiding social function in the local landscape—a suffocating city/town. Admittedly, Narayan's desire to preserve and protect the local flair of Malgudi is often expressed in his distaste for other Indian cities; Madras, for instance, is portrayed as "notoriously cold-blooded" (Narayan 1981b [1952]: 166) and "the boys were ragged street-urchins with matted hair and sun-scorched complexions" (ibid., 172). It is, thus, unsurprising that Narayan's penchant for mapping a fabulist topography outside of, yet within, Indian social reality was inspired by his deep commitment to what critics have called "empathetic humanism," "Indian humanism," or "Hindu humanism."[10] If Western humanism concerns the transcendence of difference (alterity, oppression, dissent) through secularism, liberalism, and other rational tenets of post-enlightenment reason, Narayan's "ethno-humanism" resorts to the ethno-specific cosmologies of myth and mysticism as the "other" enlightenment. If human rights, civil society, and multi-lateral institutions are the instruments of liberal humanism, "ethno-humanism" operates in the absence of all institutional and restitutional governance. For unlike the liberal metropolitan and cosmopolitan humanism which inherits its "polity" from the legacies of colonial dominance, Malgudi's "ethno-humanism" lacks the structural privileges of the "metro," the "polis," or the "politan." Invariably, this leaves the mystic and the mythic, often tainted by the rational ideologies of colonialism, as the proper source of "ethno-humanism" that is inherent to the native cosmos.

Consider, for instance, "A Willing Slave," where a mythical character, Old Fellow, meets his own uncanny double in order to diffuse the conflictual nature of real-life characters. Ayah is a "willing slave" who works as a domestic servant in the house of a rich Malgudian master. Graceful, strong, and domineering, she becomes a maternal figure for the four-year-old Radha, the youngest of the master's daughters. As their relationship unfolds further, Ayah introduces Radha to a scary figure called Old Fellow who will carry people off (1984b [1943]: 139–40), but who will remain locked up in a dog kennel in the front yard.[11] Of course, this is only a ruse contrived to keep young Radha under control. This trick, however, springs to life once the real Old Fellow, who is none other than Ayah's "old man," returns from the tea gardens of Ceylon demanding "'I want Thayi [Ayah]. She is to cook for me. She must go with me'" (ibid., 141). For young Radha, the loss of Ayah is both inconsolable and irrevocable. But for Ayah, the ruse is her only means of escape. Here, on the narrator's account, the reader is further contrived to believe that Ayah leaves the door of the dog kennel open and claims innocence. "Is the Old Fellow carrying you off?" (ibid.), Radha cries out. "'Yes dear, bad fellow.' … 'He wants to carry me off'" (ibid.), Ayah responds. In Narayan's genius, real human predicaments find mythic resolutions: the "willing slave" must be freed, but without arousing oppression or repression in this conflictual human drama where rational humanist instruments cannot find "non-conflictual" solutions.

In "A Horse and Two Goats," the deliberate miscommunication between the Malgudian peasant and the New York tourist reaches an impossible consensus. The New Yorker approaches a destitute peasant, resting under a horse sculpture. Assuming that it is owned by the peasant, the tourist initiates a conversation about the price of the statue. The peasant, nonplussed by the encounter of this "Parangi language" (1987c [1985]: 24), understands that the New Yorker is actually making an offer for his goats lying in the grass. He accepts the offer; the statue is bought, the goats are sold. The New Yorker loads the statue in his truck, the peasant rushes to the village with the money, to buy "[d]hall, chili, curry leaves, mustard, coriander, gingelly oil, and one large potato" (ibid., 15) for a drumstick curry he had been craving for a long time. The goats return home soon after.

Like "A Horse and Two Goats," where one man's false acquisition becomes another man's salvation from hunger, "A Career" is a moving tale where one man's curse becomes another man's boon. The 20-year-old Ramu arrives in Malgudi from Trinchnopoly hunting for his next prey. The victim is none other than the once well-to-do talkative man of Malgudi. Ramu robs him in a cleverly laid out con-scheme and disappears from Malgudi, hoarding "much money in Hyderabad, Delhi, Benares, or some-where" (Narayan 1987b [1985]: 49). Years later, the talkative man finds him begging at a temple with his companion, who is an armless beggar himself. For one anna, the armless beggar reveals the doomed fate of Ramu:

"[…] His wife, a bad sort, deserted him. He is vexed with the world. Some Pilgrims coming from the North brought him here…" (Narayan 1987b [1985]: 49). The talkative man, shaken by a fit of rage and anger, walks up to Ramu, but silently places a rupee on his outstretched palm. Despite the redemptive justice of this ill-fated tale, Narayan's "ethno-humanism" is not all about "transcending difference" in the "consensual" spirit of "perpetual peace" (Popke 2007: 509–11). Ethno-humanism (and Malgudi) may lack the institutional bases of liberal humanism, but it is certainly not prone to anarchy or lawlessness. When all attempts to retain the spirit of Malgudi's social order fail, asceticism and mythic realism become the only outlets for all sorts of human pathos and predicaments. In either case, Narayan creates a mythical world of *sannyasis* where dead spirits coexist with the real-world, where irrational events and elements bring an abrupt end to his narratives and characters. In *The Guide*, Raju is left to die as an unwilling *sannyasi* for eloping with another man's wife. Chandran, the Bachelor of Arts suffers a near-similar fate for denying the authority of his parents. Krishna, the English teacher, finds salvation in the mysterious second life of his dead wife. Jagan, the vendor of sweets, returns to his ascetic "master" as a victim of the criminal schemes played out by his son, Mali. In *The Dark Room* (1981c [1938]), Savitri discovers her "true self" in her self-appointed ascetic exile in a temple. Vasu, the man-eater of Malgudi, is deservedly punished in an accidental suicide, though it is the mosquito on his temple, which should have taken the fatal beating.

Unlike the "rootless" or "imperially rooted" liberal cosmopolitanism(s), Malgudian "hospitality" unfolds deep "within" its cultural peculiarities, physical landscapes, social function of community, and a strong awareness of tradition and its limits. In the absence of a state or other institutional functionaries that demarcate civil and civic duties of citizenship or sovereignty, Malgudi represents a boundless cartography where the notion of "hospitality" cannot be reduced to conditional/unconditional idioms: the *sannyasis* like Raju and Chandran are openly embraced by the villagers. Despite the troubles they bring (as in Kant's notion of "threat to sovereignty" and "perpetual peace") foreigners and strangers, such as Ramu, Grace, Rosy, Dr Rann, and Daisy are welcomed by Malgudi one and alike. And despite the fact that its topography is studded with signs, symbols, and activities that resemble towns, cities, and both Indian and Western metropolises, Malgudi remains loyal to its agrarian roots. In essence, Malgudi can best be described as a "locopolis" as it refutes the "metro-glorification" of the Western "polis," including its paternalism, homogeneity, urban vogue, or even the imperial shades of the postcolonial cities themselves.

Malgudi breeds all sorts of postcolonial cosmopolitan(ism)s. Grace, the American-Korean girl from Michigan is an exemplary figure of Bhabha's "vernacular cosmopolitan" (2000b); she embraces Hindu tradition without having to renounce her American habit(u)s. The talkative man, who encounters eccentrics, foreign travelers, intruders, and adventurers, resembles the interlocutor-figure of Clifford's "discrepant cosmopolitan." Then there are "patriotic cosmopolitans"—the likes of Jaggu and Raman— who struggle to defend their rural roots and urban promise. Because Malgudi is neither reproducible nor representable, it is both a "rooted" and a "plural" cosmopolitan space. Even in its quasi-fabulist formulation, Narayan succeeds in forging a cosmopolitan narrative because, as in Lazarus's (2011: 133) view, the success of such an undertaking would entail the writer's "ability to find the words, concepts, figures, tropes, and narrative forms to mediate between and thread together—in ways that are not merely plausible but, more importantly, *intelligible* and *transmissible*" (emphasis in original).

Conclusion

In 1967, Narayan wrote a condemnatory review of the Bollywood adaptation of *The Guide*, having learnt that the film was set in the Western Indian city of Jaipur:

> My story takes place in South India … It is South-Indian in costume, tone and content. Although the whole country is one, there are diversities and one has to be faithful in delineating them. You have to stick to my geography and sociology. Although it is a world of fiction, there are certain inner veracities. (Narayan 2001)

Much to Narayan's credit, it is in light of this "faithful delineation" of the "veracities," "diversities," "costume," and "geography" that Malgudi's local character remains all the more isonomic. And to reduce Malgudi to an Indian "microcosm" means not only to deny its local character, but to attribute it to a "larger-than-life" national(ist) trope. Yet such reductionisms are not immune to the admirers of Narayan who go on to equate Malgudi with "Hindu upper-caste pan-India, resistant to change, eternal and immutable" (Mukherjee 2000: 171). In this chapter, I have tried to demonstrate that Malgudi, both as a postcolonial topography and a topography of the postcolony, breeds cosmopolitanism by way of seeing, desiring, imagining, and receiving the world "through the local" as opposed to a passive absorption and/or reception of global modernity, metropolitan urbanity, worldly rhetoric, imperial imports, and other pedantic schemes of universal humanism. Although it is not my intention to suggest that the various "exilic," "diasporic," or "minority" cosmopolitanisms in contemporary postcolonial discourse have no conceptual merit, they simply fail to register the local as an active site of cultivating cosmopolitan ethics and experience. And any cosmopolitanism uninspired by geography and "geographical specificity," as Harvey (2000: 557–58) reminds us, "is either mere heterotopic description or a passive tool of power for dominating the weak."

Notes

1. This quote is an excerpt from Mahasweta Devi's inaugural lecture at the Frankfurt Book Festival in 2006. Devi's words are adapted from Shankardas Kesarilal's lyrics written for the film *Sree 420* (1955).

2. *Lungi* is a distinctly Tamil costume, though Narayan's reference to Singapore is a deliberate invocation of the diasporic context of the Tamil settlers outside of India. I would like to thank Dieter Riemenschneider, Birte Heidemann, Ines Detmers, and Lucienne Loh for commenting on earlier drafts of this chapter.

3. The parenthetical prefix "proto" is adopted from Spivak's reading of Marx as a "proto-deconstructionist," one who is "not" unaware of the representational failures of "class consciousness" among the French peasants (Spivak 1988b: 271–313). By the same token, Narayan's Malgudi man is "not" unaware of the "world" outside of Malgudi.

4. See Gikandi (2010: 22–35) and Spencer (2010: 36–47) for a recent summary of the relevant debates in postcolonial studies.

5. There are, however, a few notable exceptions: Shompa Lahiri's (2010) depiction of Brahmo Cosmopolitanism based on Tagore's writing; Julie Mullaney's (2002) analysis of transnational feminism in Arundhati Roy's *God of Small Things*. Nonetheless, there is a general lack in registering the postcolonial "local" as a site for producing cosmopolitan imagination outside of the "transnational" and "diasporic" enclaves, see Black (2006: 45–65); Knowles (2007: 1–11).

6. This is analogous to Bill Ashcroft's notion of "transnation" as a site of diasporic encounters within the cultural spheres of a nation-state (2010: 72–85).

7. Narayan (1984a [1972]: 8); my citations in this chapter are drawn from the 1984 edition.

8. I am aware of the fact that Harvey is not a postcolonial theorist per se, but his writings have had a considerable impact on the emergence of "postcolonial geography" in the late 1990s, see Popke (2007).

9. This observation is based on the map of Malgudi in *Malgudi Days* (1984a [1972]).
10. Though I am wary of the "Hindu-centrist" or "anti-secular" undertones of this approach to Narayan's work, there is enough defense for Narayan's well-intended, anti-essentialist, anti-astheist reception of Hinduism; see Riemenschneider (2005: 164–228).
11. This observation is based on Shankar Nag's television series *Malgudi Days* (1986).

7

(An)other Way of Being Human: Indigenous Alternatives to Postcolonial Humanism*

Introduction

In *The Wretched of the Earth*, Frantz Fanon writes, "[f]or Europe, and for humanity, comrades, we must grow a new skin, we must work out new concepts, and try to set afoot a new man" (1968 [1961]: 316).[1] Arguably, Fanon's apocalyptical vision of the "other man" is a crucial moment in postcolonial theory's pursuit for an alternative to Eurocentric humanism.[2] Variously proclaimed as the *missão civilizadora* (civilizing mission) and the White Man's Burden by the European colonizers, the abuses of Euro-humanism are again best captured in Fanon's famous exhortation: "leave this Europe where they are never done talking of Man, yet murder men everywhere they find them" (1968 [1961]: 311). Fittingly, postcolonial discourse opposes the Universal Declaration of Human Rights (Universal Declaration hereafter) of 1948 as an ideological extension of colonial humanism;[3] the "benevolence and rationality advanced by colonial apologists" therein, who (ab)used humanist narratives to "promote social hierarchies and the violence necessary to maintain them" (De Gennaro 2003: 54).

Yet postcolonial theory's silence in addressing the Declaration on the Rights of Indigenous Peoples in 2007 ("Declaration" hereafter), albeit its selective deployment of the terms "native" and "indigene" to refer to the

---

* This chapter was previously published in *Third World Quarterly - Journal of Emerging Areas*, 2011. This text has been edited for typographical errors, stylistic consistency, and sequential organization in order to make it suitable for inclusion in this book.

victims of all colonialisms, does not lend itself to an easy explanation or justification. Naively or unwittingly, postcolonial theory conflates the "native" figure of the now-postcolonial national cultures with some 370 million indigenous and tribal populations scattered all around the world. This leads to a bi-fold problem in the context of the Declaration in particular, and the manner in which postcolonial theory denounces Eurocentric humanism in general. First, the Declaration of 2007 appealed to a distinct humanist provision for collective rights and self-determination of the indigenous peoples, both within and outside the national cultures. In the latter, the native figure comes to efface its own uncanny double—the native to the colonizer, and then native to the colonizer's colonized—the indigene, the tribal, the *adivasi* (indigenous, original inhabitant), and so on. Second, if the Declaration concedes a special provision for the indigenous populations in relation to "the other" (conventional) natives of colonialism who now occupy the majoritarian-national cultures as dominant ethnic groups(s), how can then postcolonial theory rescue "the" native—"the" indigene—from just "another" native in its challenge to Euro-humanism? The sheer significance of the Declaration for postcolonial discourse and its humanist critique notwithstanding, it is somewhat puzzling that indigenous rights find no place in the elaborate debates on postcolonial theory's "introspections" and "retrospections."[4] For a more substantive theoretical account on the indigenous rights movement, one has to look outside the postcolonial field; political science, sociology, and international law (Anaya 2004; Kymlicka 1999; Wright 2001). Evidently, the many illuminating studies to have emerged on the prospects, promises, and reflections on the Declaration since 2007 have come from indigenous scholars themselves, who continue to operate on the "decolonization" theories and methodologies that inspired postcolonial discourse in the first place.[5]

As this chapter suggests, the Declaration of 2007 remains faithful to Fanon's notion of "growing new skin" of a "different mankind," though the existing strands of postcolonial humanism may relegate such allegorical subversion to essentialist politics.[6] Yet the inadequacies of contemporary postcolonial discourse in addressing the Declaration or the indigenous rights, in general, cannot be salvaged by simply re-orienting postcolonial theory's approach to humanism or its critique, but by drawing upon the ideological lessons imparted by the successes of the Indigenous Peoples Movement (IPM, hereafter) leading to the Declaration in 2007. In essence, this chapter contends that the IPM succeeds in what postcolonial theory has conventionally set out to do, that is, to provide an alternative understanding of being human.

Postcolonial Humanism and Rights

Postcolonial approaches to humanism reveal two distinct currents. First, in what I would call the foundations of an alter-humanist thought—a humanism that positively enables the colonizer's ascribed otherness—can be traced to the early postcolonial thinkers, such as Frantz Fanon, Albert Memmi, and Aimé Césaire. Second, a "consolidating," "residual," or "inclusive" humanism (Hassan 1996; Karavanta and Morgan 2008) ("critical humanism" hereafter) that is neither averse to nor fully complicit with the European humanism as found in the writings of Edward Said, Dipesh Chakrabarty, Gayatri Spivak, and Homi Bhabha.

In his critique of the European philosophy of humanity, Fanon calls for a radically new humanist paradigm which portrays the African as the alter-human. There is a distinctly redemptive quality to this counter-humanism in Fanon's argument, which pits the native subjects against the colonizer(s) as ontologically ("ontological resistance") other humans (Fanon 1967 [1952]: 110). Evidently, as in the title of his book *Wretched of the Earth*, Fanon attributes this new human quality to "all" the "wretched" of the "earth." The "Algerian Revolution," for Fanon, is "the oxygen" (1965 [1959]: 13) for national liberation, not only in Africa but for the entire "wretched" humanity. Lazarus terms Fanon's liberationism "a 'new' humanism," which is "predicated upon a formal repudiation of the degraded European form and borne embryonically in the national liberation movement" (Lazarus 1993: 93). In what critics have called "revolutionary" and "radical humanism," Fanonian humanism is oriented toward (re)creating a "new" man "outside" Eurocentrism—"elsewhere than in Europe" (Fanon 1968 [1961]: 315).

As Hiddleston (2010) argues, like Fanon, Césaire's concept of *Négritude*, which, despite the criticism that it (negatively) reinforces the very binary essentialism it opposes, is essentially humanist. While Césaire's *Négritude* is popularly conceived as a pan-African cultural movement, with an emphasis on black culture(s) and its cosmos, Hiddleston argues that it is not a "unidirectional movement" for its implied "reconfiguration of geographical space, which, far from simply returning the black man to Africa, brings him into contact with territories across the world" (ibid., 90). Hence, Césaire's diasporic solidarity servers as "a halting step on the road to the construction of a postcolonial ethical criticism" (ibid., 102), one that also anticipates the inclusive humanism of Said, and the oppositional humanism of Fanon (ibid., 89). Although Césaire rejects European humanism as "corrupt" racialism, he is not dismissive of a universalism that is "removed" from its "abuses" (De Gennaro 2003: 58). In fact, as Mara De Gennaro observes, Césaire's fictional accounts are deeply immersed in "plumbing the depths" of an "unknowable," "natural," "primitive," yet a "profound" state of "being" human "over whom all sorts of ancestral layers and alluviums had been deposited" (Césaire cited in De Gennaro 2003: 60).

Albert Memmi, too, belongs to the same breed of radical humanists as Fanon and Césaire. In his influential work—*The Colonizer and the Colonized* (2003 [1957])—Memmi provides a provocative commentary on the pathologies of inhumanity in colonial discourse. Memmi observes: "to expect the colonized to open his mind to the world and be a humanist and internationalist would seem to be ludicrous thoughtlessness" (2003 [1957]: 179). Thus, even at "the risk of falling into exclusionism and chauvinism" (ibid.), Memmi advocates that the colonized must set "national solidarity against human solidarity—and even ethnic solidarity against national solidarity" (ibid.). Of course, Memmi's "ethnocentrism" may well be a rhetorical assertion at best, but his account of the almost "inalienable" relationship between the colonizer and the colonized reconfigures itself as a catachrestic ideological device for the latter to dislocate, disfigure, and decenter the received humanism of the colonizer. Despite the "egocentric" and "ethnocentric" (Yetiv 1989: 128) responses to colonial tyranny, Memmi's work appeals "to all nations of the world, of all religions and ethnicities, to … conjugate their efforts and pool their resources to combat human suffering, poverty, and disease that lead to the only certainty, death" (ibid., 131).

Taken together, the humanist critiques of Fanon, Césaire, and Memmi have remained central to the writings on postcolonial theory during the 1980s and 1990s, which argued that colonial discourse canonized European humanism as a rhetorical device to transform the raw man (native as animal) into a real man (Armstrong 2002: 413–15). Against this view, postcolonial theory generally held that the colonized native has always already been "human," and is simply disfigured (Orientalism, for instance) as the "not-yet-human" in the discourses of European humanism. As this perspective yields the supplemental political position that the colonized native person is the "other human" in relation to the European human, the postcolonial view asserts that the Universal Declaration is part and parcel of a "residual humanism," one that is set out to rescue the (non)human other in almost "heroic or mystical language" (Charlesworth 1994: 59). Indeed, as Pheng Cheah observes, the presumption of the grandiose notions in the preamble of the Universal Declaration Article 1 that all human beings are "rational" beings, born with "dignity" are not only "contentless" (Cheah 2004: 153), but they have no credible philosophical or theological meanings in the non-European cultures (ibid.).

Despite their radical assertions—perhaps precisely for that reason—the alter-humanist narratives of Fanon, Memmi, and Césaire have been gradually refashioned and reapplied by later postcolonial theorists.[7] This has led to an uneasy coexistence of "the anti-humanist developments of post-structuralism and multiculturalism with humanisms articulated in varying degrees and explicitness" (De Gennaro 2003: 62) *within* postcolonial cultural theory. A case in point, Anthony Appiah proclaims that while there "are *different* local human ways of being," it is possible to "live with" humanism's "deadening urge to uniformity" (1997: 621; emphasis in original). Such conflating accounts of humanism and localism, universalism and culturalism, and globalism and nativism have often amounted to what critics call "residual humanism"—one that recedes into the very liberal humanist thought it strives to exit from (Lazarus 2011a: 193).

Although Said frequently (and strategically) drew upon human rights language in defense of Palestine, Iran, and Iraq, his appeal for "critical" and "contrapuntal" humanism entails the paradoxical undertones of humanism in the absence of universalism. Said's homogenization of the West, for instance, is considered as thoroughly essentialist for its ensuing "third worldism," and the woeful negation of many nation states in the Western world that themselves were the victims of imperial domination (Lazarus 2011a: 190–96). In addition to this, Said's incessant deification of criticism and intellectual activity—"[n]ever solidarity before criticism" (Said 1994b: 32)—suffers from the same elitist pedagogies (of humanism) it seeks to dismantle. Yet, Said's refusal to treat Palestine as a special case, wherein he places "solidarity" before criticism, clearly reaffirms his commitment to humanism by means of a contrapuntal critique. Consider, for instance, Said's conflation of national identity, rights, and universalism in his last public address in February 2003 at the University of California Berkeley:

> So, far from Israel and the Palestinians being a special case of unusual circumstances, I think the exact opposite is true – that because Palestine is perhaps of all places on earth the most densely saturated with cultural and religious significance, precisely that reality makes it an instance of universality thwarted and flouted. The universality of human co-existence, human acceptance of the Other, and the human construction of a just and fair society for all – and certainly not only for some of its residents – are all relevant principles. (Said 2003)

In spite of this, Dipesh Chakrabarty, too, endorses Said's sympathetic reception of metropolitan humanism: "the most trenchant critic of the institution of 'untouchability' in British India refer us back to some originally European ideas about liberty and human equality" (2008 [2000]: 5). Situating himself as a postcolonial theorist "within this inheritance," Chakrabarty rereads Fanon in an identical fashion to Said:[8] "Fanon's struggle to hold on to the Enlightenment idea of the human—even when he knew that European imperialism had reduced that idea to the figure of the settler-colonial white man—is now itself a part of the global heritage of all postcolonial thinkers" (ibid.).

Arguing that there is no more pure "indigenous theory" uncontaminated 19th-century colonialism (Spivak cited in Morton 2007a: 7), Gayatri Spivak devles into the representational impasse of humanism (and the humanities) in her critique of essentialist politics. As Jill Didur and Teresa Heffernan suggest, for Spivak, it is possible to construct "an ethics of alterity that is not reducible to identity politics" (2003: 11), since the (gendered) subaltern is "not" fully detached from the forces of global capitalism. In her deconstructed reading of rights and responsibilities, Spivak writes that "the usual thing is to complain about the Eurocentrism of human rights. I have no such intention" (2004: 524). Accordingly, Spivak revokes the heuristic distinction between rights-based societies in the North, and responsibilities-based societies in the South, about which she concedes, "[t]he former need supplementation for entry into democratic reflexes just as the latter need supplementation into the call of the other" (2005: 131). While acknowledging the hegemonic role of human rights discourse, Spivak maintains that responsibility-based cultures keep their subjectivity "alive" largely because "parts of the[ir] mind [are] not accessible to reason" (Spivak 2004: 542) and therefore "inaccessible to us as objects and instruments of knowledge" (ibid., 545). At the same time, Spivak is not dismissive of the human rights doctrine, as stated in her aversion to Eurocentrism which, in her view, "has turned out to be the breaking of the new nations, in the name of their breaking-in into the international community of nations" (ibid., 525). To that end, Spivak calls for an enabling vision (against "violation") through language-based ("vernacular") humanities and teaching, which have the capacity to produce qualitatively different ("plural") kind of pedagogies for both humanist ethics and human rights activists when they broach "other" spaces and their subjects with humility and caution (2004; 2005; Didur and Heffernan 2003). For Spivak (2003: 72–73), then, the very idea of being human means "to be intended toward the other" (Spivak 2003: 73), one that is not derivative of reason, but of an "alterity" that is unnamed and "discontinuous."

In much the same way, Bhabha argues that the "European" and the "indigenous" cannot be conceived as isonomic categories given that the colonizer's attempts to forge "discriminatory identities" were met by constant "disruptions" and "disavowals" by the colonial subjects themselves (2004 [1994]; 110, 162). Thus, in responding to Okin's (1997) critique that "minority rights" are harmful to multiculturalism since they perpetuate patriarchal practices in the name of "tradition," Bhabha (1997) argues that there are no "pure minorities" who do not embody liberal ideologies of rights inasmuch as there is no "pure" dominant/West (liberal) that is devoid of sexism and patriarchal values. Bhabha further contends, "I do not wish to press the tired and overused charge of 'Eurocentrism' against such an argument" (ibid.). Against this, in his essay "On Minorities: Cultural Rights," Bhabha writes:

> The creation of new minorities reveals a liminal, interstitial public sphere that emerges *in-between* the state and the non-state, *in-between* individual rights and group needs .... In fact, the prevailing school of legal opinion specifically describes minority cultural rights as assigned to 'hybrid' subjects who stand somewhere in-between individual needs and obligations, and collective claims and choices, in partial cultural milieux. (Bhabha 2000a: 4–5; emphasis in original)

For Bhabha, then, if being human is essentially a multicultural category, minority and cultural rights belong to a hybrid realm consisting of the new wave of immigrants, refugees, and diasporic populations who fall outside the national cultures. Accordingly, Bhabha (2000a: 3) goes on to invoke Article 27 of the Universal Declaration,[9] reaffirming that minority and cultural rights have a place within (liberal) human rights discourse.

Unlike the critical humanist approaches of Said, Bhabha, Spivak, and Chakrabarty, the IPM shares more in common with alter-humanist critique. As such, the IPM is opposed to the Universal Declaration as it is premised on the pervasion and preservation of individual rights (for example, right to education, health, water), while categorically undermining the special status of the indigenous peoples for "collective rights" (Henderson 2009; Wright 2004). In fact, as nation-states deemed the Universal Declaration as an adequate proxy for individual equality for all ("turning everyone to be a lawful citizen"), it has led to a forcible assimilation of indigenous peoples into the modern state systems in recent times (Henderson 2009: 1–20). Until recently, both humanism and human rights discourses were used in defense of the integrationalist policies deployed by the states in the post-rights era (for example, Indian and Northern Affairs of Canada, Australia's Aboriginal Protection Board). Indeed, it comes as no surprise that most indigenous scholars regard European human rights as "missionary in the best sense of the term" (Donnelly 1998: 15), comparable to that of the "civilizing mission": "[d]espite the fatal tainting of the language of 'civilization' by abuses carried out under (and by the exponents of) the classic standard of civilization, internationally recognized human rights share a similar legitimating logic" (ibid., 16).

Accordingly, the proponents of indigenous rights hold that the ethical imperatives of the Universal Declaration derive from select historical and ideological moments, specific to European cultures. The departure point of the indigenous critique of human rights is the doctrines of natural rights and natural law in European political thought. Rooted in the biblical mythologies of the Garden of Eden, Western thought emphasizes that individuals exist in a state of nature isolated from organic society (Clinton 1990). Hence, in the absence of a compact with the state or an organized government, it is individuals' natural right to defend themselves against other such individuals—a situation that nevertheless lacks the sociality and governance necessary for civic existence.[10] In "natural law doctrine," then, all members of an organized society delegate their sovereign right to the state to exist freely, independent of law or custom, in exchange for peace, security, governance, and civic organization (ibid., 740–41). As Western political thought is based on the assumption that "the individual antedates the state," it focuses primarily on the relationships ("compact") of the state with that of the "individual" (ibid., 740). Ironically, this had led to a distorted perception of the indigenous cultures as having existed in a "disorganized state of nature" that lacked social organization (ibid.). In Clinton's view, "rights are legal constructs that limit state action. At core, most modern western conceptions of human rights owe their existence to some pattern of thought of this type, whether derived from Locke, Hobbes, Rousseau, Rawls, or, possibly, Dworkin" (ibid.,740–41).

In the Western world, the American Declaration of Independence and Bill of Rights, and the French Declaration of the Rights of Man and Citizens in the late 18th century laid the grounds for the modern rights movement. A defining feature of the rights movement has been to both reinstate the natural rights doctrine by realigning the state's role with that of individual autonomy. These developments were fuelled by the rapid shifts in the political climate of the Western hemisphere between the mid-19th and 20th centuries: the abolition of slavery; the rise and fall of the World Wars; the formal end of colonialism; the Holocaust; and the Nuremburg Trials. Not only did these events evoked a renewed interest in the humanist ideals set forth by the Enlightenment project, but they ensured that the right to secure individual freedoms became a poster child for the anti-totalitarian campaign in the West (Henderson 2009; Wright 2001).

With its distinct Western legacy, Canada's human rights scholar Shelly Wright argues, the human rights doctrine is "coterminous with corporate capitalism" and individual emancipation initiative (Wright 2001: 11). According to Wright, apart from the significant shifts in the socio-political institutions in Europe and America, multilateral financial institutions flourished at the behest of the Universal Declaration. Following the Great Depression of the 1930s, in 1944, the United Nations (UN) Monetary and Financial Conference in Bretton Woods featured the agenda for a Keynesian economic model with the IMF/World Bank at its head (ibid., 22). Consequently, the Bretton Woods institutions developed a global economic model, fixed exchange rates, including the economic stimulation required to set the US dollar a reserve currency for the world (ibid., 22–23). Weighed voting in at the UN allowed the World Bank to promote the Right to Development (1986) as a universal right (ibid., 23). With the direct intervention of financial institutions in the language of human rights, Wright argues that the reformed natural rights doctrine for individual autonomy was gradually shifted from the domestic sphere (of the West) to the international law with an alleged global consensus. In the aftermath of the Cold War in the late 1980s, which marked the end of the second wave of the rights movement (Messer 1997: 293–317), international law championed the human rights doctrine more aggressively than ever, pitting any normative categories or notions that resembled collectively or communitarianism against individuality and civic freedom. As Wright emphatically states: "Individualism is seen as axiomatic to human rights, essential to the competitive nature of 'man,' and any reference to collective or co-operative values is dismissed as a laughable or even dangerous degeneration into romanticism, socialism or cultural relativism" (2001: 11).

Correspondingly, the key bone of contention for the indigenous scholars is that, by and large, indigenous conceptions of humanity are discredited for their presumed lack of institutional foundations. Indeed, much to the dismay of postcolonial theorists who contend that humanism is a distinctly European phenomenon, Wright claims that "[i]deas about 'humanness' … developed in European debates on the meaning of civil society [which are] borrowed from indigenous sources while genocide, slavery and misogyny flourished" (Wright 2001: 10). Yet seen through the prism of the natural rights doctrine, "whenever the rights of Native indigenous people are raised, [it] really represents a clash over views about the nature of organized society" (Clinton 1990: 743). Admittedly, not only are indigenous societies irreducible to the logic of the natural rights, but as social beings indigenous people never existed "in isolation from others in some mythic, disorganized state of nature" (ibid., 742). On the contrary, indigenous traditions reveal that a human being is recognized as a social being by virtue of his or her social roles, functions and obligations (Messer 1997: 298–99). If critics find such achieved personhood through society and community somewhat abstract, it is possibly because rationalism cannot conceive the indigenous conceptions of communitarianism. On the contrary, for some, it is in fact the Western "concept of self that is normatively undesirable" (Walzer cited in Franck 2001: 196) since, for the most part, it "generates a radical individualism" that strips off all "communal responsibility" (ibid.). Such notions find parallels among many indigenous communities in the world today, where the legal enforcement of "individual rights" presents grave economic and cultural consequences to individuals who are expected to fulfill communal responsibilities, and where, in cases, individuals are integrated into communities before they are deemed legal subjects under law.[11]

Thus, as a countermovement to the Universal Declaration, the ratification of the Declaration is particularly noted for its political victory in the legitimization of collective rights. Such rights include, but are not restricted to, significant historical attachments to territory, ownership of land and resources, the establishment of distinct political and economic institutions, national and territorial integrity, self-determination, and a resolve to preserve both place ("territory") and culture as a means of achieving the collective good of community (Henderson 2009). This achievement further exemplifies the success of the IPM in negotiating a language that would legitimize other ways of being human without being adversarial or antithetical to European human(ism). In effect, the 2007 Declaration does not override the entitlement of individual rights endowed to all human persons, including the indigenous peoples, by the Universal Declaration in 1948. Article 1 of the Declaration ensures a dual, in that sense a separable, right to indigenous peoples, both as individuals and collective members of their respective traditions.

Unlike the postcolonial project, which is predominantly literary and academic in its anticolonial critiques, the IPM holds the unique distinction of being a "soft" and "invisible" movement, and Henderson (2009) hails the case of the Declaration as the success of a diplomacy network. Correspondingly, the origins of the IPM date back to the early 20th century, when the "[t]reaties were broken with impunity" (Sanders 1998: 73) by the settler colonialists as well as the newfound postcolonial states in an attempt to assimilate and regulate the indigenous populations under the "domestic" law. The Indian leaders from British Columbia traveled to London in 1906 and again in 1909 to redress the dishonoring of the treaties. In 1919, the formation of the League of Nations in Paris served as a global platform for the indigenous peoples to table their grievances for the first time. In 1923, Iroquois patriot Deskaheh of the Six Nations (representing Mohawk, Oneida, Onondaga, Cayuga, Seneca, and Tuscarora) traveled to Geneva to speak at the League of Nations much to the world's attention. However, after the League of Nations collapsed in the 1930s, indigenous concerns were quickly overshadowed by World War II, which presented new challenges and new set of priorities for the rights movement. In the process, between 1945 and 1948, indigenous peoples were excluded from the UN and its regulatory bodies that shaped the Universal Declaration. However, the growing pressure from the indigenous advocates notwithstanding, in 1945 the International Labour Organization (ILO) led a study commissioned by the UN to document the socio-economic and cultural rights, fair working conditions, standard of living, health care, and well-being of the indigenous populations. The ILO report concluded that the conditions of indigenous peoples, both in the settler colonies and the postcolonial states, were particularly oppressive (Anaya 2004).

Subsequently, a number of human rights instruments emerged during the 1960s to address the plight of indigenous peoples, including the International Convention on the Elimination of All Forms of Racial Discrimination (1965) and the two international human rights covenants (1966). In 1957, the ILO adopted Convention No. 107 on Indigenous Tribal Peoples, with directives to independent countries to initiate a progressive integration of indigenous populations into the national society as a whole. Indigenous peoples of the American continent, including those of the other settler-colonial states, regarded the ILO convention akin to internal colonialism, and demanded a political space to govern themselves (Willemsen-Diaz 2009: 31). Although the ILO 107 was ratified by 27 countries, the question of self-determination posed a daunting challenge to the advocates of indigenous rights during the 1970s:

[w]hile human rights in the Universal Declaration of Human Rights concern the relationship between state authorities and the individuals who are subject to the exercise of their authority, the right to self-determination brought in an entirely different perspective: who should govern whom, and who should exercise authority and control over territory and natural resources? (Eide 2009: 37)

Between the 1970s and 1980s, the continued efforts of NGOs, indigenous scholars, community elders, and representatives of indigenous nations from over 20 countries culminated in the creation of the Working Group on Indigenous Populations (WGIP) within the Human Rights Commission, as a UN Sub-Commission on Prevention of Discrimination and Protection of Minorities. From 30 people in the first session in 1982, the Working Group grew to over 700 representatives in 1999 (Daes 2009: 66). In 1995, the WGIP and the Prevention of Discrimination and Protection of Minorities developed a Draft Declaration on the Rights of the Indigenous Peoples with some reasonable demands: prevention of forced assimilation; preservation of indigenous cultures; restitution of cultural property (including human remains) and languages; and the right to self-determination (ibid.). Accordingly, Article 3 of the Draft Declaration defined self-determination as indigenous peoples' right "to freely determine their political status and freely pursue their economic, social and cultural development" (cited in Anaya 2004: 320).

Parallel to these developments at the WGIP, in 1989, the ILO issued a revised version of Convention No. 107 (as No. 169), which was

> based on the new perspective of greater autonomy for indigenous peoples, recognition of their collective control over land and natural resources, educational rights based on their own cultural orientation and needs, and labour protection and vocational training more geared to the assumption that they would serve their own society and find employment there, *not only in the non-indigenous part of society*. (Eide 2009: 37; emphasis added)

Both the Draft Declaration and the Convention No. 169 have had a tremendous impact on the events leading to the Declaration in 2007, which was voted in favor by 143 countries, four against and eleven abstaining during the 62nd Session of the UN General Assembly. Countries, such as the United States, Australia, Canada, and New Zealand, initially opposed the Declaration, claiming that the provision for self-determination was potentially unjust if not discriminatory.[12] They argued that rights to lands, territories, and resources are particularly unworkable and unacceptable, since they are owned by other non-indigenous citizens "lawfully" (ibid., 40).

Bearing the potential divisive interests in mind, in the subsequent drafts, the provision on the right to self-determination in Article 3 was left unchanged but its significance and scope was curtailed with the introduction of Article 46(1), emphasizing that the Declaration cannot challenge the integrity of the political unity of a state. In Asbjørn Eide's observation, indigenous representatives fully consented to the amended language by which "[d]emands for autonomy under the heading of self-determination under Articles 3 and 4 of the Declaration will have to respect the political unity of the state, the implication of which may be difficult to determine in the abstract" (Eide 2009: 42). Thus, indigenous humanism, divisive as it may be, is also non-integrationalist in intent, unlike the revisionist humanism of postcolonial discourse.

Again, contrary to the postcolonial project that sees Eurocentric humanism as both inadequate and indispensable, the indigenous movement does not relate to Euro-humanism in any indispensable sense. It acknowledges the existence of the European human while willfully distancing from it. As noted earlier, the Declaration's Article 1 ensures that indigenous peoples have the right to full enjoyment, as a collective and as individuals, of all human rights provisions found in the Universal Declaration. This ensures the added privilege that indigenous peoples have "a right to determine the content of their own education, in addition to the right to have access to the general education of the state in which they live; the right to have *their own* media *and* to have access to the wider, national media; and the right to retain their cultural heritage" (ibid., 44; emphasis added). In that respect, the Declaration of 2007 neither supersedes nor intercedes with the Universal Declaration; it merely annexes to the existing human rights provisions, while reasserting the notion that there are other ways of being human "alongside" European ways.

Postcolonial Theory, Indigenous Rights, and the Humanist Alternative

As the aforementioned accounts reveal, despite the fact that the two movements are inspired by a common concern to repudiate euro-humanism, the IPM yields a more strategic, viable, and evidently more instrumental humanist alternative than that of postcolonial theory.[13] In the latter, as John Noyes observes, the manifest disjuncture between the alter-humanist and critical humanism "looks like a simple confusion of two very different states: the philosophical move that opposes the hegemonic force of universalization on the one hand and, on the other, a politics of difference aimed at empowering minorities" (2002: 274). In other words, unlike the early postcolonial humanism which posits the colonized native as authentically alter-human, the humanist alternatives advanced by Said's "contrapuntality," Spivak's "humanities pedagogies," and Bhabha's "cultural rights" relapse into the very liberal humanist discourses that alter-humanism has sought to battle. In essence, while denouncing the notion of an authentic or pure indigenism, the critical humanists refute any radical possibility of difference other than "a discursive and epistemic relationship that will be 'noncolonizing', that will make possible 'a mutual exploration of difference'" (Mohanty 1995: 109).

The IPM, on the contrary, holds that an authentic indigenous humanism cannot be forged through, or sustained by, a mutual effacement with the colonizer's model of humanity. In that respect, the IPM remained faithful to the repudiation of Euro-humanism and its natural rights doctrine in the path it paved to the Declaration. A case in point, the IPM rejected the ILO Convention No. 107 as assimilationist and neo-colonialist, and amended the Draft Declaration to reflect its demands for collective rights accordingly. In spite of that, the IPM succeeded in maintaining a nonadversarial relationship with the Universal Declaration by rightfully claiming its provisions as legal entitlements. But it rejected the Universal Declaration only when the latter threatened their traditional way of life by means of the assimilationist tactics used by the States. Hence, for the indigenous communities around the world, "Group Rights are every bit as important to human dignity and well-being as individual rights" (Clinton 1990: 747).

By virtue of its arms-length relationship with the Universal Declaration, the IPM holds a strategic advantage that postcolonial humanism lacks. Even Fanon's radical assertions about the emergence of the "other" man, which stem from his own redemptive reasoning that "violence" may be the only answer to the colonizer's "violence," unwittingly reduces the native person into a caricatured imprint of the colonizer's image—as one who cannot be imagined in his own terms, but only in oppositional violence to the latter.[14] This is certainly not the case with indigenous peoples, who do not seek a redemptive or restorative humanity in any sense of the term, but a self-authorizing humanity by means of: (1) collectivity that is inherent to their cultures and (2) resistance to assimilationist forces that continue to threaten their traditional ways of living. In Will Kymlicka's view, indigenous peoples' claims for the preservation of traditional ways of life are convincingly different from the other minority cultures in the world. In his essay "Theorizing Indigenous Rights" (1999), Kymlicka goes on to correct James Anaya's tactical fallacy in dividing indigenous rights into remedial rights and substantial rights. According to Anaya,[15] remedial rights are only temporary in nature, and they are required only to the point that they can restore the historical injustices of the past. Substantial rights, on the other hand, are more permanent, and they derive from the indigenous peoples' inherent right to self-determination. For Kymlicka, however, the argument for remedial rights does not hold much weight because it cannot distinguish the historical injustices against the indigenous peoples from other stateless minorities (for example, the Catalans, Puerto Ricans, Flemish, Scots, and Quebecois). Instead, indigenous rights based on the need for cultural isolation, distinction, and preservation from modern societies is a more viable argument, as has been the case with the IPM (Kymlicka 1999: 281–93).

Apropos of Kymlicka's caution, Bhabha's defense of cultural rights in the face of minorities and diasporic populations cannot address indigenous peoples' concerns over assimilation and forcible integration. Moreover, indigenous peoples cannot be considered as "minorities," and they are not necessarily identical to the "hybrid subjects" of the national states who stand between individual rights and obligations. Although Bhabha is careful to separate cultures from nations and nation-states, his argument for "cultural rights" undermines the fact that indigenous peoples remain "doubly" marginalized in the postcolonial national cultures; and as a result, they are far less prone to the forces of modernization than their surrogate natives, including the diasporic and other religious minorities. While Spivak is careful to recognize the double marginalization of the "subaltern," her argument for the mutual effacement of rights-based and responsibility-based societies is untenable to say the least, since the "mental structures" of the indigenous peoples appear to be more "inaccessible" to the "rational mind" than any other responsibility-based society in existence today.

Last but not the least, perhaps, the most striking distinction between postcolonial theory and the IPM's road to a humanist alternative is the question of representation. As Dirlik (1994) has argued, the celebration of diversity, hybridity, and difference in global capitalism assumed a theoretical status only with the arrival of third world intellectuals in the Western academy. Dirlik's charge notwithstanding, by and large, the IPM leading to the Declaration is representative of the indigenous scholars, lawyers, and educationalists as activists themselves (James Anaya of Apache

Nation, Marie Battiste of Mi'kmaw, Bimal Bikkhu of Chamka People, to name a few). Hence, in contrast to postcolonial theory's interlocutors, as Ronald Niezen remarks, "[t]he development of an international movement of indigenous peoples in recent decades reflects a changing alignment of political advocacy and shows some indigenous leaders to be, despite their limited power and resources, among the most effective political strategists on the contemporary national and international scenes" (2003: 16).

Conclusion

If, for Hiddleston, "[h]umanism remains a defining concept in postcolonial thought, despite the bagginess of this ageing term" (2010: 102), for Noyes, "from Frantz Fanon through to Edward Said, postcolonial theory has been able to sustain a strange combination of a politics of engagement with a theoretical humanism that borders on the philosophically naive" (2002: 274). Thus, despite the early promises in the alter-humanist imaginings of Fanon, Césaire, and Memmi, postcolonial humanism falls short where the IPM succeeds. Instead, the gradual refashioning of postcolonialism humanism into "anti-essentialist," "anti-foundationalist" categories in the guise of contrapuntality, hybridity, and "unnamable alterity" has only served the detractors of indigenous rights and its theory. Since the Draft Declaration in 1995, the IPM has been subject to attacks that range from breeding "fascism," "idiosyncratic traditions" to "reverse racism," and even "terrorism" (Picq 2011), despite the fact that it is a peaceful, non-antagonistic movement which opted for "a remedy both to assimilation and the possibility of an armed revolution" (Henderson 2009: 33).

Nevertheless, the IPM continues to challenge the notion of *homo europaeus* as a universal constant, paving the way to self-determination, and re-author(iz)ing the "other" human that the indigene already is, without being overtly antithetical to Euro-humanism or the Universal Declaration. Whereas postcolonial theory sees nativism somewhat uneasily as ethno-centric and essentializing, the indigenous movement regards difference not as an ideology or label, nor as a matter of alterity that is "unnamable," but as a collective right to the lands its people came from, the lands they lived in, and the lands they must reclaim. At the same time, the continued use of the terms "native" and "indigenous" in postcolonial theory as universal constants for the victims of all colonialism is not only misleading, but also leaves the ethics and human agency implied by those terms at bay.

Notes

1. Fanon's phrase *il faut faire peau neuve* is often translated as "turn over a new leaf" (Alessandrini 2009: 72).
2. For a detailed account of postcolonial humanism, see Gikandi (2004: 141–62) and Lazarus (2004b: 19–40).
3. See Oreford (2003), Poe and Tate (1994), Robbins and Stamatopoulou (2004), Venn (2006), and Wright (2001) for a critique of the Eurocentric legacy of the human rights discourse in contemporary world politics.
4. These include the critical assessment of postcolonial studies in the works of Lazarus, ed. (2004a), Parry (2004), Quayson and Goldberg (eds) (2000). Notable exceptions that make a case for a postcolonial reading of human rights are Donaldson and Pui-Lan (2002), Battiste (2000), Byrd and Rothberg (2011), and Pratt (2008 [1992]).
5. Some recent examples are Allen and Xanthki (2010), Blaser et al. (2010), Charter and Stavenhagen (2009), and Adolfo de Oliveria (2009).
6. I am aware of the fact that this position conflates governing one's relations (Indigenous Peoples) with the discursive responses of the postcolonial humanism. Mbembe's notion of "illicit cohabitation" of power relations in the postcolony is a good example of how colonial discourses were enacted through institutional governance; see Mbembe (1992, 2001), and see also and Dirks (1999) for a similar line of argument.
7. For a detailed account on the pitfalls of postcolonial humanism, see Gikandi (2004: 112–14) and Wynter (1987).
8. See Chapter 4 for Said's reading of Fanon's humanism.
9. See Huddart's (2006) chapter "Cultural Rights" (83–99) for a more elaborate discussion of Bhabha's interventions into the discourses on rights.
10. I am aware of the fact that Western legal discourse is neither homogenous nor static, but this discussion is framed in the context of "natural rights" and "natural law" doctrine, which were fundamental to the early Euro-American legal discourses and the ensuing colonization of the non-Western societies (Maine 1861).
11. For more elaborate examples, see Barkel (1976), Goodale (2009), and Sardar (1998).
12. As of today, the four countries which voted against the Declaration in 2007 have signed the Declaration.
13. See Quayson (2000) for a critique of postcolonial theory's limitations in addressing "instrumental" or "practical" issues. For more general critiques of this aspect, see Chowdhury (2006), Ganguly (2002), and Parry (2004: 16–17).
14. Here, it is important to note that Fanon's thesis on redemptive violence (as outlined in his chapter "Concerning Violence" in *Wretched of the Earth*) is based on the view that violent response (to the colonizer's Manichean logic) can instill self-determination, empowerment, and even a sense of psychological liberation among the colonized populations.
15. This position reflects Kymlicka's reading of Anaya.

8

Margins of India: Kancha Ilaiah's Postcolonial "Nationalogues"

Introduction

Kancha Ilaiah is arguably one of the leading indigenous thinkers in India today. Although a number of postcolonial commentators such as Ania Loomba (2000), Diana Brydon (2000), and Dipesh Chakrabarty (2005)[1] have cited Ilaiah's work as a necessary interruption to the homological discourse[2] on subalternity and indigeneity, it has not succeeded in achieving a fully transformative impact outside the Indian subcontinent. Added to this, Ilaiah's own proactive role in the DalitBahujan[3] politics has earned him the tag of a hateful polemicist who promotes casteism, communalism, and anti-Hinduism (Singh 2011). For his interlocutors, however, *Why I am Not a Hindu* (1996) is nothing short of a DalitBahujan political manifesto; for his admirers, though, Ilaiah is no less an earthy pundit than a Phule, a Mahasewta Devi. His essay "Reservations: Experience as Framework of Debate" (1990) sparked a heated debate on the question of narrative authority during the 1990s. His argument that "experience-based" narration carries greater empirical validity than traditional ethnological accounts posed a daunting challenge to the already vexed issue of ethnographic authority. Although a number of critics have pointed out Ilaiah's own uncritical treatment of DalitBahujans as a collective category, his own identity as a non-Dalit, and his sweeping generalizations about the gods, rituals, and political allegiances of non-DalitBahujan castes (Sastry 2012), had little impact on the principle veracity of his argument in refuting the Hindu religious doctrine at large.

The task of this chapter, however, is to move away from these populist polemics, and in doing so, rescue the politics of Ilaiah's work—including its formal aesthetics and representational politics—that are glossed over by the seemingly overstated critiques of its perceived anti-Hinduism. Consider, for instance, Meera Nanda's (2012) remark that *post-Hindu India* (2009) "boasts of a 'unique methodology' that seems to lie in the total absence of any reference to published work: the entire 295 pages of text appear to have emerged straight from Ilaiah's own mind." Nanda's observation holds true for its prequel *Why I am Not a Hindu*, which might as well be read as "Why I am Not an Indian," depending on how one reads the complicity and collusion of populism, religion, and nationalism in the subcontinent. Yet, *Why I am Not a Hindu* resists any generic categorizations that precondition textual and narrative authority. Even if the entire text "appears to have emerged straight from Ilaiah's own mind" (Nanda 2012), it is neither an autobiography nor an auto-ethnography. And its sequel *Post-Hindu India* reads like a Foucauldian genealogy of caste vis-à-vis a DalitBahujan political manifesto. However, it remains an unfinished manifesto because of its complicity with the very discourse it seeks to dismantle. Instead of a complete overhaul of the Hindu national doctrine, Ilaiah proposes, in a Spivakian sense, to ab-use ("using from below") its ideological genesis from an indigenous point of view. For instance, in his "Acknowledgements" to *Post-Hindu India* Ilaiah writes, "I am thankful to God for having let me be born in this country" (Ilaiah 2009), despite the fact that he goes to great lengths in its prequel to uncover how Indian history is consumed by oppressive Hindu doctrine (hence the justification *Why I am Not a Hindu*). It takes a "civil war," Ilaiah exclaims, not a national liberation struggle, to overthrow Hindu national hegemony (Ilaiah 2009: 263–64). This double bind of "not being a Hindu" on the one hand, and "wanting to be an Indian" on the other, poses a curious challenge to the positioning of (narrative) selfhood in the existing literary genres today. Hence, my contention that Ilaiah's work pioneers a new sub-genre of "nationalogue" requires a careful treatment of its conceptual precedents in literary studies. This includes, but is not restricted to, the theories of postcolonial nationalism, autobiography, life writing, national autobiography, parabiography, testimonio, and minor writing.

The Nation and Its Margins: From Autobiography to Nationalogue

Like Bhabha's caveat of performative nationalism, Kathy Burrel's thesis on the "personal" trajectories of nationalism (2006: 65–66) points out the way nationalism cements itself through personalized acts of rehearsing national symbols, rituals, and traditions by which other individuals are connected, even in the absence of an implicit knowledge of a nation or its geographical affinity (Burrel 2006: 66–67). This personal–community nexus, Burrell maintains, finds an even more pronounced expression among immigrants and minority populations. Accordingly, in the past two decades, postcolonial discourse has been largely preoccupied with theorizing nationalism and post-nationalism from a diasporic perspective (Goonewardena 2004; Lie 2008). This is accompanied by the prolific output of third world literature in recent times, owing largely to writers with diasporic origins, which has led to the undue canonization of select modes of cosmopolitanism and cultural globalization. The advent of post-nationalist discourse, and its relegation of nationalist concerns to a host of fissured, differed, and deferred narratives of longing and belonging, has further obfuscated the unresolved questions of cultural nationalism and the growing resistance to popular nationalism and globalization in the former colonies (Parry 2004: 39–42; Pershai 2010: 379–98). Today, most theories on postcolonial nationalism are concerned with the ways in which nationalist ideologies invent, institute, and perform forms of difference (McClintock 1993: 61) as opposed to unifying them. Homi Bhabha, for instance, points to the clash between the "pedagogic" (state, bourgeois institutions) and "performative" (gender, ethnic, class subjectivities) narratives of nationalism that open up space for women, minorities, workers, peasants, and other marginalized groups to interrupt the homogenous narration of national identities (2004 [1994]: 51, 207–08).[4] For Partha Chatterjee (1993), anticolonial nationalism is essentially a "derivative" discourse, one that is rallied by the Western-educated national elite, and therefore fails to register the nationalist aspirations and articulations of the indigenous masses. In the absence of an authentic indigenous discourse that is "generative" as opposed to "derivative," Chatterjee holds that postcolonial nationalism is an incomplete, fragmented, yet an inevitable discourse (ibid.). Although most postcolonial critiques are apt to register the antinomies of bourgeois nationalism, populism, and indigenous aspirations, they say very little about how and where, and if at all, a counter-discourse to derivative nationalism takes place. As John McLeod questions, "Does the agency for resistance derive from the acts of representation by those from the nation's margins, or is it found mystically within nationalism itself? If it is the latter, then why have nationalist discourses been so powerful?" (2000: 120). While it is possible to argue that nationalist ideologies remain powerful largely due to their pedagogic appropriation by the national elite, it is the "margins" (Bhabha), "fragments" (Chatterjee), and "performative narratives" (Bhabha) that prove to be too elusive to most postcolonial critics. Thus, if one is allowed to distinguish between postcolonial nationalism as a failed political project and as a failed literary project, though it is possible to suggest that both failures coincide, I argue that the "nationalogue" is one such marginal site where literary resistance to derivative nationalism takes place.

The source of my optimism is the revival of cultural nationalism among the Marxist postcolonial critics who have been reluctant to concede that the sort of nationalitarianism—nationalism as an emancipatory narrative—that is originally conceived by Fanon should be abandoned altogether. Neil Lazarus (2011: 93–97), for instance, defends Fredric Jameson's asseveration that much of third world literature is burdened by the nationalist aspirations that find a collective expression in the individual author.[5] Considering the fact that Jameson's thesis on "third world national allegory" derives from the (socialist) realist technique of Lu Xun's short story "Diary of a Madman" (1918), it is not entirely surprising that "literary" failures of nationalism have found a renewed expression in the genre of autobiography. In line with Jameson's view of the collective character of third world realism, Philip Holden defines autobiography as "the narrative of a collective subject from that of an individual life" (2008: 17). While Jameson accedes that autobiography has always been akin to Bildungsroman, he denies the aesthetic status attributed to Bildungsroman as "'natural' form[s]" (Jameson 1981: 145) for it valorizes the immediacy of political representation.[6] Apropos of its educational character, Roy Pascal defines autobiography as "the product of maturity"; it deals with how "one has found the way to the realised self" (1960: 175).[7] Conceivably, early accounts of autobiography reveal that it was a prerogative of kings, noblesse, imperial agents, and social elites who had an easy access to literacy and the written word. A leisurely vocation at its best, autobiographical writing embodies both the Platonic and Victorian traits of the autonomous and adventurous self-subject. Accordingly, the imperial autobiography constructed its own literary canon (Holden 2008: 16–38) through the writings of William Henry Sleeman (*Rambles and Recollections* 1844), Frederick Lugard (*The Dual Mandate* 1922), and Cecil Rhodes (*Last Will and Testament* 1902), among others. Most of these canonical works, as critics argue, are characterized by a deep commitment to imperialism and colonialism, and a reassertion of Victorian and Edwardian masculinities and their "gentlemanly traits" (Holden 2008: 16–38; Moore-Gilbert 2009: 111–12). Although Bart Moore-Gilbert delineates a non-canonical autobiography under the guise of "life writing", he wonders whether all canonical autobiographies expressed a deep commitment to the prevailing social order or if heretic and radical voices can be found within the canon (2009: 111–12). The sub-genre of national autobiography that emerged during the post-independent era (1940s–60s) was seen as a proper response to the imperial canon of autobiography. Typically, national autobiography was characterized by a certain celebratory moment in which the birth of new nations coincided with the birth of new national heroes such as Jawaharlal Nehru, Mohandas Gandhi, Nelson Mandela, Kwame Nkrumah, Le Kwan Yew, among others. According to Holden (2008: 17), the departure point of most national autobiographies is the political exile of the authors, which progresses from a retrospective engagement with colonial struggles to the formation of the modern nation. The nationalistic representations in the autobiographies of these figures could even be read as parabiography, which, in Tobias Döring's terms (1998: 149–51), functions as a parallel biography to the imperial canonical autobiography.

However, the "deferred achievement" of nationalism (Laursen 2010: 87) in these works has led critics, such as Elleke Boehmer and Philip Holden, to argue that all national autobiographies are inherently masculine like their imperial counterparts, and that they constitute "a dense intertextual network of emulative self-fashioning that is frequently fraternal or filial in nature" (Holden 2008: 5).[8] In what Boehmer calls the "syntax of nationalist life writing" (2005: 70), the narratives of national heroes typically begin with their exile in the West where they learn the grammar of modernity, followed by a return to the homeland where they rediscover their native roots and remap their national boundary by embarking on a "national *journey*" (ibid.; emphasis in original). The ensuing autobiographical narratives, as Boehmer contends, are invariably shaped by their "*modes of address*" (ibid., 71; emphasis in original) (typically through the association with a masculine pronoun), which conflates individual development with that of national development, and signifies a seamless blend of modernity, tradition, enterprise, and even "pioneering spirit" (ibid.). The constitutive grammar of such national autobiographies is often distinguished from the "intellectual autobiographies" of C.L.R. James (*Beyond a Boundary* 1963), Michael Ondaatje (*Running in the Family* 1993), and Edward Said (*Out of Place* 1999). While most of these works themselves have become canonized, they bear greater resemblance to parabiography than that of national autobiography. Here, as Döring shows in his analysis of V.S. Naipaul's and David Dabydeen's texts, the presence of the authorial "I" in the European autobiographical canon is strategically replaced by an absent "eye."

This situation, Döring argues, enables the parabiographical authors to invoke their representative community while maintaining a certain degree of authorial "desire for invisibility" (1998: 164) and anonymity. For instance, while comparing Naipaul's *The Enigma of Arrival* (1988) with Dabydeen's *Disappearance* (1993), Döring demonstrates how Dabydeen's project follows the trajectory of a parabiography by "fragmenting the passage into Englishness that Naipaul's personae compulsively perform" (1998: 163). Against Naipaul's visual technique of witnessing life through travels, Dabydeen's narrative is driven by a "desire for invisibility" exerted by the author's own autobiographical personae (ibid.). The I/eye distinction of Döring is also central to the generic boundaries that separate selfhood from the individual in autobiography, life writing, testimonio, and travel writing. According to C.L. Innes, "[w]hereas European autobiographies traditionally map a journey through life to a point of completion or arrival, many postcolonial autobiographies ... accept a concept of identity which embraces 'contingency, indeterminacy, and conflict'" (Anderson in Innes 2007: 70–71). By extension, in life writing, the recovery of lost identity becomes a proxy narration of selfhood through one's own originary community. If, therefore, autobiographical narratives are constitutive of an individuality that is assertive and complete, life writing, as it were, points to a construction of incomplete selfhood in the sphere of an imagined collective. Sally Morgan's *My Place* (1988), for instance, is considered as a prime example of life writing that is written with the perspective of a future belonging in a deeply radicalized Australian society (Moore-Gilbert 2009: 3–8). Correspondingly, Moore-Gilbert argues that if autobiography is defined by a retrospective gaze, life writing "looks forward as much as it does to the past, to a future where its aspirations will be realised" (ibid., 112).

Travel writing, on the other hand, is characterized by a certain ideological innocence of selfhood that is inflected by its generic commitment to a factual present (for example, from Mark Twain's *The Innocents Abroad* [1869] to Naipaul's *India: A Wounded Civilization* [1977]). Both in travel writing and autobiography, the narrative perspective of author/narrator/protagonist is eliminated to accommodate space for factual mediation. Unlike autobiographical genres, however, the stability of the self in travel writing is categorically undermined (Clark 1999: 64) due to its presumed ideological innocence. This has led to what Mary Louise Pratt calls the ideology of "anticonquest" in the European travel writing of the 19th century, which was driven by a "planetary consciousness" (Pratt 2008 [1992]: 29) that sought to export Eurocentric humanism to the traveled domains. This is particularly the case with scientific travel writers such as Alexander von Humboldt whose penchant for naturalizing "local knowl-edge into European forms of relocations of power" (Fontinha de Alcantara 2009: 5) has led to the "utopian image of a European bourgeois subject simultaneously innocent and imperial, asserting a harmless hegemonic vision that installs no apparatus of domination" (Pratt 2008 [1992]: 33). However, in the absence of a viable alternative to travel writing, the new-found genre of testimonio is often played out as its postcolonial variant. Invoking Raymond Williams's distinction between the canonical novel and the British working-class novel, John Beverley argues that testimonio is closely affiliated to the working-class autobiography and its mutations into other less recognized literary forms. Accordingly, testimonio is a synthesis of oral history, memoir, confession, non-fiction novel, or what Beverley calls "facto-graphic literature" (2011: 17). With its roots in Latin American autobiographies of the early 20th century, testimonio originally developed as what Barbara Harlow (1987) terms "resistance literature," in which the narrator's account of events is often mediated by a translator. Because testimonio arises out of an urgency to communicate a problem of repression, persecution, subalternity, or imprisonment (ibid., 18), it is "usually presented without any literary or academic aspirations" (ibid.). Beverley argues that the narrator in testimonio "speaks for, or in the name of, a community or group, approximating in this way the symbolic function of the epic hero without at the same time assuming his hierarchical and patriarchal status" (ibid., 19). This view also corres-ponds to Deleuze and Guattari's notion of "minor literature" (1986), which is characterized by both a deterritorialized language and a deterritorialized national consciousness. Writing from the margins of a dominant language, minor literature is constitutive of a vernacular awareness that constantly defines signification, therefore territorialization. The minor writer, then, belongs to a domain that is physically deterritorialized from the "vehicular" modulation (institutional, governmental language) of the dominant lan-guage, therefore its national character. This enables the writer to forge the sensibilities of a "vernacular" language into the "vehicular" code (Deleuze and Guattari 1986: 23). Yet it is "not" the shortage of linguistic or literary talent, as Lazarus's defense of Jameson would have it, but the historical exclusion of the minor writer from the dominant literary field that both "obliges" and "necessitates" him/her to speak on behalf of his/her entire community (familial, communal, and national).[9] Thus, in line with Jameson's view on the implied anonymity of the working-class pro-tagonist, the function of the lead character in minor literature is politically charged with the function of the collective (Deleuze and Guattari 1986). Unlike autobiography and life writing, then, the linguistic "I" in testimonio functions as the "shifter" (Beverley 2011: 26), implicating the entire social field of the author/narrator through individual predicament. Some recent examples of this include Satnam's *Janglenama* (2010), Niromi de Soyza's *Tamil Tigress* (2011), and Pascal Khoo Thwe's *From the Land of Green Ghosts* (2003)—all of which feature first person accounts of collective struggles over ethno-nationalism and self-determination.

While it is certainly overstating to say that a nationalogue is made up of all these elements, it would be equally misleading to suggest that it does not borrow from the various sub-genres outlined earlier. Although a nationalogue distances itself from the self-centered subject of autobiography, including its restrictive retrospective gaze, it inherits from life writing's negation of coherency and chronology. The non-linear narration of the nationalogue, like a life history, is inlaid by the author's penchant for the visionary and emancipatory, taking precedence over the past and present alike. For a nationalogue replaces the self-evident "I" with the subject-centered "eye," the discovery of the self is leveraged through an imagined collective of the narrator. Because this requires the author of a nationalogue to be acquainted with the "vehicularity" of the dominant language, it is reasonable to assume that he/she is a petit-subaltern who invests in a certain aesthetic education, one who is equivalent to the fictional author who, in Beverley's view (2011: 18–21), attempts a pseudo-autobiography of a subaltern or working-class individual.[10] Yet like testimonio, a nationalogue is committed to factual representation; in most cases, however, independent or verifiable facts assume a collective form, as in Ilaiah's description of caste customs in the Indian villages. Unlike testimonio, however, it mimics travel writing's penchant for the visual, factual, and the picturesque without assuming its ideological innocence. But given that a nationalogue is not based on a direct participation in events, it is the "narrative" that travels rather than the narrator himself/herself, just as in Edward Said's notion of "traveling theory" (1983: 226–47). In other words, a nationalogue's assertion belongs to a mental space rather than to a physical one. By virtue of this, a nationalogue accounts for one's generational struggle of a fractured nation against the pedagogical narratives of a collective nation. As the narrating subject of a nationalogue lacks the vantage point of the national elite, it allows for the rediscovery of the suppressed self and self-fashioning of one's national community simultaneously. In other words, in the absence of a "filial or fraternal network," the author of a nationalogue turns to his/her own community members who assume the role of the "emulative" and "self-fashioning" (Holden 2008: 190) subjects of the national autobiography.

Kancha Ilaiah's Nationalogues

Why I am Not a Hindu opens like a typical autobiographical account: "I was born in a small South Indian Telangana village in the early fifties and grew up in the sixties" (2002 [1996]: x). But it soon resumes its life-writing mode, as anointed by Ilaiah in his *Preface*, by way of proxy interlocution that invokes the plight of his entire community:

> This book is an outcome of my constant interaction with the Dalitbahujans … who kept telling me, in a variety of ways, about their culture, economy and politics. What I have done is to put their ideas down in a systematic way. Apart from my personal experiences all the ideas in this book are picked up from illiterate and semi-literate Dalitbahujans and also from a few formally educated Dalitbahujan organic intellectuals. (ibid., vi)

Presumably, the organic knowledge collected and (re)presented therein is mediated through the author's own translation (from his mother tongue Telugu) into the language of his choice—English. While this translator-like authorial positioning resembles the formative aspects of testimonio, the reasons for Ilaiah's choice are somewhat extra-literary. In spite of their Eurocentric biases, Ilaiah claims that English texts exposed him to a language of "equality" and "inequality" (ibid., 55) that has been kept conspicuously silent in the Indian Brahminical texts. Here, Ilaiah's refusal to write a critique in the same language as its oppressor's exudes a process of double deterritorialization that is endemic in minor writing.[11] Sure enough, Ilaiah threads a painful account of his progression from childhood to college days in his opening chapter (ibid., 1–19), detailing how his encounters with the Telugu educational system and the English curriculum contradicted everything he had experienced and learned from his community. While the early autobiography's diary-like form is kept intact in the first two chapters, "Childhood Formations" and "Marriage, Market and Social Relations," Ilaiah breaks away from this "retrospective" narrative mode in the subsequent chapters that engage with the ideological contingencies of his oppressor's discourse—mainstream Hinduism. Here, Ilaiah devotes as much energies to re-narrating the history of Hindu domination as to the historical oppression of the DalitBahujan community. Such a contrapuntal approach clearly differs from recent examples of political life writing, such as Suad Amiry's *Sharon and My Mother-in-law: Ramallah Diaries* (2004) and Christina Asquith's *Sisters in War: A Story of Love, Family, and Survival in the New Iraq* (2009), that are primarily concerned with collective suffering narrated through the life trajectories of the authors. Though, by Ilaiah's own concession, much of his narrative is based on his own life trajectory and the state of the DalitBahujans in post-independence India, he uses his auto-ethnographic moment as an anchor not only to reconstruct a "timeless collective" of the DalitBahujan past, but to deconstruct the mythical genealogies of the oppressor's discourse. For instance, he writes:

> By and large the Scheduled Castes have retained the tribal notion of property as "public" for thousands of years. Whatever the Dalitbahujans procure—a dead cow or bull—or when they cut a living sheep or goat, they divide equally among themselves. ... The Dalitbahujans have never believed that power is embodied in property. (Ilaiah 2002 [1996]: 41–42)

And he later explains: "This is one of the main reasons why welfare inputs disappear into collective consumption within no time" (ibid., 118). Counterpoising this view to the Hindu notion of private property, Ilaiah writes:

> In Hinduism God is private, prayer is private, family is private and wife and children are personal. The Baniyas operate on similar principles in business. Their families being absolutely brahminical and patriarchal, they apply the principle of 'manipulating the mind' to control business and the market perpetually. Here again personal and private are two conditioning factors. Business is private as much as priesthood is. If one is the private property of Brahmins, the other is the private property of Baniyas. Operating in the same ideological domain, classical Kshatriyas structured political power as their private property. (ibid., 45)

In much the same way, the four core chapters of Ilaiah's book alternate between cataloging every conceivable aspect of both DalitBahujan and Hindu lives, from eating, drinking, working, and childbearing to conceptions of death. As the very titles (and subtitles) of his chapters "Hindu Gods and Us; Our Goddesses and Hindus" and "Hindu Death and Our Death" reveal, the contrasting auto-narration of the collective histories of both the oppressor and the oppressed aids the transition of Ilaiah's authorial positioning into a monologic mode. In other words, the conspicuous, if not self-appointed, double deterritorialization enables Ilaiah to narrate a life history of two antithetical communities just as in a dramatic monologue that interrupts the dramaturgic consciousness of the actors in the presence of an expectant audience. And Ilaiah has no qualms in singling out his staged audience: "For about three thousand years you people learnt only how to teach and what to teach others—the DalitBahujans. Now in your own interest and in the interest of this great country you must learn to listen and to read what we have to say" (Ilaiah 2002 [1996]: xii). This ethical imperative to "learn to listen," like Spivak's (2012) notion of "learning to play double bind" with an unwavering commitment to both the political and the ethical, sets Ilaiah's work apart from the existing genres of autobiographical studies, while turning it into a performative monologue at the behest of his entire national community:

> The only way to historicize the past and safeguard the future is to create an army of organic intellectuals – men and women – from Dalitbahujan forces. … Just as they are shouting from their rooftops (and they have very big houses) "Hinduize India," we must shout from our toddy palms, from the fields, from treetops and from Dalitbahujan waadas, "Dalitize India." We must shout "we hate Hinduism, we hate Brahminism, we love our culture and more than anything, we love ourselves." (ibid., 132)

Consequently, the communal estrangement exerted through the individual predicament in the very title of *Why I am Not a Hindu* translates into a quest for "belonging" in non-belonging (a Hindu) as in Deleuze and Guattari's (1986: 20–24) notion of "becoming a minor" outside of one's imposed norms. In the process, the language of narration itself assumes a minor form by way of its botched syntax, circumlocution, stylistic irregularity, absence of metaphors (Hunter 2007: 139), abrogation, and appropriation. The only occasions when Ilaiah uses metaphors, they are laced with catechetical force, which renders them almost meaningless: "Hinduism runs as a thread in a garland in shaping all institutions as 'upper' caste preserves" (Ilaiah 2002 [1996]: 48). Here, Ilaiah's metaphorical signification fails, or rather turns it into an over-metaphor, largely because both its tenor ("Hinduism") and vehicle ("a thread in a garland"—largely associated with gods and deities) are drawn from the same donor field of the Hindu cultural lexicon. This holds true for Ilaiah's most curious acclamation that the "[Brahmin] child pretends to be as obedient as Gandhi pretended to be poor" (ibid., 11). Again, the metaphorical enunciation of this claim fails to achieve its intended effect for the sheer improbability it poses in disrupting the chain of signification between Gandhi, poverty, and disobedience. If anything, "poverty" and "disobedience" compliment Gandhi's fakir-like ascetic image given his own proactive role in the "civil disobedience movement," and his proven disdain for material wealth.

On other occasions, to prove that dominant cultural language cannot articulate the "productive" metaphors of community, Ilaiah finds even more creative ways of mutilating English: "their alienation from the people is total" (Ilaiah 2002 [1996]: 101); "her [Hindu Goddess Saraswati] alienation from nature is total" (ibid., 76); "Both languages [Telugu and English] are alien to us, and the alienness is equally striking in both cases" (ibid., 56). In contrast to Brahminical terminology, Ilaiah claims that DalitBahujan caste language "is structured by its own grammar. It is a flexible and alert grammar, designed for production-based communication" (ibid., 5). But because the writer chooses to write in a foreign language in the absence of rhetoric or metaphor or nonfunctional lexicon, the narrative form mimics that of testimonio by virtue of the writer's own translation of his originary (re)source:

> As I struggled through the educational institutions, I began to learn that the structures of the state, the country and the world are far larger than those of our village. Later, as I pushed my way into the institutions of higher education at various levels, education began to appear more and more alien to me, more and more brahminical and anglicized. (ibid., 54)

While the fusion of the formative aspects of autobiography, life writing, and testimonio are evident throughout *Why I am Not a Hindu*, it resists a fixed generic categorization for the "ethical bind" it forges upon its implied reader—the non-DalitBahujan Hindu. In the process, Ilaiah implicates his reader(s) active participants of his manifesto by contending that the only way they can learn about DalitBahujan society is by simultaneously unlearning their own learning of Hinduism. This ethical conditioning is exerted[12] through a series of soliloquy-like exclamations that reoccur throughout Ilaiah's book:

> Those who say that all of us are Hindus must tell us which morality is Hindu morality? Which values do they want to uphold as right values? The "upper" caste Hindu unequal and inhuman cultural values or our cultural values? What is the ideal of society today? What shall we teach the children of today? Shall we teach them what the Hindus or what the Dalitbahujan masses of this country want to learn? Who makes an ideal teacher? Who becomes a good hero? (ibid., 18)

On other occasions, he goes on to muse: "But where does the concept of *prasaadam* (food offered to God) exist in our homes?" (Ilaiah 2002 [1996]: 26); or "But how does one spend this very short life here?" (ibid., 103).

Unlike *Why I am not a Hindu*, his sequel *Post-Hindu India* bears the features of parabiography and travel writing. In the first chapter of the book, for instance, Ilaiah begins with a subsection titled "Starting the Journey," claiming that he has "a few questions" (2009: 2) to explore: "Who constructed the humanness of our being, sharpened our sensibilities and continues to teach us vital lessons?" (ibid.). The answer, Ilaiah exclaims, is "based on my own long journey across the vast territories of India, [which] is unusual or rather unexpected—for it is the 'tribals'" (ibid.). Though this "journey" metaphor is recurrent throughout the book—on almost every occasion he introduces a new place and a new community—his empirical reference point remains his own native turf of Andhra Pradesh. On one occasion, for instance, Ilaiah argues that the Madigas are Chamars of North India (ibid., 32), even though they are not "the same" but share similar cultural traits. Yet in his preface to the book, Ilaiah provides a lengthy justification about the limitations of such comparisons: "[e]ach chapter in this book is written around the cultural and scientific knowledge that each caste possesses within the context of Andhra Pradesh .... But it draws general conclusions, as the religious experiences of all Indian productive castes is the same" (ibid., xxvi). Yet, his appeal for "sameness," as opposed to "similarity," "difference," or even "differential sameness" is based on the implied ethics of narration that "one has to make an effort in that direction" (ibid., 1), for, while suffering of the masses may be different, the structures of oppression are the same. Hence, Ilaiah has no qualms in declaring his authorial (mis)intentions: "it is important to liberate Dalit-Bahujan masses from the clutches of Brahmanism and from their own ignorance" (ibid.).

Here, despite the nobility of the cause or the ethics of narration, the petit-subalternity of the presumably "non-innocent" author is staged as a necessary rhetorical ploy, one that allows the author to turn his life writing into a meta-life writing of his community. If we are allowed to set aside the author–narrator representational impasse for the moment, Ilaiah's authorial narrator can be compared to that of Kafka's anonymous narrator in minor literature, who in Deleuze and Guattari's characterization, is "positively charged with the role and function of the collective" (Deleuze and Guattari 1986: 17). Thus, it is no surprise that Ilaiah's journey-like narration takes greater liberties in generalizing caste cultures across the spectrum than, say, a conventional travel account would do. While such narration does not necessarily discredit the authenticity of Ilaiah's travel, it does raise questions about the polyvalence of his hypothetical evidence. As most of Ilaiah's examples are auto-ethnographic—"[m]y discussions with the Madiga tanners" (Ilaiah 2009: 32); "my journey" (ibid., 2); or "[m]y assumption" (ibid., 93)—the travel aspect of his narrative remains more or less symbolic, fulfilling the opposite function of imperial travel writing. In other words, instead of exporting "planetary consciousness" into the traveled domains, Ilaiah's imaginary journey assembles the ruins of local knowledge against the cognitive colonialism of an already universalized domain—the Hindu religious doctrine. In essence, as Ilaiah's "journeys" are driven by the daunting task of uncovering the indigenous scientific inventions that are discredited by the Hindu doctrine—from Kammari's melting hearth to Madiga's drum, and to Chakali's soap and Mangali's knife—they gesture toward a counter–canonical move that repudiates the imperial travel canon. For instance, by retracing the "universality" (pan-Indian) of a subaltern science (see Chapter 2, "Subaltern Scientists") on the basis of his own "living" (Telangana) tradition, Ilaiah's travel narration reverses the universalization of scientific aesthetics based on the naturalist perception of foreign lands in the European travel canon (Pratt 2008 [1992]).[13] Given Ilaiah's penchant for subverting generic conventions, it is no surprise that *Post-Hindu India* assumes a parabiographical narrative form:

> This book was born out of a gut feeling that the Indian nation is on the course for a civil war; a civil war that has been simmering as an undercurrent of the caste-based cultural system that Hinduism has constructed and nurtured for centuries. (Ilaiah 2009: ix)

Implicitly, Ilaiah takes upon himself the task of narrating the other side of this self-proclaimed civil war. This situation allows him to challenge the official national autobiographies of Gandhi and Nehru by way of a parallel autobiographical narration that forges the means of another national community. Thus, the term "post-Hindu" does not signify a temporal moment of after-Hinduism, but the existence and survival of a community in the absence of Hinduism. The entire book, for instance, reads like a testimonial to the DalitBahujan contributions to the Indian nation—from the invention of the wheel to the recipe of a beef curry—that were either appropriated by the Hindu doctrine or suppressed by the anticolonial nationalism that collided with the latter.

Ilaiah provides ample examples to substantiate his claims, beginning with the very anticolonial nationalism that iconicized select individual figures as tribal national heroes even though they were not tribals (Alluri Sita Rama Raju in Andhra Pradesh being his prime example). In Ilaiah's (2009: 233) view, the 1857 Sepoy Revolt is a vegetarian-eating, upper-caste revolt because no historical accounts make a mention of the role of the meat-eating DalitBahujans in the event. Thus, in Ilaiah's claim, a mutiny based on the Brahminical sentiments against cow-fat or pig-fat says nothing about the mass humanity of DalitBahujans who ate dead carcasses to save the upper castes from deadly epidemics. It is the Gandhian vegetarianism, Ilaiah acclaims, that "destroyed the general health of the nation" (ibid., 10). In what Ilaiah calls "Baniya Nationalism" (ibid., 174), he argues that as community leader of *Baniyas* (a caste of traders), "Gandhi himself constructed a powerful modern Hindu vegetarian idiom that went against the historical tradition of meatarianism of the Shudras, Chandalas, Adivasis and the pan-Indian masses" (ibid., 176). In a curious way, Ilaiah's theory of "vegetarian nationalism" espouses Bhabha's observations on the indigenous challenge to the forced (yet failed) religious conversions in colonial India: "words of the Christian god do not come from the mouths of meat eaters" (Bhabha cited in Mitchell 1995b). Counterpoising the Gandhian ideals of asceticism, celibacy, and nonattachment philosophy, Ilaiah invokes the notions of collectivity and productivity:

> [I]n the Dalit-Bahujan *wadas*, a *sanyasi* is not viewed as a respectable being but an idle creature, a parasite who consumes commodities produced by the productive society constituted of the Sudras and the Chandalas.... According to the Dalit-Bahujan discourse, the main social source of all forms of knowledge is *samsaram* or familyhood, not *sanyasam* or sainthood. (Ilaiah 2009: 91; emphasis in original)

While Ilaiah's frequent invocation of Gandhi and Nehru throughout the pages of *Post-Hindu India* may be a conscious one, in line with the notion of parabiography, consider, for instance, Gandhi's own autobiographical account of Hinduism:

> Only Christianity was at that time an exception. I developed a sort of dislike for it. And for a reason. In those days Christian missionaries used to stand in a corner near the high school and hold forth, pouring abuse on Hindus and their gods. I could not endure this. (Gandhi 1940: 67)

Here, it is important to note that while both Gandhi's and Ilaiah's appeal for indigenism is based on a similar principle of anti-religious colonization, they are shaped by two distinct yet parallel autobiographical moments—anti-Christianity and anti-Hinduism. The same holds true for the unassuming clash between Ilaiah's vision for a "spiritual democratization" of India and Nehru's vision for a "secular modernization" of India as expressed in Nehru's own dissonance with Gandhian nationalism in his autobiography:

> "India's salvation consists", he [Gandhi] wrote in 1909, "in unlearning what she has learned during the last fifty years. The railways, telegraphs, hospitals, lawyers, doctors, and suchlike have all to go; and the so-called upper classes have to learn consciously, religiously, and deliberately the simple peasant life, knowing it to be a life giving true happiness". ... All this seems to me utterly wrong and harmful doctrine, and impossible of achievement. ... Personally I dislike the praise of poverty and suffering. I do not think they are at all desirable, and they ought to be abolished. (1942: 136–38)

If the filial and fraternal nationalism of Gandhi's and Nehru's autobiographies becomes evident through such intertextual mediation, then it is in the individual–collective nexus that Ilaiah's nationalogue finds a parabiographical expression. For instance, challenging the fraternal relations of the national elite, Ilaiah turns to the mediation of subaltern knowledge among DalitBahujan and castes, such as Mangalis and Madigas, which might have resulted in the invention of knife and needle, among other agrarian products of use, due to their close relationship to the domains of labor and production (Ilaiah 2009: 35–40; 90–95). It is for this reason that, just as in parabiography's "desire for invisibility," *Post-Hindu India* is replete with collective pronouns such as "we," "our," "their" (ibid., 1–190) as opposed to the personification of the national allegory in the autobiographies of Gandhi and Nehru. And Ilaiah does not hesitate to take his critique to the crux of the matter: if Gandhian vegetarianism destroyed the physical health of the Indian nation, Ilaiah argues, Nehruvian modernity destroyed its spiritual health. The source of this spiritual health, he contends, derives from his childhood formations in a community that embraced "labour as an integral aspect of spirituality" (Ilaiah 2009: 269). In what Ilaiah calls a "spiritual democracy" (ibid.) DalitBahujan society is built on egalitarian principles of work and fulfillment (*pani* and *paata*—work and song, ibid., 42) as opposed to the Hindu-bourgeoisie doctrine of meritocracy and inequality (*chaduvu* and *sandhya*—reading and praying [ibid.]). To that end, Ilaiah holds Nehru responsible for the blind modernization of India based on a Hindu-inspired, sanskritized cultural ethos. If Gandhian asceticism was the principle reason why Brahminical castes are alienated from the domain of work forces, Nehruvian modernity, Ilaiah argues, was the catalyst for the emergence of national bourgeoisie: "after the independence, the construction of a so-called 'modern' India took place with the strategic enrichment of the Brahmins and the Baniyas" (Ilaiah 2009: 166) because Nehru, "realized that the modernist post-independence national economy can accommodate Brahmans in the bureaucratic capital and Baniyas in the business capital" (ibid., 165).

Conclusion

Taken together, *Why I am Not a Hindu* and *Post Hindu India* are unique texts that exhibit the features of a variety of literary genres from autobiography to testimonio, and from parabiography to minor literature. But I have preferred to term them as nationalogues not only for the difficulties they present to a singular characterization, but for their sheer innovative dynamics of form, style, and a language that sets out to articulate forms of political agency. While *Why I am Not a Hindu* is a geographically restricted narrative, it introduces the ethics of reading and readership by tactfully appropriating various genres of authorship and authorial ethics—autobiography, life writing, testimonio—in the name of emancipatory politics. *Post-Hindu India*, on the other hand, features an intricate fusion of generic conventions from parabiography to travel writing, as well as minor writing. Although the sort of nativism advocated by Ilaiah may not be unfamiliar to readers in postcolonial studies, it is certainly not the sort of mythical nativism that is associated with ethnic chauvinism and identity politics. If anything, Ilaiah's political allegiances are as post-Eurocentric as they are modernist. *Post-Hindu India*, for instance, is replete with examples where Ilaiah makes a case for learning lessons from the civil wars of France, China, America, and Russia in order to avoid one in India. Even in the Indian context, he goes to great lengths to prove that it is among the subalterns and working classes that the shared values of humanity are continually nurtured and tested due to their close relationship to nature and production. Citing the example of the rice dish Biryani, which was "originally standardized by the DalitBahujans who converted into Islam, [and later] spread across the country as a special dish of India" (Ilaiah 2009: 111), Ilaiah claims that the invention of Biryani is a sign of inter-religious, intercaste solidarity between DalitBahujans and Muslims in a nation that is born out of religious dissent. Thus, it is entirely possible to read Ilaiah's work as a narrative of "disconsolatory" modernism, which in Lazarus's view (2011: 29–33) resists the assimilatory forces of institutionalized modernism that valorizes third world collectivity.

Notes

1. Despite his misgivings about postcolonial discourse at large, Ilaiah contributed an essay to the subaltern studies collective (see Ilaiah 1996).
2. This refers to the standard view of the subaltern figure based on the South Asian examples of peasants, illiterate landless laborers, and women in postcolonial discourse, which is challenged by recent critics, such as Dabashi (2012).
3. DalitBahujan is Ilaiah's neologism, which includes Dalits (untouchable castes) and Bahujans (in literal translation "other such people" consisting of a whole host of artisan and working castes). In *Why I am Not a Hindu*, Ilaiah uses the run-on "Dalitbahujans," while in *Post-Hindu India* he places an emphasis on Bahujans with a capital letter preceded by a hyphen—"Dalit-Bahujans." Excluding direct quotations, I use the non-hyphenated "DalitBahujan" to avoid unforeseen conflation between the author's emphasis and my own.
4. For a critical review of the debates on postcolonial nationalism, see McLeod's (2000) two chapters "Nationalist Representations" and "The Nation in Question" (66–101). See also Sivanandan's (2004) essay: "Anticolonialism, National Liberation, and Postcolonial Nation Formation" (41–65); and Chrisman's (2004) essay: "Nationalism and Postcolonial Studies" (183–98).
5. Objecting to Aijaz Ahmad's critique of Jameson's generalizations on third world realism (against first world modernism) and its national allegory, Lazarus suggests that Jameson's observations are based on the need to expose and challenge, not to reassert, the reception and treatment of third world literature in the first world educational curriculum (Lazarus 2011a: 93–97).
6. Here it is possible to argue that there is a conflation of Bildungsroman and autobiography in non-canonical texts, as in Jameson's treatment of the British working class novel. This conflation can also be read as a form of modernism outside of canonical modernism. Inspired by Jameson—as inflected in the very title of his book, *The Postcolonial Unconscious*, that mimics Jameson's *The Political Unconscious*—Lazarus advances the notion of "disconsolation," one that accounts for the resurgence of modernism in the postcolonial literatures *outside* of (unconscious) institutionalized modernism. See Lazarus (1999; 2011a).
7. I have benefitted from discussions with Ole Birk Laursen, the Open University, and I am thankful to him for sharing the draft of his doctoral thesis and other relevant work with me. See Laursen. 2012."Black and Asian British Life Writing: Race, Gender and Representation in Selected Novels from the 1990s," Ph.D. dissertation, the Open University, UK.

8. The terms "fraternal" and "filial" refer to the way most national autobiographers ground their past in a self-appointed manner that appeals to a heroic national origin which legitimizes their place in the independence movements as "nationalist pioneer[s]" (Boehmer 2005: 79). The fraternal aspect further alludes to the mutual self-fashioning of the national autobiographers such as Nehru, Gandhi, Nkrumah, Mandela, and Kaunda, whose "national journeys" are modeled after each other, both through direct and indirect exchange of their respective nation-building experiences (ibid., 78–79).

9. For a detailed discussion of the politics of community and collectivity, see Jan Mohammad and Lloyd (1990).

10. Aravind Adiga's The *White Tiger* (2008) is a recent literary example.

11. In Kafka's "minor literature," this double deterritorialization operates at the linguistic level, Kafka being a German-speaking Jew living in Prague, and at a political level as a national minority—deterritorialized from both canonical German and its national consciousness exerted by its vehicular code (Deleuze and Guattari 1986: 23–25). In Ilaiah's case, this translates into his self-appointed deterritorialization from mainstream Hinduism, and his (rhetorical) refusal to write in his mother tongue Telugu.

12. This is intensified by Ilaiah's frequent deployment of imperative terms such as "must," "the only way," "never," and so forth.

13. This canon consists of European scientific explorers of the Americas such as Alexander von Humboldt, Captain William Betagh and Charles-Marie de la Condamine.

Bibliography

Books, Journals, and Other Publications

Abuza, Zachary. 2003. *Militant Islam in Southeast Asia: Crucible of Terror*. Boulder CO: Lynne Rienner.

Achebe, Chinua. 1994 [1959]. *Things Fall Apart*. New York: Anchor Books.

Adiga, Aravind. 2008. *The White Tiger*. New York: Free Press.

Afzal-Khan, Fawiza. 2000. "At the Margins of Postcolonial Studies," in Fawiza Afzal-Khan and Kalpana Seshadri-Crooks (eds), *The Pre-Occupation of Postcolonial Studies*, pp. 24–36. Durham, NC: Duke University Press.

Agamben, Giorgio. December 17, 2010. "Metropolis," *The Funambulist Architectural Archives*. Available online at http://thefunambulist.net/2010/12/17 (downloaded on January 7, 2011).

Agnani, Sunil, Fernando Coronil, Gaurav Desai, Mamadou Diouf, Simon Gikandi, Jennifer Wenzel, Patricia Yaeger, and Susie Tharu. 2007. "Editor's Column: The End of Postcolonial Theory? A Roundtable with Sunil Agnani, Fernando Coronil, Gaurav Desai, Mamadou Diouf, Simon Gikandi, Susie Tharu, and Jennifer Wenzel," *PMLA* 122(3): 633–51.

Ahmad, Aijaz. 1987. "Jameson's Rhetoric of Otherness and the 'National Allegory'," *Social Text*, 17: 3–25.

———. 1991. "Between Orientalism and Historicism," in A.L. Macfie (ed.), *Orientalism: A Reader*, pp. 285–97. Edinburgh: Edinburgh University Press.

———. 1992. *In Theory: Classes, Nations, Literatures*. London and New York: Verso.

Al-Dabbagh, Abdulla. 2010. *Literary Orientalism, Postcolonialism, and Universalism*. New York: Peter Lang.

Alessandrini, Anthony C. 2009. "The Human Effect: Fanon, Foucault, and Ethics without Subjects," *Foucault Studies*, 7: 64–80.

Al-Kassim, Dina. 2002. "The Face of Foreclosure," *Interventions*, 4(2): 168–75.

Allen, Steve and Alexandra Xanthaki. 2010. *Reflections on the UN Declaration on the Rights of Indigenous Peoples*. London: Hart Publishing.

Almond, Ian. 2007. *The New Orientalists: Postmodern Representations of Islam from Foucault to Baudrillard*. London and New York: I.B. Tauris.

Amiry, Suad. 2004. *Sharon and My Mother-in-Law: Ramallah Diaries*. New York: Pantheon Books.

Anand, Mulk Raj. 1939. *The Village*. London: Jonathan Cape.

Anaya, S. James. 2004. *International Peoples in International Law* (second edition). Oxford and New York: Oxford University Press.

Apostel, Léo, Guy Berger, Asa Briggs, and Guy Michaud (eds). 1972. *Interdisciplinarity: Problems of Teaching and Research in Universities.* Paris: OECD.

Appiah, Anthony. 1997. "Cosmopolitan Patriots," *Critical Inquiry,* 23(3): 617–39.

Apter, Emily. 2004. "Saidian Humanism," *Boundary 2,* 31(2): 35–53.

Armstrong, Philip. 2002. "The Postcolonial Animal," *Society & Animals,* 10(4): 413–19.

Asad, Talal (ed.). 1974. *Anthropology and the Colonial Encounter.* London: Ithaca.

Ashcroft, Bill. 2009. "Beyond the Nation: Postcolonial Hope," *Journal of the European Association of Studies on Australia,* 1: 12–22.

———. 2010. "Transnation," in Janet Wilson, Cristina Sandru and Sarah Lawson Welsh (eds), *Rerouting the Postcolonial: New Directions for the Millennium,* pp. 72–85. London and New York: Routledge.

Ashcroft, Bill and Pal Ahluwalia. 1999. *Edward Said.* London and New York: Routledge.

Ashcroft, Bill, Gareth Griffiths, and Helen Tiffin. 2002 [1989]. *The Empire Writes Back: Theory and Practice in Postcolonial Literatures.* London and New York: Routledge.

Asquith, Christina. 2009. *Sisters in War: A Story of Love, Family, and Survival in the New Iraq.* New York: Random House.

Baber, Zaheer. 2001. "Modernization Theory and the Cold War," *Journal of Contemporary Asia,* 31(1): 71–85.

———. 2002. "Orientalism, Occidentalism, and Nativism: The Culturalist Quest for Indigenous Science and Knowledge," *European Legacy,* 7(6): 747–58.

Baden-Powell, B.H. 1896. *The Indian Village Community.* London: Longmans, Green & Co.

Baer, Robert. 2006. *Blow the House Down.* New York: Crown.

Bahri, Deepika. 2003. *Native Intelligence: Aesthetics, Politics, and Postcolonial Literature.* Minneapolis, MN: University of Minnesota Press.

Ballantyne, R.M. 1986 [1858]. *The Coral Island.* London: Puffin Classics.

Barber, Benjamin R. 2003. *Fear's Empire: War, Terrorism, and Democracy.* New York: Norton.

Baudrillard, Jean. 2003. *The Spirit of Terrorism and Other Essays.* Translated by Chris Turner. London and New York: Verso.

Brathwaite, Edward Kamau. 1977. "Caliban, Ariel, and Unprospero in the Conflict of Creolization: A Study of the Slave Revolt in Jamaica in 1831–32," *Annals of the New York Academy of Sciences,* 292(1): 41–62.

Barkel, S.J. 1976. "American Indian Tribal Courts, Separate? 'Yes'. Equal, 'Probably Not'," *American Bar Association Journal,* 62(3): 1001–06.

Bates, Crispin. 1995. "Race, Caste and Tribe in Central India: The Early Origins of Indian Anthropometry," *Edinburgh Papers in South Asian Studies,* 3: 3–35. Available online at http://www.csas.ed.ac.uk/__data/assets/pdf_file/0005/38426/WP03_BATES_RaceCaste_and_Tribe.pdf (downloaded on February 11, 2015).

Battiste, Marie (ed.). 2000. *Reclaiming Indigenous Voice and Vision.* Vancouver: University of British Columbia Press.

Beck, Richard A. 2003. "Remote Sensing and GIS as Counterterrorism Tools in the Afghanistan War: A Case Study of the Zhawar Kili Region," *Professional Geographer,* 55(2): 170–79.

Behdad, Ali. 1993. "Traveling to Teach: Postcolonial Critics in the American Academy," in Cameron McCarthy and Warren Crichlow (eds), *Race, Identity and Representation in Education,* pp. 40–49. London and New York: Routledge.

———. 1999. *Belated Travelers: Orientalism in the Age of Colonial Dissolution.* Durham, NC: Duke University Press.

Benaissa, Slimane. 2004. *The Last Night of a Damned Soul*. Translated by Janice and Daniel Gross. New York: Grove Press.

Beverley, John. 2011. "The Margin at the Center: On Testimonio (Testimonial Narrative)," in Robert P. Marzec (ed.), *Postcolonial Literary Studies: The First Thirty Years*, pp. 15–34. Baltimore, MD: The Johns Hopkins University Press.

Bhabha, Homi K. 1985. "Signs Taken for Wonders: Questions of Ambivalence and Authority Under a Tree in Delhi, May 1817," *Critical Inquiry*, 12(1): 144–65.

——— (ed.). 1990. *Nation and Narration*. London and New York: Routledge.

———. 1991. "Race, Time and the Revision of Modernity," *Oxford Literary Review*, 13(1): 193–219.

———. 1997. "Liberalism's Sacred Cow," *Boston Review*. Available online at http://www.bostonreview.net/BR22.5/bhabha.html (downloaded on August 20, 2011).

———. 2000a. "On Minorities: Cultural Rights," *Radical Philosophy: A Journal of Socialist and Feminist Philosophy*, 100: 3–6.

———. 2000b. "The Vernacular Cosmopolitan," in Dennis Ferdinand and Naseem Khan (eds), *Voices of the Crossing: The Impact of Britain on Writers from Asia, the Caribbean, and Africa*, pp. 133–42. London: Serpent's Tail.

———. 1994. "In a Spirit of Calm Violence," in Gyan Prakash (ed.), *After Colonialism: Imperial Histories and Postcolonial Displacements*, pp. 332–36. Princeton, NJ: Princeton University Press.

———. 2004 [1994]. *The Location of Culture*. London and New York: Routledge.

Bhagat, Chetan. 2004. *Five Point Someone: What Not to Do at IIT!* New Delhi: Rupa & Co.

Bhambra, Gurminder. 2007. *Sociology and Postcolonialism: Another Missing Revolution*. Basingstoke: Palgrave Macmillan.

Biccum, April. 2010. *The Legacy of Empire: Marketing Development*. London and New York: Routledge.

Black, Shameem. 2006. "Cosmopolitanism at Home: Amitav Ghosh's *The Shadow Lines*," *Journal of Commonwealth Literature*, 41(3): 45–65.

Blaser, Mario, Ravi de Costa, Deborah McGregor, and William D. Coleman (eds). 2010. *Indigenous Peoples and Autonomy: Insights for a Global Age*. Vancouver: University of British Columbia Press.

Bloom, Clive. 1996. *Cult Fiction*. Basingstoke: Palgrave Macmillan.

———. 2008 [2002]. *Bestsellers: Pulp Fiction since 1990*. Basingstoke: Palgrave Macmillan.

Blunt, Alison and Cheryl McEwan (eds). 2002. *Postcolonial Geographies*. London: Continuum.

Boehmer, Elleke. 1993. "Transfiguring the Colonial Body into Narrative," *NOVEL: A Forum on Fiction*, 26(3): 268–77.

———. 2005. *Stories of Women: Gender and Narrative in the Postcolonial Nation*. Manchester: Manchester University Press.

Bowman, Isaiah. 1928. *The New World: Problems of Political Geography*. New York: World Book Company.

Breckenridge, Carol A., Sheldon Pollock, Homi K. Bhabha, and Dipesh Chakrabarty (eds). 2002. *Cosmopolitanism*. Durham, NC: Duke University Press.

Brennan, Timothy. 1988. "India, Nationalism, and Other Failures," *South Atlantic Quarterly*, 87(1): 131–46.

———. 2000. "The Illusion of a Future: 'Orientalism' as Traveling Theory," *Critical Inquiry*, 26(3): 558–83.

Brennan, Timothy. 2001. "Cosmopolitanism and Internationalism," *New Left Review*, 7: 75–84.

Brontë, Charlotte. 2006 [1847]. *Jane Eyre*. London: Penguin.

Brown, Cody. 2007. "The New Terrorism Debate," *Alternatives: Turkish Journal of International Relations*, 6(3–4): 28–43.

Brydon, Diana. 2000. *Postcolonialism: Critical Concepts in Literary and Cultural Studies Volume 1*. London and New York: Routledge.

———. 2004. "Postcolonialism Now: Autonomy, Cosmopolitanism and Diaspora," *University of Toronto Quarterly*, 73(2): 691–706.

———. 2013. "Modes and Models of Postcolonial Cross-Disciplinarity," in Graham Huggan (ed.), *The Oxford Handbook of Postcolonial Studies*, pp. 427–48. Oxford: Oxford University Press.

Brzezinski, Zbigniew. 1997. *The Grand Chessboard: American Primacy and its Geostrategic Imperatives*. New York: Basic Books.

Burnett, Jonny and Dave Whyte. 2003. "Embedded Expertise and the New Terrorism," *Journal for Crime, Conflict and the Media*, 1(4): 1–18.

Burrell, Kathy. 2006. *Moving Lives: Narratives of Nation and Migration among Europeans in Post-War Britain*. Aldershot: Ashgate.

Byrd, Jodi A. and Michael Rothberg. 2011. "Between Subalternity and Indigeneity: Critical Categories for Postcolonial Studies," *Interventions*, 13(1): 1–12.

Césaire, Aimé. 1986 [1969]. *A Tempest*. Translated by Richard Miller. New York: Ubu Repertory.

Chakrabarty, Dipesh. 1992. "Postcoloniality and the Artifice of History: Who Speaks for "Indian" Pasts?" *Representations*, 37: 1–26.

———. 2000. "Subaltern Studies and Postcolonial Historiography," *Nepantla: Views from South*, 1(1): 9–32.

———. 2002. *Habitations of Modernity: Essays in the Wake of Subaltern Studies*. Chicago, IL: University of Chicago Press.

———. 2005. "Legacies of Bandung: Decolonisation and the Politics of Culture," *Economic and Political Weekly*, 40(46): 4812–18.

———. 2008 [2000]. *Provincializing Europe: Postcolonial Thought and Historical Difference*. Princeton, NJ: Princeton University Press.

———. 2012. "Postcolonial Studies and the Challenge of Climate Change," *New Literary History*, 43(1): 1–18.

Chalk, Peter. 2001. "Separatism and Southeast Asia: The Islamic Factor in Southern Thailand, Mindanao, and Aceh," *Studies in Conflict & Terrorism*, 24(4): 241–69.

Charlesworth, Hilary. 1994. "What are Women's International Human Rights?" in Rebecca J. Cook (ed.), *Human Rights of Women: National and International Perspectives*, pp. 58–84. Philadelphia, PA: University of Pennsylvania Press.

Charters, Claire and Rodolfo Stavenhagen (eds). 2009. *Making the Declaration Work: the United Nations Declaration on the Rights of Indigenous Peoples*. Copenhagen: IWGIA.

Chatterjee, Partha. 1993 [1986]. *Nationalist Thought and the Colonial World: A Derivative Discourse*. Minneapolis, MN: University of Minnesota Press.

———. 1997. *Our Modernity*. Rotterdam: SEPHIS.

Chatterjee, Partha and Pradeep Jeganathan (eds). 2000. *Subaltern Studies No. XI: Community, Gender and Violence*. New York: Columbia University Press.

Cheah, Pheng. 2004. *Inhuman Conditions: On Cosmopolitanism and Human Rights*. Cambridge, MA: Harvard University Press.

Cherland, Meredith Rogers and Helen Harper. 2007. *Advocacy Research in Literacy Education: Seeking Higher Ground.* Mahwah, NJ: Lawrence Erlbaum Associates.

Chew, Matthew. 2001. "An Alternative Metacritique of the Postcolonial Cultural Studies from a Cultural Sociological Perspective," *Cultural Studies*, 15(3–4): 602–20.

Chowdhury, Kanishka. 2006. "Interrogating 'Newness': Globalization and Postcolonial Theory in the Age of Endless War," *Cultural Critique*, 62: 126–61.

Chrisman, Laura. 2004. "Nationalism and Postcolonial Studies," in Neil Lazarus (ed.), *The Cambridge Companion to Postcolonial Literary Studies*, pp. 183–98. Cambridge: Cambridge University Press.

Chua, Amy. 2003. *World on Fire: How Exporting Free Market Democracy Breeds Ethnic Hatred and Global Instability.* London: William Heinemann.

Clark, Stephen H. (ed.). 1999. *Travel Writing and Empire: Postcolonial Theory in Transit.* London: Zed Books.

Clarke, Richard. 2006. *The Scorpion's Gate.* New York: Putnam.

Clifford, James. 1988. *The Predicament of Culture: Twentieth-Century Ethnography, Literature, and Art.* Cambridge, MA: Harvard University Press.

———. 1992. "Traveling Cultures," in Lawrence Grossberg, Cary Nelson, and Paula Treichler (eds), *Cultural Studies*, pp. 96–116. London and New York: Routledge.

Clifford, James and George E. Marcus (eds). 1986. *Writing Culture: The Poetics and Politics of Ethnography.* Berkeley, CA: University of California Press.

Clinton, Robert N. 1990. "The Rights of Indigenous Peoples as Collective Groups Rights," *Arizona Law Review*, 32(4): 739–44.

Codell, Julie F. and Dianne Sachko Macleod (eds). 1989. *Orientalism Transposed: The Impact of the Colonies on British Culture.* Aldershot: Ashgate.

Comaroff, Jean and John Comaroff. 2003. "Ethnography on an Awkward Scale: Postcolonial Anthropology and the Violence of Abstraction," *Ethnography*, 4(2): 291–324.

Conell, Liam. 2004. "Post-Colonial Interdisciplinarity," *Critical Survey*, 16(2): 1–7.

Connors, Michael. 2006. "War on Terror and the Southern Fire: How Terrorism Analysts Get it Wrong," *Critical Asian Studies*, 38(1): 151–75.

Cook, Ian and Harrison, Michelle. 2003. "Cross Over Food: Re-materializing Postcolonial Geographies," *Transactions of the Institute of British Geographers*, 28(3): 296–317.

Coetzee, J.M. 1986. *Foe: A Novel.* London: Secker & Warburg.

Cooper, James Fenimore. 2008 [1826]. *The Last of the Mohicans.* New York: Pocket Books.

Crush, Jonathan. 1994. "Post-colonialism, De-colonization, and Geography," in Anne Godlewska and Neil Smith (eds), *Geography and Empire*, pp. 333–50. Oxford: Blackwell.

Cutter, Susan L., Douglas B. Richardson, and Thomas J. Wilbanks (eds). 2003. *The Geographical Dimensions of Terrorism.* London and New York: Routledge.

Dabashi, Hamid. 2009. *Post-Orientalism: Knowledge and Power in Time of Terror.* New Brunswick and London: Transaction Publishers.

———. August 3, 2011. "Norway: Muslims and Metaphors, Part Two," *Aljazeera Online.* Available online at http://www.aljazeera.com/indepth/opinion/2011/07/201173110360249386.html (downloaded on January 14, 2012).

———. 2012. *The Arab Spring: The End of Postcolonialism.* London: Zed Books.

———. January 15, 2013. "Can Non-Europeans Think?" *Aljazeera Online.* Available online at http://www.aljazeera.com/indepth/opinion/2013/01/2013114142638797542.html (downloaded on February 11, 2014).

Dabydeen, David. 1993. *Disappearance.* London: Secker & Warburg.

Daes, Erica-Irene A. 2009. "The Contribution of the Working Group on Indigenous Populations to the Genesis and Evolution of the UN Declaration on the Rights of Indigenous Peoples," in Claire Charters and Rodolfo Stavenhagen (eds), *Making the Declaration Work: The United Nations Declaration on the Rights of Indigenous Peoples*, pp. 48–77. Copenhagen: IWGIA.

Das, Veena. 2007. *Life and Worlds: Violence and the Descent into the Ordinary*. Berkeley, CA: University of California Press.

Davis, Fergal, Nicola McGarrity, and George Williams (eds). 2014. *Surveillance, Counter-Terrorism and Comparative Constitutionalism*. London and New York: Routledge.

Defoe, Daniel. 2003 [1719]. *Robinson Crusoe*. Harmondsworth: Penguin.

De Gennaro, M. 2003. "Fighting Humanism in its Own Terms," *Difference*, 14(1): 53–73.

De Oliveria, Adolfo (ed.). 2009. *Decolonising Indigenous Rights*. London and New York: Routledge.

De Oto, Alejandro J. 2003. *Frantz Fanon: Plíticay Poética del Sujeto Poscolonial*. Mexico City: El Colegio de México, A.C.

De Soyza, Niromi. 2011. *Tamil Tigress: My Story as a Child Soldier in Sri Lanka's Bloody Civil War*. Sydney: Allen & Unwin.

Deleuze, Gilles and Felix Guattari. 1986. *Franz Kafka: Toward a Minor Literature*. Minneapolis, MN: University of Minnesota Press.

Deleuze, Gilles and Michel Foucault. 1977. "Intellectuals and Power," in Donald F. Bouchard (ed.), *Language, Counter-Memory and Practice*, pp. 205–17. Ithaca, NY: Cornell University Press.

DeLillo, Don. 2007. *Falling Man*. New York: Scribner.

Desai, Kiran. 2006. *The Inheritance of Loss*. New York: Atlantic Monthly Press.

Desani, G.V. 2007 [1948]. *All About H. Hatterr*. New York: The New York Review of Books.

Devi, Mahasweta. October 6, 2006. "The Republic of Dreams," *Tehelka Online*. Available online at http://archive.tehelka.com/story_main20.asp?filename=hub102106The_republic.asp (downloaded on February 25, 2014).

Dhillon, Pradeep A. 1999. "Dis(locating) Thoughts: Where Do the Birds Go after the Last Sky?" in Thomas S. Popkewith and Lynn Fendler (eds), *Critical Theories in Education: Changing Terrains of Knowledge and Politics*, pp. 191–208. London and New York: Routledge.

Didur, Jill and Teresa Heffernan. 2003. "Revisiting the Subaltern in the New Empire," *Cultural Studies*, 17(1): 1–15.

Dirilik, Arif. 1994. "The Postcolonial Aura: Third World Criticism in the Age of Global Capitalism," *Critical Inquiry*, 20(2): 328–56.

Dirks, Nicholas B. 1993 [1987]. *The Hollow Crown: Ethnohistory of an Indian Kingdom*. Ann Arbor, MI: University of Michigan Press.

———. 1999. "The Crimes of Colonialism: Anthropology and the Textualization of India," in Peter Pels and Oscar Salemink (eds), *Colonial Subjects: Essays on the Practical History of Anthropology*, pp. 153–79. Ann Arbor, MI: University of Michigan Press.

———. 2001. *Castes of Mind: Colonialism and the Making of Modern India*. Princeton, NJ: Princeton University Press.

Donaldson, Laura and Kwok Pui-Lan (eds). 2002. *Postcolonialism, Feminism and Religious Discourse*. London and New York: Routledge.

Donnelly, Jack. 1998. "Human Rights: A New Standard of Civilization?" *International Affairs*, 74(1): 1–23.

Döring, Tobias. 1998. "The Passage of the Eye/I: David Dabydeen, V.S. Naipaul and the Tombstones of Parabiography," in Alfred Hornung and Ernstpeter Ruhe (eds), *Postcolonialism & Autobiography*, pp. 149–66. Amsterdam and Atlanta: Rodopi.

Doyle, Arthur Conan. 1982 [1890]. *The Sign of Four*. London: Penguin.

Drew, Julie. 1999. "Cultural Composition: Stuart Hall on Ethnicity and the Discursive Turn," in Gary A. Olson and Lynn Worsham (eds), *Race, Rhetoric, and the Postcolonial*, pp. 205–39. Albany, NY: The State University of New York Press.

Driver, Felix. 2000. *Geography Militant: Cultures of Exploration and Empire*. Oxford: Blackwell.

Driver, Felix and Rose Gillian (eds). 1992. *Nature and Science: Essays in the History of Geographical Knowledge*. Cheltenham: Historical Geography Research Group Series.

Dumont, Louis. 1966. "The Village Community from Munro to Maine," *Contributions to Indian Sociology*, 9: 67–89.

———. 1970. *Homo Hierarchicus: The Caste System and its Implications*. London: Weidenfeld and Nicolson.

During, Simon. 2012. "Empire's Present," *New Literary History*, 43(2): 331–40.

Duyvesteyn, Isabelle. 2004. "How New Is the New Terrorism?" *Studies in Conflict & Terrorism*, 27(5): 439–54.

Eagleton, Terry. 1999. "In the Gaudy Supermarket," *London Review of Books*, 21(10): 3–6.

Eide, Asbjørn. 2009. "The Indigenous Peoples, the Working Group on Indigenous Populations and the Adoption of the UN Declaration on the Rights of Indigenous Peoples," in Claire Charters and Rodolfo Stavenhagen (eds), *Making the Declaration Work: the United Nations Declaration on the Rights of Indigenous Peoples*, pp. 32–46. Copenhagen: IWGIA.

Elliot, Henry M. 1869. *Memoirs on the History, Folk-lore, and Distribution of the Races of the North Western Provinces of India*. London: Trübner & Co.

Elphinstone, Mountstuart. 1838 [1821]. *Report on the Territories Conquered from the Paishwa*. Submitted to the Supreme Government of British India. Bombay: Government Central Press.

———. 1966 [1841]. *The History of India: The Hindu and Mahomatan Periods*. Allahabad: Kitab Mahal.

Engseng, Ho. 2004. "Empire through Diasporic Eyes: A View from the Other Boat," *Comparative Studies of Society and History*, 46(2): 210–46.

Escobar, Arturo. 1992. "Imagining a Postdevelopment Era? Critical Thought, Development and Social Movements," *Social Text*, 31(32): 20–56.

Fabian, Johannes. 1983. *Time and the Other: How Anthropology Makes its Object*. New York: Columbia University Press.

———. 1990. "Presence and Representation: The Other and Anthropological Writing," *Critical Inquiry*, 16(4): 753–72.

Fanon, Frantz. 1965 [1959]. *A Dying Colonialism*. Translated by Haakon Chevalier. New York: Grove Press.

———. 1967 [1952]. *Black Skin, White Masks*. Translated by Charles Lam Markmann. New York: Grove Press.

———. 1968 [1961]. *The Wretched of the Earth*. Translated by Constance Farrington. New York: Grove Press.

Featherstone, Mike. 2002. "Cosmopolis: An Introduction," *Theory, Culture & Society*, 19(1–2): 1–16.

Fesperman, Dan. 2004. *The Warlord's Son*. Berkshire: Transworld.

Firminger, W.K. (ed.). 1917–1918 [1812]. *The Fifth Report From the Select Committee of the House of Commons on the Affairs of the East India Company: Dated 28th July 1812* (3 volumes). Calcutta: R. Cambray & Co.

Flint, Colin. 2003. "Terrorism and Counterterrorism: Geographic Research Questions and Agendas," *Professional Geographer*, 55(2): 161–69.

Fontinha de Alcantara, Christiane. 2009. "Imperial Eyes: A Second Look," *Palimpsesto*, 8(8): 1–6.

Foucault, Michel. 1977. *Discipline and Punish: The Birth of the Prison*. Translated by A.M. Sheridan Smith. New York: Vintage Books.

Franck, Thomas. 2001. "Are Human Rights Universal?" *Foreign Affairs*, 80(1): 191–204.

Fraser, Nancy. 1989. "Foucault on Modern Power: Empirical Insights and Normative Confusions," *PRAXIS International*, 3: 272–81.

Freitag, Sandria B. 1991. "Crime in the Social Order of Colonial North India," *Modern Asian Studies*, 25(2): 227–61.

Furphy, Joseph. 1903. *Such is Life*. Sydney: The Bulletin Newspaper Company.

Gandhi, Leela. 1998. *Postcolonial Theory, a Critical Introduction*. New York: Columbia University Press.

Gandhi, Mohandas. 1940. *Autobiography: The Story of My Experiments with Truth*. Auckland: The Floating Press.

Ganguly, Keya. 2002. "Adorno, Authenticity, Critique," in Crystal Bartolovich and Neil Lazarus (eds), *Marxism, Modernity, and Postcolonial Studies*, pp. 240–56. Cambridge: Cambridge University Press.

Gaonkar, Dilip Parameshwar. 1999. "On Alternative Modernities," *Public Culture*, 11(1): 1–18.

Garratt, Dean and Heather Piper. 2010. "Heterotopian Cosmopolitan Citizenship Education?" *Education, Citizenship and Social Justice*, 5(1): 43–55.

Gearson, John 2002. "The Nature of Modern Terrorism," *Political Quarterly*, 73(1): 7–24.

George, Rosemary. 2004. "Of Fictional Cities and Diasporic Aesthetics," in Katharyne Mitchell, Sallie A. Marston, and Cindi Katz (eds), *Life's Work: Geographies of Social Reproduction*, pp. 141–62. Oxford: Blackwell.

———. 2013. *Indian English and the Fiction of National Literature*. Cambridge: Cambridge University Press.

Gikandi, Simon. 2004. "Poststructuralism and Postcolonial Theory," in Neil Lazarus (ed.), *The Cambridge Companion to Postcolonial Literary Studies*, pp. 97–119. Cambridge: Cambridge University Press.

———. 2010. "Between Roots and Routs: Cosmopolitanism and the Claims of Locality," in Janet Wilson, Cristina Sandru, and Sarah Lawson Welsh (eds), *Rerouting the Postcolonial: New Directions for the Millennium*, pp. 22–35. London and New York: Routledge.

Gilmartin, Mary and Lawrence D. Berg. 2007. "Locating Postcolonialism," *Area*, 39(1): 120–24.

Gilroy, Paul. 2001. "After the Great White Error… The Great Black Mirage," *Transformation*, 47: 28–49.

Glissant Edouard. 1997. *Poetics of Relation*. Translated by Besty Wing. Ann Arbor, MI: University of Michigan Press.

Godlewska, Anne and Neil Smith (eds). 1994. *Geography and Empire*. Oxford: Blackwell.

Goldberg, David Theo. 2009. *The Threat of Race: Reflections on Racial Neoliberalism*. Oxford: Blackwell.

Goodale, Mark. 2009. *Surrendering to Utopia: An Anthropology of Human Rights*. Stanford, CA: Stanford University Press.

Goodwin, Jeff. 2006. "A Theory of Categorical Terrorism," *Social Forces*, 84(4): 2027–46.

Goonewardena, Kanishka. 2004. "Postcolonialism and Diaspora: A Contribution to the Critique of Nationalist Ideology and Historiography in the Age of Globalization and Neoliberalism," *University of Toronto Quarterly*, 73(2): 657–90.

Gopal, Priyamvada and Neil Lazarus. 2006. "Editorial," *New Formations*, 59: 7–9.

Gopal, Rupa. February 20, 2011. "The Malgudi that is Agumbe," *The Hindu*. Available online at http://www.hinduonnet.com (downloaded on July 27, 2011).

Greedharry, Mrinalini. 2008. *Postcolonial Theory and Psychoanalysis: From Uneasy Engagement to Effective Critique*. Basingstoke: Palgrave Macmillan.

Gregory, Derek. 2007. "Vanishing Points," in Derek Gregory and Allan Pred (eds), *Violent Geographies: Fear, Terror, and Political Violence*, pp. 205–36. London and New York: Routledge.

Griffin, Michael. 2013. *Enlightenment in Ruins: The Geographies of Oliver Goldsmith*. Lewisburg, PA: Bucknell University Press.

Grovogui, Siba. 2005. "The New Cosmopolitanisms: Subtexts, Pretexts and Context of Ethics," *International Relations*, 19(1): 103–13.

Guha, Ranajit. 1982. "On Some Aspects of the Historiography of Colonial India," in Ranajit Guha (ed.), *Subaltern Studies I: Writings on South Asian History and Society*, pp. 1–7. Delhi: Oxford University Press.

———. 1983. *Elementary Aspects of Peasant Insurgency in Colonial India*. Delhi: Oxford University Press.

———. 1988. "The Prose of Counter-Insurgency," in Ranajit Guha and Gayatri Chakravorty Spivak (eds), *Selected Subaltern Studies*, pp. 45–88. New York: Oxford University Press.

———. 1997. *Dominance without Hegemony: History and Power in Colonial India*. Cambridge, MA: Harvard University Press.

Guha, Ranajit and Gayatri Chakravorty Spivak (eds). 1988. *Selected Subaltern Studies*. New York: Oxford University Press.

Gunaratana, Rohan. 2005. "Understanding al-Qaeda and Its Network in Southeast Asia," in Paul J. Smith (ed.), *Terrorism and Violence in Southeast Asia: Transnational Challenges to States and Regional Stability*, pp. 62–78. New York: M.E. Sharpe.

Gupta, Akhil. 1998. *Postcolonial Developments: Agriculture in the Making of Modern India*. Durham, NC: Duke University Press.

Habib, Irfan. 2005. "In Defence of Orientalism: Critical Notes on Edward Said," *Social Scientist*, 3(1): 40–46.

Hafeznia, M.R. 1994. "Geopolitical Analysis of the Kashmir Crisis," *South Asian Studies*, 11: 125–30.

Hamid, Mohsin. 2007. *The Reluctant Fundamentalist*. New York: Houghton Mifflin.

Hannerz, Ulf. 1990. "Cosmopolitans and Locals in World Culture," in Mike Featherstone (ed.), *Global Culture. Nationalism, Globalisation and Modernity*, pp. 237–51. London: SAGE.

Hardt, Michael and Antonio Negri. 2000. *Empire*. Cambridge, MA: Harvard University Press.

Harlow, Barbara. 1987. *Resistance Literature*. New York: Methuen.

Harris, Wilson. 1996. *Jonestown*. London: Faber & Faber.

———. 2005 [1999]. "Tradition and the West Indian Novel," in Andrew Bundy (ed.), *Selected Essay of Wilson Harris*, pp. 139–48. London and New York: Routledge.

Harvey, David. 1982. *The Limits to Capital.* Chicago, IL: University of Chicago Press.

———. 2000. "Cosmopolitanism and the Banality of Geographical Evils," *Popular Culture,* 12(2): 560–80.

Hassan, Ihab. 1996. "Negative Capability Reclaimed: Literature and Philosophy Contra Politics," *Philosophy and Literature,* 20(2): 305–24.

Hatch, William John. 1928. *The Land Pirates of India: An Account of the Kuravers, a Remarkable Tribe of Hereditary Criminals, their Extraordinary Skill as Thieves, Cattle-lifters & Highwaymen & their Manners & Customs.* London: Seeley, Service & Co. Ltd.

Hawthorne, Nathaniel. 2010 [1844]. *Rappaccini's Daughter.* Whitefish, MT: Kessinger Publishing.

Henderson, James Youngblood. 2009. *Indigenous Diplomacy and the Rights of the Peoples.* Saskatoon: Purich Publishers.

Hepple, Leslie W. 1986. "The Revival of Geopolitics," *Political Geography Quarterly,* 5(4): 21–36.

Hiddleston, Jane. 2010. "Aimé Césaire and Postcolonial Humanism," *Modern Language Review,* 105(1): 87–102.

Highmore, Ben. 2002. *Everyday Life and Cultural Theory.* London and New York: Routledge.

Hoeveler, Diane and Jeffery Cass. 2006. *Interrogating Orientalism: Contextual Approaches and Pedagogical Challenges.* Columbus, OH: Ohio State University Press.

Holden, Philip. 2008. *Autobiography and Decolonization: Modernity, Masculinity, and the Nation-State.* Madison, WI: University of Wisconsin Press.

Huddart, David. 2004. "Postcolonial Piracy: Anxiety and Interdisciplinarity," *Critical Survey,* 16(2): 7–27.

———. 2006. *Homi K. Bhabha.* London and New York: Routledge.

———. 2008. *Postcolonial Theory and Autobiography.* London and New York: Routledge.

Huggan, Graham. 2002. "Postcolonial Studies and the Anxiety of Interdisciplinarity," *Postcolonial Studies,* 5(3): 245–75.

———. 2005. "(Not) Reading Orientalism," *Research in African Literatures,* 36(3): 124–36.

———. 2008. *Interdisciplinary Measures: The Future of the Postcolonial Studies.* Liverpool: Liverpool University Press.

Hulme, Peter. 1989. "Subversive Archipelagos: Colonial Discourse and the Break-Up of Continental Theory," *Dispositio,* 14(36/38): 1–23.

Hunter, Adrian. 2007. "Introduction: a 'Minor' Literature?" in Adrian Hunter (ed.), *The Cambridge Introduction to Short Story in English,* pp. 138–41. Cambridge: Cambridge University Press.

Ilaiah, Kancha. 1990. "Reservations: Experience as Framework of Debate," *Economic and Political Weekly,* 25(41): 2307–10.

———. 1996. *Why I am Not a Hindu: A Shudra Critique of Hindutva Philosophy, Culture and Political Economy.* Calcutta: Samya.

———. 2000. "Productive Labour, Consciousness and History: the Dalitbahujan Alternative," in Samir Amin and Dipesh Chakrabarty (eds), *Subaltern Studies IX,* pp. 165–200. Delhi: Oxford University Press.

———. 2009. *Post-Hindu India: A Discourse on Dalit-Bahujan, Socio-Spirtual and Scientific Revolution.* New Delhi: SAGE.

Inden, Ronald B. 1986. "Orientalist Constructions of India," *Modern Asian Studies,* 20(3): 401–46.

———. 1990. *Imagining India.* Bloomington, IN: Indiana University Press.

Innes, C.L. 2007. *The Cambridge Introduction to Postcolonial Literatures in English*. Cambridge: Cambridge University Press.

Irwin, Robert. 2006. *For a Lust of Knowing: The Orientalists and Their Enemies*. Harmondsworth: Penguin.

———. August 19, 2011. "How and Why the West Misrepresents the East," *The Times Literary Supplement*. Available online at http://www.the-tls.co.uk/tls/public/article703888.ece (downloaded on January 1, 2012).

Iwamura, Jane Naomi. 2010. *Virtual Orientalism: Asian Religions and American Popular Culture*. Oxford: Oxford University Press.

Iyer, N. Sharada. 2002. "Malgudi—A Vision, a Waking Dream, a Reality," in Amar Nath Prasad (ed.), *Indian Writing in English: Critical Explorations*, pp. 37–45. New Delhi: Sarup & Sons.

Jabri, Vivienne. 2013. *The Postcolonial Subject: Claiming Politics/Governing Others in Late Modernity*. London and New York: Routledge.

Jackson, Richard. 2007. "The Core Commitments of Critical Terrorism Studies," *European Political Science*, 6(3): 244–51.

Jacobson, Matthew F. 2002. "Post-Orientalism," *American Quarterly*, 54(2): 307–15.

James, C.L.R. 1993 [1963]. *Beyond a Boundary*. Durham, NC: Duke University Press.

Jameson, Fredric. 1981. *The Political Unconscious: Narrative as a Socially Symbolic Act*. Ithaca, NY: Cornell University Press.

———. 1986. "Third-World Literature in the Era of Multinational Capitalism," *Social Text*, 15: 65–88.

Jan Mohammad, A.R. and David Lloyd (eds). 1990. *The Nature and Contact of Minority Discourse*. New York: Oxford University Press.

Kanakasabhai, V. 1965. *The Tamils Eighteen Hundred Years Ago*. Tinnevelly: Saiva Siddhanta Works Publishing Society.

Kapila, Shruti. 2007. "Race Matters: Orientalism and Religion, India and Beyond c.1770–1880," *Modern Asian Studies*, 41(3): 471–513.

Kapoor, Ilan. 2003. "Acting in a Tight Spot: Homi Bhabha's Postcolonial Politics," *New Political Science*, 25(4): 561–77.

———. 2008. *The Postcolonial Politics of Development*. London and New York: Routledge.

———. 2013. *Celebrity Humanitarianism: The Ideology of Global Charity*. London and New York: Routledge.

Karavanta, Mina and Nina Morgan (eds). 2008. *Edward Said and Jacques Derrida: Reconstellating Humanism and the Global Hybrid*. New Castle: Cambridge Scholars Publishing.

Kemp, Geoffrey and Robert E. Harkavy. 1997. *Strategic Geography and the Changing Middle East: Carnegie Endowment for International Peace*. Washington, DC: Brookings Institution Press.

Keown, Michelle. 2005. *Postcolonial Pacific Writing: Representations of the Body*. London and New York: Routledge.

Khadra, Yasmina. 2006. *The Attack*. Translated by John Cullen. London: Vintage Books.

Khair, Tabish. 2004. "Postcolonial Studies: a Paradigm for Interdisciplinarity?" *The Object of Study in the Humanities*, pp. 101–12. Copenhagen: Museum Tusculanum.

Khatri, Chhote Lal. 2006. *R.K. Narayan: Reflections and Re-Evaluation*. Delhi: Sarup.

Khoo Thwe, Pascal. 2003. *From the Land of Green Ghosts: A Burmese Odyssey*. London: Flaming.

Kim, Julie H. 2005. "Introduction: Murder and the Other," in July H. Kim (ed.), *Race and Religion in the Postcolonial British Detective Story*, pp. 1–12. Jefferson, NC: McFarland Publishers.

Kipling, Rudyard. 2010 [1901]. *Kim*. London: Vintage Classics.

Klein, Julie Thompson. 1990. *Interdisciplinarity: History, Theory, and Practice*. Detroit, MI: Wayne State University Press.

———. 2005. *Humanities, Culture, and Interdisciplinarity: The Changing American Academy*. Albany, NY: The State University of New York Press.

Klein, Julie Thompson and William H. Newell. 1997. "Advancing Interdisciplinary Studies," in Jerry G. Gaff and James L. Ratcliff (eds), *Handbook of the Undergraduate Curriculum: A Comprehensive Guide to Purposes, Structures, Practices, and Change*, pp. 393–415. San Francisco, CA: Jossey-Bass.

Knowles, Sam. 2007. "Macrocosm-opolitanism? Gilroy, Appiah, and Bhabha: The Unsettling Generality of Cosmopolitan Ideas," *Postcolonial Text*, 3(4): 1–11.

Koshy, Susan. 2008. "Postcolonial Studies after 9/11: A Response to Ali Behdad," *American Literary History*, 20(1 2): 300–03.

Krishna, Sankaran. 2008. *Globalization and Postcolonialism: Hegemony and Resistance in the Twenty-First Century*. London: Rowman and Littlefield.

Kymlicka, Will. 1999. "Theorizing Indigenous Rights," *University of Toronto Law Journal*, 49(2): 281–93.

Lahiri, Shompa. 2010. "At Home in the City, at Home in the World: Cosmopolitanism and Urban Belonging in Kolkata," *Contemporary South Asia*, 18(2): 191–204.

Lal, Vinay. 1995. "Introduction," in Naidu Bahadur M. Pauparao (ed.), *The History of Railway Thieves, with Illustrations and Hints on Detection*, pp. i–xxvii. Gurgaon: Vintage Press.

Lamming, George. 1953. *In the Castle of My Skin*. New York: McGraw Hill.

———. 2005 [1960]. *The Pleasures of Exile*. London: Pluto Press.

Latham, Andrew. 1999. "Response to Woo-Cumings," *Macalester International*, 7(1): 200–206.

Lau, Lisa and Ana Cristina Mendes (eds). 2011. *Re-orientalism and South Asian Identity Politics: The Oriental Other Within*. London and New York: Routledge.

Laursen, Ole Birk. 2010. "Review of Bart Moore-Gilbert's *Postcolonial Life-Writing: Culture, Politics and Self-Representation* (2009) and Philip Holden's *Autobiography and Decolonization: Modernity, Masculinity, and the Nation-State* (2008)," *Wasafiri*, 25(3): 86–88.

———. 2012. PhD Dissertation. "Black and Asian British Life Writing: Race, Gender and Representation in Selected Novels from the 1990s," UK: Open University.

Lattuca, Lisa R. 2011. *Creating Interdisciplinarity*. Nashville, TN: Vanderbilt University Press.

Lazarus, Neil. 1993. "Disavowing Decolonization: Fanon, Nationalism, and the Problematic of Representation in Current Theories of Postcolonial Discourse," *Research in African Literatures*, 24(4): 69–98.

———. 1999. *Nationalism and Cultural Practice in the Postcolonial World*. Cambridge: Cambridge University Press.

——— (ed.). 2004a. *The Cambridge Companion to Postcolonial Literary Studies*. Cambridge: Cambridge University Press.

———. 2004b. "The Global Dispensation since 1945," in Neil Lazarus (ed.), *The Cambridge Companion to Postcolonial Literary Studies*, pp. 19–40. Cambridge: Cambridge University Press.

———. 2006. "Postcolonial Studies After the Invasion of Iraq," *New Formations*, 59: 10–22.

———. 2011a. *The Postcolonial Unconscious*. Cambridge: Cambridge University Press.

Lazarus, Neil. 2011b. "Cosmopolitanism and the Specificity of the Local in World Literature," *Journal of Commonwealth Literature*, 46(1): 119–37.

Leclerc, Gérard. 1972. *Anthroplogie et Colonialisme*. Paris: Fayard.

Lennon Joseph. 2004. *Irish Orientalism: A Literary and Intellectual History*. Syracuse, NY: Syracuse University Press.

Lentin, Ronit. 2007. "Ireland: Racial State and Crisis Racism," *Ethnic and Racial Studies*, 30(4): 610–27.

Leonard, Philip. 2005. *Nationality between Poststructuralism and Postcolonial Theory*. Basingstoke: Palgrave Macmillan.

Levin, Lennart and Ingemar Lind (eds). 1985. *Interdisciplinarity Revisited*. Stockholm: OECD.

Lewis, Bernard. 2002. *What Went Wrong? Western Impact and Middle Eastern Response*. Oxford: Oxford University Press.

Lewis, Herbert S. 2007. "The Influence of Edward Said and Orientalism on Anthropology, or: Can the Anthropologist Speak?" *Israel Affairs*, 13(4): 774–85.

Lie, John Zainichi. 2008. *Koreans in Japan: Diasporic Nationalism and Postcolonial Identity*. Berkeley, CA: University of California Press.

Little, Douglas. 2002. *American Orientalism: The United States and the Middle East since 1945*. Chapel Hill, NC: University of North Carolina Press.

Livingstone, David N. 1991. "The Moral Discourse of Climate: Historical Considerations on Race, Place and Virtue," *Journal of Historical Geography*, 17(4): 413–34.

Loomba, Ania. 2005. *Colonialism/Postcolonialism*. London and New York: Routledge.

Lowe, Lisa. 1991. *Critical Terrains: French and British Orientalisms*. Ithaca, NY: Cornell University Press.

Ludden, David. 2001. *Reading Subaltern Studies*. New Delhi: Permanent Black.

———. 2003. "Presidential Address: Maps of Mind and the Mobility in Asia," *Journal of Asian Studies*, 62(4): 1057–78.

Lugard, Frederick D. 1965 [1922]. *The Dual Mandate in British Tropical Africa*. London: Cass.

Luttwak, Edward N. 1990. "From Geopolitics to Geo-Economics, Logic of Conflict, Grammar of Commerce," *National Interest*, 20: 17–24.

———. 1993. *The Endangered American Dream: How to Stop the United States from Becoming a Third World Country and How to Win the Geo-economic Struggle for Industrial Supremacy*. New York: Simon and Schuster.

MacKenzie, John M. 1995. *Orientalism: History, Theory and the Arts*. Manchester: Manchester University Press.

Maeda, Donna. 1997. "The Other Woman: Irreducible Alterity in Feminist Theologies," *Religion*, 27: 123–28.

Maine, Henry Sumner. 1861. *Ancient Law: Its Connection with the Early History of Society and its Relation to Modern Ideas*. London: John Murray.

———. 1876. *Village Communities in the East and West*. London: John Murray.

Makos, Jeff. February 16, 1995. "Rethinking Experience of Countries with Colonial Past," *The University of Chicago Chronicle*. Available online at http://chronicle.uchicago.edu/ (downloaded on June 7, 2011).

Malreddy, Pawan Kumar. 2015. "Introduction," in Pavan Kumar Malreddy, Birte Heidemann, Ole Birk Laursen, and Janet Wilson (eds). *Reworking Postcolonialism: Globalization, Labour Rights*, pp 1–15. Basingstoke: Palgrave Macmillan.

Mamadouh, V.D. 1998. "Geopolitics in the Nineties: One Flag, Many Meanings," *GeoJournal*, 46: 237–53.

Marcus, George E. and Michael Fisher. 1986. *Anthropology as Cultural Critique: An Experimental Moment in the Human Sciences*. Chicago, IL: University of Chicago Press.

Marder, Michael. February 8, 2013. "Marginalising Europe," *Aljazeera Online*. Available online at http://www.aljazeera.com/indepth/opinion/2013/02/2013239733423939. html (downloaded on March 9, 2014).

———. 2013. "A Post-colonial Comedy of Errors," *Aljazeera Online*. April 13, 2013. Available online at http://www.aljazeera.com/indepth/opinion/2013/03/2013314112255761369. html (downloaded on February 11, 2014).

Markandaya, Kamala. 2010 [1954]. *Nectar in a Sieve*. New York: Signet Classics.

Martel, André. 1991. *La Libye 1835–1990, essai de géopolitique historique*. Paris: PUF.

Marx, John. 2004. "Postcolonial Literature and the Western Literary Canon," in Neil Lazarus (ed.), *Cambridge Companion to Postcolonial Literary Studies*, pp. 83–95. Cambridge: Cambridge University Press.

Mazumdar, Sucheta, Vasant Kaiwar, and Thierry Labica (eds). 2009. *From Orientalism to Postcolonialism: Asia, Europe and the Lineages of Difference*. London and New York: Routledge.

Mbembe, Achille. 1992. "Provisional Notes on the Postcolony," *Africa: Journal of the International African Institute*, 62(1): 3–37.

———. 2001. *On the Postcolony*. Berkeley, CA: University of California Press.

———. 2003. "Necropolitics." Translated by Libby Meintjes. *Public Culture*, 15(1): 11–40.

McAlister, Melani. 2001. *Epic Encounters: Culture, Media, and US-Interests in the Middle East since 1945*. Berkeley, CA: University of California Press.

McBratney, John. 2005. "Racial and Criminal Types: Indian Ethnography and Sir Arthur Conan Doyle's *The Sign of Four*," *Victorian Literature and Culture*, 33(1): 149–67.

McClintock, Anne. 1993. "Family Feuds, Gender, Nationalism and the Family," *Feminist Review*, 44: 61–80.

McEwan, Cheryl. 2003. "Material Geographies and Postcolonialism," *Singapore Journal of Tropical Geography*, 24(3): 340–55.

———. 2009. *Postcolonialism and Development*. London and New York: Routledge.

McEwan, Ian. 2005. *Saturday*. London: Jonathan Cape.

McFarlane, Colin. 2004. "Geographical Imaginations and Spaces of Political Engagement: Examples from the Indian Alliance," *Antipode*, 36(5): 890–916.

McFarlane, Colin and Stephen Legg. 2008. "Guest Editorial," *Environment and Planning A*, 40(1): 6–14.

McLaren, Peter. 1992. "Collisions with Otherness: 'Traveling' Theory, Post-Colonial Criticisms and the Politics of Ethnographic Practice—the Mission of the Wounded Ethnographer," *Qualitative Studies in Education*, 5(1): 77–92.

McLeod, John. 2000. *Beginning Postcolonialism*. Manchester: Manchester University Press.

Melas, Natalie. 1999. "Humanity/Humanities: Decolonization and the Poetics of Relation," *Topoi*, 18: 13–28.

———. 2007. *All the Difference in the World: Postcoloniality and the Ends of Comparison*. Stanford, CA: Stanford University Press.

Mellor, P.A. 2004. "Orientalism, Representation and Religion: the Reality Behind the Myth," *Religion*, 34: 99–112.

Memmi, Albert. 2003 [1957]. *The Colonizer and the Colonized*. Translated by Howard Greenfeld. London: Earthscan Publications.

Messer, Ellen. 1997. "Pluralist Approaches to Human Rights," *Journal of Anthropological Research*, 53(3): 293–317.

Mignolo, Walter. 2000. "The Many Faces of Cosmo-polis: Border Think_ and Critical Cosmopolitanism," *Public Culture*, 12(3): 721–48.
———. 2010. "The Communal and the Decolonial," *Turbulence* 5. Available online at http://turbulence.org.uk/turbulence-5/decolonial/ (downloaded on March 7, 2014).
———. February 19, 2013. "Yes, We Can: Non-European Thinkers and Philosophers," *Aljazeera Online*. Available online at http://www.aljazeera.com/indepth/opinion/2013/02/20132672747320891.html (downloaded on February 10, 2014).
Miles, Franklin. 1901. *My Brilliant Career*. Edinburgh: Blackwood.
Mishra, Vijay and Bob Hodge. 2005. "What Was Postcolonialism?" *New Literary History*, 36(3): 375–402.
Mitchell, W.J.T. 1995a. "Interdisciplinarity and Visual Culture," *Arts Bulletin*, 77(4): 540–44.
———. 1995b. "Translator Translated (Interview with cultural theorist Homi Bhabha)," *Artform*. Available online at http://prelectur.stanford.edu/lecturers/bhabha/interview.html (downloaded on January 4, 2013).
Miyoshi, Masao. 1997. "Sites of Resistance in the Global Economy," in Keith Ansell-Pearson, Benita Parry, and Judith Squires (eds), *Cultural Readings of Imperialism: Edward Said and the Gravity of History*, pp. 49–87. London: Lawrence and Wishart.
———. 2000. "A Borderless World? From Colonialism to Transnationalism and the Decline of the Nation-State," in Diana Brydon (ed.), *Postcolonialism: Critical Concepts in Literary and Cultural Studies*, pp. 1867–92. London and New York: Routledge.
Mohanty, Satya. 1995. "Colonial Legacies, Multicultural Futures: Relativism, Objectivity, and the Challenge of Otherness," *Publication of the Modern Languages Association*, 110(1): 108–18.
Moore-Gilbert, Bart. 1997. *Postcolonial Theory: Contexts, Practices, Politics*. London and New York: Verso.
———. 1999. "Postcolonial Cultural Studies and Imperial Historiography: Problems of Interdisciplinarity," *Interventions*, 1(3): 397–411.
———. 2009. *Postcolonial Life-Writing: Culture, Politics and Self-Representation*. London and New York: Routledge.
Moran, Christopher R. and Robert Johnson. 2010. "In the Service of Empire: Imperialism and the British Spy Thriller, 1901–1914," *Studies in Intelligence*, 54(2): 1–22.
Morgan, D.E. 2003. PhD Dissertation. "Pulp Literature: A Re-evaluation," Murdoch University.
Morgan, Matthew J. 2004. "The Origins of the New Terrorism," *Parameters*, 34(1): 29–43.
Morgan, Sally. 1988. *My Place*. Melbourne: Penguin.
Morton, Stephen. 2007a. *Gayatri Spivak: Ethics, Subalternity and the Critique of Postcolonial Reason*. Cambridge: Polity.
———. 2007b. "Terrorism, Orientalism and Imperialism," *Wasafiri*, 22(2): 36–42.
Motyl, Alexander J. 2001. *Encyclopedia of Nationalism* (Two-Volume Set, vol. 2). San Diego, CA: Academic Press.
Moussa, Mario and Ron Scapp. 1996. "The Practical Theorizing of Michel Foucault: Politics and Counter-Discourse," *Cultural Critique*, 33: 87–112.
Mufti, Aamir R. 1998. "Auerbach in Istanbul: Edward Said, Secular Criticism, and the Question of Minority Culture," *Critical Inquiry*, 25: 95–125.
Mukerjee, Radhakamal. 1923. *Democracies of the East: A Study of Comparative Politics*. London: P.S. King and Son.
Mukherjee, Meenakshi. 2000. *The Perishable Empire: Essays on Indian Writing in English*. Delhi: Oxford University Press.

Mukherjee, S. 1996. "The Idea of the Village Community and British Administrators," *Sydney Studies in Society and Culture*, 13: 66–74. Available online at http://ojs-prod. library.usyd.edu.au/index.php/SSSC/issue/view/631 (downloaded on February 12, 2014).

Mullaney, Julie. 2002. "Globalizing Dissent? Arundhati Roy, Local and Postcolonial Feminisms in the Transnational Economy," *Journal of Postcolonial Writing*, 40(1): 56–69.

Munro, Thomas. 1881. *Major-General Sir Thomas Munro, Governor of Madras: Selections from His Minutes and Other Official Writings, 1*. London: Kegan Paul.

Mustafa, Daanish. 2005. "The Terrible Geographicalness of Terrorism: Reflections of a Hazards Geographer," *Antipode*, 37(1): 72–92.

Naidu, Bahadur M. Pauparao. 1915. *The History of Railway Thieves, with Illustrations and Hints on Detection*. Madras: Higginbothams Limited.

Naipaul, V.S. 1987. *The Enigma of Arrival: A Novel in Five Sections*. London: Penguin.

———. 2001 [1961]. *A House of Mr Biswas*. New York: Vintage Books.

———. 2003 [1977]. *India: A Wounded Civilization*. New York: Vintage Books.

Nanda, Meera. 2010. "Are we 'Post-Hindu' yet?" *Himal South Asian Magazine*, May. Available online at http://himalmag.com/component/content/article/168-.html (downloaded on November 4, 2012).

Narayan, R.K. 1978 [1935]. *Swami and Friends*. Oxford: Oxford University Press.

———. 1980a [1937]. *The Bachelor of Arts*. Chicago, IL: University of Chicago Press.

———. 1980b [1945]. *The English Teacher*. Chicago, IL: University of Chicago Press.

———. 1981a [1949]. *Mr. Sampath: The Printer of Malgudi*. Chicago, IL: University of Chicago Press.

———. 1981b [1952]. *The Financial Expert*. Chicago, IL: University of Chicago Press.

———. 1981c [1938]. *The Dark Room*. Chicago, IL: University of Chicago Press.

———. 1982 [1976]. *The Painter of Signs*. New York: Penguin.

———. 1983a [1967]. *The Vendor of Sweets*. New York: Penguin.

———. 1983b [1961]. *The Man-Eater of Malgudi*. New Delhi: Penguin.

———. 1984a [1972]. *Malgudi Days*. New York: Penguin.

———. 1984b [1972]. "A Willing Slave," *Malgudi Days*, pp. 136–41. New York: Penguin.

———. 1984c [1972]. "God and the Cobbler," *Malgudi Days*, pp. 224–31. New York: Penguin.

———. 1984d [1982]. *A Tiger for Malgudi*. New York: Penguin.

———. 1987a [1985]. *Under the Banyan Tree*. New York: Penguin.

———. 1987b [1985]. "A Career," *Under the Banyan Tree*, pp. 43–49. New York: Penguin.

———. 1987c [1985]. "A Horse and Two Goats," *Under the Banyan Tree*, pp. 14–30. New York: Penguin.

———. 1987d [1985]. "The Roman Image," *Under the Banyan Tree*, pp. 31–38. New York: Penguin.

———. 1988 [1958]. *The Guide*. New York: Penguin.

———. 2001. "Imaginary Homeland," the *The Hindu*, June 3. Available online at http://www.hinduonnet.com (downloaded on June 7, 2011).

———. 2002 [1999]. "Talkative Man," in S Krishnan (ed.), *A Town Called Malgudi*, pp. 257–376. New Delhi: Penguin.

Nash, Catherine. 2002. "Cultural Geography: Postcolonial Cultural Geographies," *Progress in Human Geography*, 26(2): 219–30.

Nehru, Jawaharlal. 1936. *Toward Freedom: The Autobiography of Jawaharlal Nehru*. London: The Bodley Head.

Ngugi wa Thiong'o. 2002 [1967]. *A Grain of Wheat*. London: Penguin.

Niezen, Ronald. 2003. *The Origins of Indigenism, Human Rights and the Politics of Identity*. Berkeley, CA: University of California Press.

Niu, Greta Aiyu. 2008. "Techno-Orientalism, Nanotechnology, Posthumans, and Post-Posthumans in Neal Stephenson's and Linda Nagata's Science Fiction," *Multi-Ethnic Literature of the United States*, 33(4): 73–96.

Niyogi De, Esha. 2004. "Decolonizing Universality: Postcolonial Theory and the Quandary of Ethical Agency," *diacritics*, 32(2): 42–59.

Noyes, John. 2002. "Nature, History, and the Failure of Language," in Ato Quayson and David Theo Goldberg (eds), *Relocating Postcolonialism*, pp. 270–81. Oxford: Blackwell.

Nussbaum, Martha C. 1996. "Patriotism and Cosmopolitanism," in Joshua Cohen (ed.), *For Love of Country: Debating the Limits of Patriotism*, pp. 3–20. Boston, MA: Beacon Press.

Nyers, Peter. 2003. "Abject Cosmopolitanism: The Politics of Protection in the Anti-Deportation Movement," *Third World Quarterly*, 24(6): 1069–93.

Obeidat, Marwan M. 1998. *American Literature and Orientalism*. Berlin: Klaus Schwartz.

Okin, Susan. 1997. "Is Multiculturalism Bad for Women?" *Boston Review*. Available online at http://www.bostonreview.net/forum/susan-moller-okin-multiculuralism-bad-women (downloaded on August 20, 2011).

Okri, Ben. 1991. *The Famished Road*. London: Jonathan Cape.

Omvedt, Gail (ed.). 1982. *Land, Caste, and Politics in Indian States*. Delhi: Authors Guild Publications.

Ondaatje, Michael. 1993. *Running in the Family*. London: Vintage Books.

O'Neill, Joseph. 2008. *Netherland*. London: Fourth Estate.

Orford, Anne. 2003. *Reading Humanitarian Intervention: Human Rights and the Use of Force in International Law*. Cambridge: Cambridge University Press.

Palat, Ravi Arvind. 2004a. "Areas Studies after-9/11, Requiescat in Pace," *APSI*. Available online at http://www.duke.edu/APSI/ pdf/asiaconf/Ravipalat.pdf (downloaded on August 22, 2007).

———. 2004b. *Capitalist Restructuring and the Pacific Rim*. London and New York: Routledge.

Parry, Benita. 2004. *Postcolonial Studies: A Materialist Critique*. London and New York: Routledge.

———. 2012. "What is Left in Postcolonial Studies?" *New Literary History*, 43(2): 341–58.

Pascal, Roy. 1960. *Design and Truth in Autobiography*. London: Routledge and Kegan Paul.

Payne, Michael. 2005. "Humanism After Theory: Or, the Last Words of Edward Said," *The Review of Education, Pedagogy, and Cultural Studies*, 27: 87–93.

Pearson, Nels and Marc Singer. 2009. "Open Cases: Detection, (Post)Modernity, and the State," in Nels Pearson and Marc Singer (eds), *Detective Fiction in a Postcolonial and Transnational World*, pp. 1–14. Farnham: Ashgate.

Pels, Peter and Oscar Salemink (eds). 1999. *Colonial Subjects: Essays on the Practical History of Anthropology*. Ann Arbor, MI: University of Michigan Press.

Perry, Nick. 1995. "Traveling Theory/Nomadic Theorizing," *Organization*, 2(1): 35–54.

Pershai, Alexander. 2010. "Minor Nation: The Alternative Modes of Belarusian Nationalism," *East European Politics and Societies*, 24(3): 1–20, 379–98.

Persram, Nalini (ed.). 2007. *Postcolonialism and Political Theory*. Plymouth: Lexington Books.

Petersen, R.A. 1997. "The Rise and Fall of Highbrow Snobbery as a Status Marker," *Poetics*, 25: 75–92.

Pickles, John. 2005. "'New Cartographies' and the Decolonization of European Geographies," *Area*, 37(4): 355–64.

Picq, Manuela. August 20, 2011. "Indigenous Resistance is the New 'Terrorism,'" *Aljazeera English Online*. http://english.aljazeera.net/indepth/opinion/2011/06/201162995115833636. html (downloaded on October 23, 2011).

Poe, Steven C. and C. Neal Tate. 1994. "Repression of Human Rights to Personal Integrity in the 1980s: A Global Analysis," *The American Political Science Review*, 88(4): 853–72.

Pollock, Sheldon, Homi K. Bhabha, Carol A. Breckenridge, and Dipesh Chakrabarty. 2000. "Cosmopolitanisms," *Public Culture*, 12(3): 577–90.

Ponzanesi, Sandra. 2004. "Beyond Postcolonial Theory? Paradoxes and Potentialities of a Necessary Paradigm," in Geoffrey V. Davis, Peter H. Marsden, Bénédicte Ledent, and Marc Delrez (eds), *Towards a Transcultural Future. Literature and Society in a 'Post'-Colonial World*, pp. 37–47. Amsterdam and New York: Rodopi.

Popke, Jeff. 2007. "Geography and Ethics: Spaces of Cosmopolitan Responsibility," *Progress in Human Geography*, 31(4): 509–18.

Porter, Patrick. 2009. *Military Orientalism: Eastern War through Western Eyes*. New York: Columbia University Press.

Power, Marcus, Giles Mohan, and Claire Mercer. 2006. "Postcolonial Geographies of Development: Introduction," *Singapore Journal of Tropical Geography*, 27(3): 231–34.

Prakash, Gyan. 1990. "Writing Post-Orientalist Histories of the Third World: Perspectives from Indian Historiography," *Comparative Studies in Society and History*, 32(2): 383–408.

———. 1992. "Postcolonial Criticism and Indian Historiography," *Social Text*, 31(2): 8–26.

———. 1994a. "Subaltern Studies as Postcolonial Criticism," *American Historical Review*, 99(5): 1475–90.

——— (ed.). 1994b. *After Colonialism: Imperial Histories and Postcolonial Displacements*. Princeton, NJ: Princeton University Press.

———. 1995. "Orientalism Now," *History and Theory*, 34(3): 199–212.

Prasad, Amar Nath (ed.). 2002. *Indian Writing in English: Critical Explorations*. New Delhi: Sarup & Sons.

Prasad, Jaya. 2006. "R.K. Narayan's Modern Heroines and the Dilemma of Men," in Chhote Lal Khatri (ed.), *R.K. Narayan: Reflections and Re-Evaluation*, pp. 76–87. New Delhi: Sarup & Sons.

Prashar, Arjuna. 2009. "Millionaire Verses Slumdogs, Creates *Economic Orientalism*," *The Indian Star*, March 9. Available online at http://www.indialink-online.com (downloaded on October 31, 2013).

Pratt, Mary Louise. 2008 [1992]. *Imperial Eyes: Studies in Travel Writing and Transculturation*. London and New York: Routledge.

Quayson, Ato. 2000. *Postcolonialism: Theory, Practice or Process?* Oxford: Blackwell.

———. 2012. "The Sighs of History: Postcolonial Debris and the Question of (Literary) History," *New Literary History*, 43(2): 359–70.

Quayson, Ato and David Theo Goldberg (eds). 2002. *Relocating Postcolonialism*. Oxford: Blackwell.

Radcliffe, Sarah. 2005. "Development and Geography: Towards a Postcolonial Development Geography," *Progress in Human Geography*, 29(3): 291–98.

Radhakrishna, Meena. 2001. *Dishonoured by History: Criminal Tribes and British Colonial Policy*. New Delhi: Orient Longman.

Radhakrishnan, Rajagopalan. 2007. "Edward Said's Literary Humanism," *Cultural Critique*, 67(1): 13–42.

Raheja, Gloria. 1996. "Caste, Colonialism, and the Speech of the Colonized: Entextualization and Disciplinary Control in India," *American Ethnologist*, 23(3): 494–513.

Ramanujam, T. 1942. *Prevention & Detection of Crimes*. Madras: Madras Book Agency.

Ramteke, S.R. 2008. "R.K. Narayan a Novelist Committed to Hindu Ideals and Beliefs," in Krishna Bhatnagar (ed.), *New Insights into the Novels of R.K. Narayan*, pp. 20–31. Delhi: Atlantic.

Raghuram, Parvati and Clare Madge. 2006. "Towards a Method for Postcolonial Development Geography: Possibilities and Challenges," *Singapore Journal of Tropical Geography*, 27(3): 270–88.

Rao, Panduranga. 1970. "The Art of R. K. Narayan," *Journal of Commonwealth Literature*, 5(1–3): 29–40.

Rao, Rahul. 2007. PhD Dissertation. "Postcolonial Cosmopolitanism: Between Home and the World." University of Oxford.

———. 2013. "Postcolonial Cosmopolitanism: Making Place for Nationalism," in Jyotirmaya Tripathy and Sudarsan Padmanabhan (eds), *The Democratic Predicament: Cultural Diversity in Europe and India*, pp. 165–87. New Delhi: Routledge.

Rao, Raja. 1989 [1938]. *Kanthapura*. New Delhi: Oxford University Press.

Rashid, Ahmed. January 14, 2002. "They Are Only Sleeping: Why Militant Islamicists in Central Asia Aren't Going to Go Away," *The New Yorker*, 34–41.

Reddy, Maureen T. 2002. *Traces, Codes, and Clues: Reading Race in Crime Fiction*. Chapel Hill, NC: Rutgers University Press.

Regev, Motti. 2011. "Pop-Rock Music as Expressive Isomorphism: Blurring the National, the Exotic and the Cosmopolitan in Popular Music," *American Behavioral Scientist*, 55: 558–73.

Rhodes, John Cecil. 1902. *The Last Will and Testament*. London: Review of Reviews Office.

Riemenschneider, Dieter. 2005. *The Indian Novel in English: Its Critical Discourse 1934–2004*. Jaipur: Rawat.

Risley, Herbert H. 1901. *Introduction to Ethnographic Appendices*. Calcutta: Government of India.

Robbins, Bruce and Elsa Stamatopoulou. 2004. "Reflections on Culture and Cultural Rights," *Southern Atlantic Quarterly*, 102(2–3): 421–36.

Robbins, Bruce, Mary Louise Pratt, Jonathan Arac, R. Radhakrishnan, and Edward Said. 1994. "Edward Said's Culture and Imperialism: A Symposium," *Social Text*, 40: 1–24.

Roberts, Susan, Anna Secor, and Mathew Spark. 2003. "Neoliberal Geopolitics," *Antipode*, 35(5): 886–97.

Roberts, Thomas J. 1990. *An Aesthetics of Junk Fiction*. Athens, GA: University of Georgia Press.

Rodell, Paul. 2005. "The Philippines and the Challenge of International Terrorism," in Paul J. Smith (ed.), *Terrorism and Violence in Southeast Asia: Transnational Challenges to States and Regional Stability*, pp. 122–44. New York: M.E. Sharpe.

Rogers, Alisdair. 1992. "The Boundaries of Reason: The World, the Homeland, and Edward Said," *Environment and Planning D: Society and Space*, 10(5): 511–26.

Roth, Philip. 2004. *The Plot Against America*. New York: Houghton Mifflin.

Rushdie, Salman. 1980. *Midnight's Children*. London: Jonathan Cape.

———. 2005. *Shalimar and the Clown*. London: Jonathan Cape.

Rhys, Jean. 2000 [1966]. *Wide Sargasso Sea*. London: Penguin

Safran Foer, Jonathan. 2005. *Extremely Loud and Incredibly Close*. New York: Houghton Mifflin.

Said, Edward W. 1983. *The World, the Text, and the Critic*. Cambridge, MA: Harvard University Press.

Said, Edward W. 1988. "Foreword," in Ranajit Guha and Gayatri Chakravorty Spivak (eds), *Selected Subaltern Studies*, pp. v–x. New York and Oxford: Oxford University Press.

———. 1989. "Representing the Colonized: Anthropology's Interlocutors," *Critical Inquiry*, 15(2): 205–25.

———. 1994a [1993]. *Culture and Imperialism*. London and New York: Verso.

———. 1994b [1993]. *Representations of the Intellectual*. London: Vintage.

———. 1997 [1981]. *Covering Islam: How the Media and the Experts Determine How We See the Rest of the World*. New York: Vintage Books.

———. 1999. *Out of Place: A Memoir*. New York: Knopf.

———. 2000. *Reflections on Exile and Other Literary Essays*. Cambridge, MA: Harvard University Press.

———. 2002 [2001]. *Power, Politics and Culture*. New York: Vintage Books.

———. 2003 [1978]. *Orientalism*. New York: Pantheon.

———. February 19, 2003. "Memory, Inequality and Power, Palestine and the Universality of Human Rights," University of California Berkeley Lecture. Available online at http://electronicintifada.net/blogs/nora-barrows-friedman/ten-years-edward-saids-passing listen-his-last-major-speech (downloaded on January 21, 2014).

———. 2004a. *Humanism and Democratic Criticism*. New York: Columbia University Press.

———. 2004b. "Orientalism Once More," *Development and Change*, 35: 869–90.

———. 2005 [August 1, 1998]. "On 'Orientalism,'" *Media Education Foundation*. Available online at www.mediaed.org/assets/products/403/transcript_403.pdf (downloaded on January 1, 2012).

Salaita, Steven. 2005. "Ethnic Identity and Imperative Patriotism: Arab Americans Before and After 9/11," *College Literature*, 32(2): 146–68.

San Juan, Jr., E. 1998. *Beyond Postcolonial Theory*. New York: St. Martin's Press.

———. 2006. "Edward Said's Affiliations," *Atlantic Studies*, 3(1): 43–61.

Sanders, Douglas. 1998. "The Legacy of Deskaheh: Indigenous Peoples as International Actors," in Cynthia Price Cohen (ed.), *Human Rights of Indigenous Peoples*, pp. 73–88. New York: Transnational Publishers.

Sardar, Ziauddin. 1998. *Postmodernism and the Other: the New Imperialism of Western Culture*. London: Pluto Press.

Sastry, Shri M.V.R. November 2012. "Kancha Ilaiah's *Why I am Not a Hindu*: A Critical Review." Available online at http://www.voiceofdharma.org/indology/Ilaiah.html (downloaded on February 25, 2013).

Satnam. 2010. *Janglenama*. New Delhi: Penguin India.

Scanlan, Margaret. 2001. *Plotting Terror: Novelists and Terrorists in Contemporary Fiction*. Charlottesville, VA: Virginia University Press.

Schneider-Mayerson, Mathew. 2010. "Popular Fiction Studies: The Advantages of a New Field," *Studies in Popular Culture*, 33(1): 21–35.

Scott, James. 1985. *Weapons of the Week: Everyday forms of Peasant Resistance*. New Haven, CT: Yale University Press.

Sebastian, Mrinalini. 2000. *The Novels of Shashi Deshpande in Postcolonial Arguments*. New Delhi: Prestige.

Sehrawat, Tarun. 2009. "A Zone of Twisted Law," *Tehelka Magazine*, December 19. Available online at http://tehelka.com/story_main43.asp?filename=Ne191209a_zone.asp (downloaded on May 9, 2012).

Sen, Krishna. 2004. *Critical Essays on R.K. Narayan's* The Guide. Hyderabad: Orient Longman.

Seth, Vanita. 2010. *Europe's Indians: Producing Racial Difference, 1500–1900*. Durham, NC: Duke University Press.

Sethi, Rumina. 1999. *Myths of the Nation: National Identity and Literary Representation*. Oxford: Clarendon Press.

Shakespeare, William. 2011 [1623]. In Virginia Mason and Alden T. Vaughan (eds), *The Tempest*, Walton-on-Thames, Surrey: Arden.

Sharp, Persram. 2010. *Geographies of Postcolonialism*. London: SAGE.

Sharp, Persram and John Briggs. 2006. "Postcolonialism and Development: New Dialogues?" *Geographical Journal*, 172(1): 6–9.

Sheshadri-Crooks, Kalpana. 2000. "At the Margins of Postcolonial Studies I," in Fawiza Afzal-Khan and Kalpana Seshadri-Crooks (eds), *The Pre-occupation of Postcolonial Studies*, pp. 3–23. Durham, NC: Duke University Press.

Simmel, Georg. 2010 [1950]. "Metropolis and Mental Life," in Gary Bridge and Sophie Watson (eds), *The Blackwell City Reader*, pp. 103–10. Oxford: Blackwell.

Simon, David. 2006. "Separated by Common Ground? Bringing (post)Development and (post)Colonialism Together," *Geographical Journal*, 172(1): 10–21.

Singh, Ranbir. February 13, 2011. "Review of Kancha Ilaiah's 'Why I am not a Hindu,'" Available online at http://www.chakranews.com/review-of-kancha-ilaiahs-why-i-am-not-a-hindu/1100 (downloaded on March 5, 2012).

Sivanandan, Ambalavaner. 2006. "Race, Terror, and Civil Society," *Race & Class*, 47(3): 1–8.

Sivanandan, Tamara. 2004. "Anti-Colonialism, National Liberation, and Postcolonial Nation Formation," in Neil Lazarus (ed.), *The Cambridge Companion to Postcolonial Literary Studies*, pp. 42–65. Cambridge: Cambridge University Press.

Slater, Gilbert. 1918. *Some South Indian Village*. Oxford: Oxford University Press.

Sleeman, William Henry. 1844. *Rambles and Recollections of an Indian Official—Volume I*. London: J. Hatchard and Son.

———. 2011 [1836]. *Ramaseeana: Or a Vocabulary of the Peculiar Language Used by the Thugs*. Cambridge: Cambridge University Press.

Sluka, Jeffrey A. 2009. "The Contribution of Anthropology to Critical Terrorism Studies," in Richard Jackson, Marie Breen Smyth, and Jeroen Gunning (eds), *Critical Terrorism Studies: A New Research Agenda*, pp. 138–55. London and New York: Routledge.

Smith, Neil. 2003. *American Empire: Roosevelt's Geographer and the Prelude to Globalization*. Berkeley, CA: University of California Press.

Smith, Paul J. 2005. *Terrorism and Violence in Southeast Asia*. New York: M.E. Sharpe.

Sorenson, Eli Park. 2010. *Postcolonial Studies and the Literary: Theory, Interpretation and the Novel*. Basingstoke: Palgrave Macmillan.

Spencer, Robert. 2010. "Cosmopolitan Criticism", in Janet Wilson, Cristina Sandru, and Sarah Lawson Welsh (eds), *Rerouting the Postcolonial: New Directions for the Millennium*, pp. 36–47. London and New York: Routledge.

———. 2011. *Cosmopolitan Criticism and Postcolonial Literature*. Basingstoke: Palgrave Macmillan.

Spivak, Gayatri Chakravorty. 1985. "Strategies of Vigilance," *Block*, 10: 5–9.

———. 1987. *In Other Worlds: Essays in Cultural Politics*. New York: Methuen.

———. 1988a. "Subaltern Studies: Deconstructing Historiography," in Ranajit Guha and Gayatri Chakravorty Spivak (eds), *Selected Subaltern Studies*, pp. 3–32. New York: Oxford University Press.

Spivak, Gayatri Chakravorty. 1988b. "Can the Subaltern Speak?" in Cary Nelson and Lawrence Grossberg (eds), *Marxism & the Interpretation of Culture*, pp. 271–313. Urbana and Chicago, IL: University of Illinois Press.

————. 1989. "In a Word: Interview with Ellen Rooney," *Differences*, 1(2): 124–56.

————. 1990. "Poststructuralism, Marginality, Postcoloniality and Value," in Peter Collier and Helga Geyer-Ryan (eds), *Literary Theory Today*, pp. 228–51. London and New York: Verso.

————. 1993. *Outside in the Teaching Machine*. London and New York: Routledge.

————. 1999. *A Critique of Postcolonial Reason: Toward a History of the Vanishing Present*. Cambridge, MA: Harvard University Press.

————. 2003. *Death of a Discipline*. New York: Columbia University Press.

————. 2004. "Righting Wrongs," *The South Atlantic Quarterly*, 103(2/3): 523–81.

————. 2005. "Addressing Human Rights: Use and Abuse of Human Rights," *Boundary 2*, 32(1): 131–89.

————. 2012. *An Aesthetic Education in the Era of Globalization*. Cambridge, MA: Harvard University Press.

Srinivas, M.N. 1987. *The Dominant Caste and other Essays*. New York: Oxford University Press.

Srinivasan, T.N. 1994. "Human Development: a New Paradigm or Reinvention of the Wheel?" *American Economic Review*, 84(2): 238–43.

Stam, Robert and Ella Shohat. 2012. "Whence and Whither Postcolonial Theory?" *New Literary History*, 43(2): 371–90.

Stowe, Harriet Beecher. 1999 [1852]. *Uncle Tom's Cabin*. London: Wordsworth Classics.

Sugirtharajah, Rasiah S. 2006. "Postcolonizing Biblical Interpretation," in Bill Ashcroft, Gareth Griffiths, and Helen Tiffin (eds), *The Post-Colonial Studies Reader*, pp. 537–39. London: Routledge.

Sylvester, Christine. 1999. "Development Studies and Postcolonial Studies: Disparate Tales of the 'Third World,'" *Third World Quarterly*, 20(4): 703–21.

Syrotinski, Michael. 2007. *Deconstruction and the Postcolonial: At the Limits of Theory*. Liverpool: Liverpool University Press.

Thomas, Nicholas. 1991a. "Against Ethnography," *Cultural Anthropology*, 6(3): 306–22.

————. 1991b. "Anthropology and Orientalism," *Anthropology Today*, 7(2): 4-7.

Tickell, Alex. 2012. *Terrorism, Insurgency and Indian-English Literature, 1830–1947*. London and New York: Routledge.

Tiffin, Helen. 1987. "Post-Colonial Literature and Counter-Discourse," *Kunapipi*, 9(3): 17–34.

Tirman, John (ed.). 2004. *The Maze of Fear*. New York: New Press.

Tolen, Rachel J. 1991. "Colonizing and Transforming the Criminal Tribesman: The Salvation Army in British India," *American Ethnologist*, 18(1): 106–25.

Turner, Bryan and June Edmunds. 2001. "The Re-invention of a National Identity? Women and 'Cosmopolitan' Englishness," *Ethnicities*, 1(1): 83–108.

Twain, Mark. 2010 [1869]. *The Innocents Abroad*. London: Wordsworth Classics.

Updike, John. 2006. *Terrorist*. New York: Knopf.

Valassopoulos, Anastasia. 2004. "Fictionalising Post-Colonial Theory: The Creative Native Informant," *Critical Survey*, 16(2): 28–44.

Van Leeuwen, Theo. 2005. "Three Models of Interdisciplinarity," in Ruth Wodak and Paul Anthony Chilton (eds), *A New Agenda for (Critical) Discourse Analysis*, pp. 3–18. Amsterdam: Benjamin.

Varisco, Daniel Martin. 2007. *Reading Orientalism: Said and the Unsaid.* Seattle, WA and London: University of Washington Press.

Varughese, Emma Dawson. 2012. *Beyond the Postcolonial: World Englishes Literature.* Basingstoke: Palgrave Macmillan.

———. 2013. *Reading New India: Post-Millennial Indian Fiction in English.* London and New York: Bloomsbury Academic.

Veness, David. 2001. "Terrorism and Counterterrorism: An International Perspective," *Studies in Conflict and Terrorism*, 24(5): 407–16.

Venn, Couze. 2006. *The Postcolonial Challenge: Towards Alternative Worlds.* London: SAGE.

Virilio, Paul. 2002. *Ground Zero.* Translated by Chris Turner. London and New York: Verso.

Walsh, William. 1972. *R.K. Narayan (Writers & Their Work).* London: Longman Higher Education.

The Wall Street Journal. January 14, 2012. "Exodus of Workers From Continent Reverses Old Patterns." Available online at http://online.wsj.com/news/ (downloaded on October 31, 2013).

Warraq, Ibn. 2007. *Defending the West: A Critique of Edward Said's Orientalism.* Amherst, MA: Prometheus Books.

Wayne, Teddy. 2010. *Kapitoil.* New York: Harper Perennial.

Weingart, Peter. 2000. "Interdisciplinarity: a Paradoxical Discourse," in Nico Stehr and Peter Weingart (eds), *Practicing Interdisciplinarity*, pp. 25–43. Toronto: Toronto University Press.

Werbner, Pnina. 2006. "Vernacular Cosmopolitanism," *Theory Culture, & Society*, 23(2–3): 496–98.

Wheeler, Ron. 2008. "Toward a Non-Normative Concept of Terrorism," *Rutgers Journal of Comparative Literature*, 9: 3–20.

Wilks, Mark. 1810. *Historical Sketches of South India, 1.* London: Longman.

———. 1817. *Historical Sketches of the South of India, in an Attempt to Trace the History of Mysore* (3 volumes). London: Longman.

Willemsen-Diaz, Augusto. 2009. "How Indigenous Peoples' Rights Reached the UN," in Claire Charters and Rodolfo Stavenhagen (eds), *Making the Declaration Work: the United Nations Declaration on the Rights of Indigenous Peoples*, pp. 16–31. Copenhagen: IWGIA.

Wilson, H. Heyman. 1855. *A Glossary of Revenue and Judicial Terms.* Delhi: Munshiram and Manoharlal.

Winant, Howard. 2004. *The New Politics of Race: Globalism, Difference and Justice.* Minneapolis, MN: University of Minnesota Press.

Winlow, Heather. 2001. Anthropometric Cartography: Constructing Scottish Racial Identity in the Early Twentieth Century," *Journal of Historical Geography*, 27(4): 507–28.

Wiser, William. 1936. *The Hindu Jajmani System.* Lucknow: Lucknow Publishing House.

Wright, Shelley. 2001. *International Human Rights, Decolonisation and Globalisation: Becoming Human.* London and New York: Routledge.

Wynter, Sylvia. 1987. "On Disenchanting Discourse: 'Minority' Literary Criticism and Beyond," *Cultural Critique*, 7: 207–44.

Xun Lu. 1990 [1918]. *Diary of a Madman and Other Stories.* Honolulu, HI: University of Hawaii Press.

Yetiv, Isaac. 1989. "From Ethnocentrism to Humanism: Albert Memmi's *Le Désert*," *The International Fiction Review*, 16(2): 128–31.

Young, Robert J.C. 2009. "What is the Postcolonial?" *ARIEL: A Review of International English Literature*, 40(1): 13–25.

———. 2012. "Postcolonial Remains," *New Literary History*, 43(1): 19–42.

Zabala, Santiago. December 26, 2012. "Slavoj Zizek and the Role of the Philosopher," *Aljazeera Online*. Available online at http://www.aljazeera.com/indepth/opinion/2012/12/2012122412215406939.html (downloaded on February 11, 2014).

Zein-Elabdin, Eiman O. 2004. "Articulating the Postcolonial (with Economics in Mind)," in Eiman O. Zein-Elabdin and S. Charusheela (eds), *Postcolonialism Meets Economics*, pp. 21–39. London and New York: Routledge.

Zeleza, Paul Tiyambe (ed.). 2006. *The Study of Africa Vol. 1: Disciplinary and Interdisciplinary Encounters*. Dakar: Codesria Book Series.

Žižek, Slavoj. 2002. *Welcome to the Desert of the Real! Five Essays on September 11 and Related Dates*. London and New York: Verso.

Movies

Abu-Assad, Hany. *Paradise Now*. 2005. Burbank, CA: Warner Independent Pictures.

Bigelow, Kathryn. *The Hurt Locker*. 2008. Burbank, CA: Warner Bros.

Greengrass, Paul. *United 93*. 2006. New York: Universal Pictures.

———. *Green Zone*. 2010. London: Working Title Films/Universal Studios.

Haggis, Paul. *In the Valley of Elah*. 2007. Burbank, CA: Warner Independent Pictures.

Hirani, Rajkumar. *3 Idiots*. 2009. Mumbai: Vinod Chopra Films.

Johar, Karan. *My Name is Khan*. 2010. Mumbai: Fox Star Studios.

Kapoor, Raj. *Sree 420*. 1955. Mumbai: R.K. Films Ltd.

Moverman, Oren. *The Messenger*. 2009. New York: Oscilloscope Laboratories.

Nag, Shankar. *Malgudi Days*. 1986. Bangalore: PADAMRAG TV International.

Redford, Robert. *Lions for Lambs*. 2007. Beverly Hills, CA: Metro-Goldwyn-Mayer.

Stone, Oliver. *World Trade Center*. 2006. Los Angeles, CA: Paramount Pictures.

Winterbottom, Michael. *The Road to Guantanamo*. 2006. London: Channel 4.

Index

About the Author

Pavan Kumar Malreddy is a Researcher at the Institute for English and American Studies, Goethe University, Frankfurt. He has previously taught at Chemnitz University of Technology, York University, Toronto (2003–04), University of Saskatchewan, Saskatoon (2009–10), and has worked with various research organizations (Canadian Council on Learning, Ottawa and Aboriginal Education Research Center, Saskatoon) as a commissioned writer and editor from 2007 to 2009. He has published numerous essays on race, postcolonialism, and indigenous politics in Canada in journals, such as *Third World Quarterly, Intertexts, Journal of Postcolonial Writing,* and *AlterNative,* among others. His co-edited collection, *Reworking Postcolonialism: Globalization, Labour and Rights* is due for publication in the spring of 2015. He is the co-editor of a special issue titled "Orientalism and Terrorism: Theory, Text, and Images after 9/11" published in the *Journal of Postcolonial Writing* (2012, vol. 48, issue 3) and of another special issue titled "Arun Joshi: Avant-Garde, Existentialism and the West" published in *ZAA: Quarterly Journal of Language, Literature and Culture* (2014). His current research work focuses on the discourses of terror, necropolitics, nationalism, and violence in India, Sri Lanka, Burma, and Nigeria. His doctoral dissertation on postcolonial theory has received the 2012 Faculty of Humanities award at Chemnitz University of Technology.